Uncle John's BATHROOM READER®

PUZZLE BOOK

Edited by
Stephanie Spadaccini

The Bathroom Readers' Institute
Portable Press
San Diego, CA, and Ashland, OR

For the twins

UNCLE JOHN'S
BATHROOM READER
PUZZLE BOOK #3

For information, write
The Bathroom Readers' Institute
P.O. Box 1117 Ashland, OR 97520
www.bathroomreader.com
email: mail@bathroomreader.com

Project Team:
Stephanie Spadaccini: Project Editor
Nancy Schuster: Design and Composition
Gordon Javna: Publisher
JoAnn Padgett: Director, Editorial and Production
Jennifer Browning: Production Editor

Cover design by Michael Brunsfeld *(brunsfeldo@comcast.net)*

ISBN 13: 978-1-59223-322-9
ISBN 10: 1-59223-322-8

Printed in the United States of America
Fourth printing: March 2011

11 12 13 14 15   9 8 7 6 5 4

CONTENTS

PUZZLES & WORDPLAY

CROSSWORDS

DROP QUOTES

CRISS-CROSS PUZZLES

WORD SEARCH PUZZLES

DOUBLE-CROSTICS

MINI-CROSTICS

CRYPTOGRAMS

QUIZZES & MORE WORDPLAY

FAMOUS PEOPLE

PLUNGING INTO HISTORY

Editor

Stephanie Spadaccini is a long-time puzzle constructor, whose crosswords and word search puzzles appear regularly in *People* and *AARP* magazine. A former managing editor of *Games* magazine and writer on TV's *Jeopardy!*, Stephanie most recently authored *The Big Book of Rules*, a complete compendium of games from Bridge and Bocce to Tiddlywinks and Stickball. This is her third Uncle John puzzle book.

Contributors

Alan Arbesfeld has been constructing crossword puzzles for over 25 years. His puzzles have appeared in the *New York Times,* the *New York Sun,* the *Los Angeles Times, Games* magazine, and *Attaché* magazine, as well as numerous crossword puzzle compilations. He lives in Brooklyn.

Michael Ashley is a widely published puzzle constructor who lives in Scottsdale, Arizona. His most recent books are *Random House Crostics by Michael Ashley Volume 9* and, with Jacqueline Byrne, *SAT Vocabulary Express: Word Puzzles Designed to Decode the New SAT.* In his spare time he takes guitar lessons from Patrick Berry.

Patrick Berry is a freelance puzzle constructor from Chapel Hill, North Carolina, whose work has appeared in numerous publications. He is also the editor of the *Chronicle of Higher Education*'s puzzle, and the author of *Crossword Puzzle Challenges for Dummies*, a how-to book on crossword construction. In his spare time he bedevils book editors by failing to send in his bio on time and then, when he finally gets around to it, including silly final sentences like this one.

Myles Callum is a former senior editor at *TV Guide* who took up puzzle making eight years ago. His puzzles have appeared in the *New York Times,* the *Wall Street Journal,* the *Los Angeles Times, USA Today*, the *Crosswords Club*, Portable Press books, and other publications. He's a regular contributor to the *Uncle John Plunges Into…* series of bathroom readers. He lives in Santa Rosa, California.

Adam Cohen is a Brooklynite who edits science and medical publications. His puzzles have appeared in the *New York Times,* the *New York Sun, Newsday, Games/World of Puzzles* magazines, and other publications. He is still aspiring to be Frank Longo.

Mark Danna is a freelance puzzle constructor whose specialty is fun-shaped word searches. He is the author of ten word search books, the *Wordy Gurdy* rhyming puzzle that is syndicated nationally to newspapers, and crosswords in the *New York Times* and many other publications. Danna's playful and unusual career has included stints as an associate editor at *Games* magazine, staff writer for a TV game show, sports director on cruise ships, and professional Frisbee player. A three-time national Frisbee champion, Danna is co-author of the *Frisbee Players' Handbook,* a round, how-to book that came packaged inside a Frisbee. He lives in Manhattan.

Chris DiNapoli, former longtime art director for *16 Magazine* and staff editor for *Dell Champion Crosswords*, is editor of *Dell Crosswords Crosswords* magazine. When she isn't laughing in the face of retirement, this native New Yorker's time is occupied with animals, gardening, and words.

Elizabeth C. Gorski is a frequent contributor to the *New York Times* and *USA Today* puzzle pages. Since February 2005 she has been in stitches—literally! That's when she founded Primrose Needleworks of New York City—the first cross-stitch pattern company to produce a line of American-style crossword puzzles for the needlework market.

Frank Longo is a freelance puzzle creator living in Hoboken, New Jersey. He has had over 2,500 puzzles published since he began constructing crosswords in 1993. His work appears regularly in a wide range of publications, including the *New York Times,* the *New York Sun,* the *Washington Post, Games* magazine, and *Games World of Puzzles*. He creates the weekly Sunday "Premier" puzzle for King Features Syndicate, as well as a biweekly "Learning Puzzle" for teens, which is published on the *New York Times* Web site. Longo is known for his wide-open, eye-popping grids and lively puzzle fills.

Nancy Mandl spends most of her time playing tennis, hiking, learning how to golf, and traveling--most recently to Hawaii and Mexico. She lives in Marin City, California, just a few miles from the Golden Gate Bridge. Her least favorite month is "Fogust."

Patrick Merrell has had over 50 crossword puzzles published in the *New York Times* over the past four years (on all days of the week, including Sundays). He is the author of *Aha! 125 Original & Amusing Word Puzzles, Punchline Puzzles*, and over a dozen maze books for children. He's a professional cartoonist, graphic designer, and writer living in Mount Vernon, New York.

Graham Meyer is a freelance puzzle constructor and writer whose work has appeared in several Uncle John's readers. He's been solving and constructing puzzles almost continuously since age 3. Even his wedding invitation had a crossword with the date of the ceremony, the site, and the names of the happy couple built into the grid. He and his new bride live in Chicago.

Andrea Carla Michaels is happy to be a new member of the Uncle John family. If she owned a car, the bumper sticker on it would read "Words are my life!" A former stand-up comic, sitcom writer, and chaperone for *The All New Dating Game*, Andrea now lives a quieter life in San Francisco as a Scrabble guru and professional namer of new products and companies. She has created word puzzles and crosswords for *Games* magazine, *TV Guide*, and the *New York Times*. She is currently working on a book of Jewish puzzles called *Who Nu?*

Trip Payne is a freelance puzzle constructor from Boca Raton, Florida, whose 5,000 puzzles have appeared everywhere from the *New York Times* to *TV Guide*. He is the author of numerous puzzle books (among them *Crosswords to Strain Your Brain, Mighty Mini Crosswords*, and the *Crosswords for Kids* series) and a contributor to many others. He is a three-time winner of the American Crossword Puzzle Tournament and an expert Scrabble player, and was the first contestant to win $32,000 on the U.S. version of *Who Wants to Be a Millionaire.*

FOREWORD

Words! Is there anything in the whole world more fun to play with? Words are the most plastic, elastic, fantastic toys under the sun. They morph, they multiply, they rhyme, and recombine. They're tricky as elves and zany as clowns. And each has a story waiting to be teased out. It's true!

If you don't believe us, just take the word *fun*. It comes from Middle English *fon*, meaning "to make a fool of" and *fonnen*, "to hoax." Yes, fun involves trickery. And nothing can amuse so deceptively as a word puzzle. It's true!

If you don't believe us, take the word *amuse*. Did you know it came from your nose? Well, it's etymologically an outgrowth of *muzzle*; an old French verb *muser* means "to stand with one's nose in the air." Think of a dog having lost a scent, sniffing the breeze with a raised snout—that's literally *amusement*. It's true!

And when we say something is true, we mean it's just like a tree! Seriously—the word *true* goes back to an ancient Sanskrit root *dreu*, meaning "wood." Long ago, when people wanted to say something was true, they compared it to the firmness of a tree; think of the saying "solid as an oak." The same root (to make optimum use of metaphor) is in *Druids*, the priestly Celts of ancient Britain who amassed great knowledge, professed magical powers, and held certain groves of trees to be sacred.

True is also one of the few English words that can be pronounced in Pig Latin so as to make another real word—*outré*. Others in this select group are *trash* and *ashtray*, *wrecks* and *X-ray*, *plunder* and *underplay*, *well* and *Elway*, *bee* and *eBay*. And there are more—you can probably think of some yourself.

See what happens when we turn to words? We play compulsively and reflexively—we just can't help it! Of course, it's our vocation, too; we write puzzles for magazines and newspapers, including the *Atlantic Monthly*, *Boston Globe*, and *New York Times* (which is itself an anagram of "monkeys write"!).

This book of verbal romps, larks, and quizzical curiosities is edited by our longtime friend Stephanie Spadaccini, which means it's particularly sharp—because her last name means *swordsmen* in Italian. Yes, her ancestors were named for swordplay, and now she's famed for wordplay. It's true!

—Emily Cox and Henry Rathvon

INTRODUCTION

When we last left you in *Uncle John's Puzzle Book #2*, you were chewing on your pencil, trying to make your way through the Entry Puzzle in our World's Hardest Crossword Puzzle Contest.

Here's how the contest worked. Entrants had to first qualify by correctly solving the Entry Puzzle. Of the 345 entry puzzles sent in to Uncle John headquarters, 309 qualified, and received in return mail a copy of the World's Hardest Crossword Puzzle. And, boy, was it hard! So hard that only 59 of the 309 sent in solutions. Of those entries, 42 managed to solve the puzzle, thereby making it to the finals: a drawing to determine the winner of the $5,000 Grand Prize.

The lucky solver was William Johnston of Watertown, Massachusetts, an editor of middle school and high school textbooks. No stranger to crossword puzzles, Johnston is the host of the *New York Times* Crossword Forum online, and is a puzzle constructor himself, specializing in later-in-the-week, tougher puzzles. When it comes to solving crosswords, he typically does them in ink, using pens from his collection of vintage Waterman, Parker, and Pelikan fountain pens. But he's only human, folks. He had to admit to us that he used a pencil to solve the World's Hardest.

Johnston called it "a monster of a puzzle" and said, "I had never solved a crossword puzzle that big that had so few black squares in it." But solve it he did. Hurrah, Will! To celebrate his win, he treated 70 of his closest crossword buddies to dinner during the weekend of the 2005 American Crossword Puzzle Tournament in Stamford, Connecticut. His guests included some of the leading lights of puzzledom, among them Frank Longo, the man who created the "monster."

This time around, we've included a brand-new Longo puzzle (see page 196). Also returning with more classic crosswords are Alan Arbesfeld, Patrick Berry, Adam Cohen, Elizabeth C. Gorski, and Trip Payne. Check out Trip's "Anything Goes" puzzle on page 198—we doubt you've ever seen anything like it.

We welcome a few new contributors to our pages: Graham Meyer, who also writes for the *Uncle John's Bathroom Readers*; Andrea Carla Michaels, our resident Scrabble and anagram expert; and Patrick Merrell, who has treated us to a crossword in the round and a crossword that uses his own cartoons as clues. And thanks to trivia man Myles Callum; Mark Danna and Chris DiNapoli for their wonderful word search puzzles; Michael Ashley for his crostics and cryptics; and again to Patrick Berry for his amazing quizzes.

Nancy Schuster quarked the book, helped immeasurably with editing, and acted as conduit to Puzzle Land. Jon Delfin, seven-time American Crossword Puzzle Tournament winner, did our proofreading. Joe Cabrera, Mac whiz, helped us over the rough spots. Many thanks to JoAnn and the two Jennifers at Portable Press.

There's a lot of fun ahead—so stop wasting your valuable puzzle time reading this silly thing and turn the page!

—Stephanie Spadaccini

FREE ADVICE

A handful of helpful hints from some high-profilers. Pay attention—you could learn something.

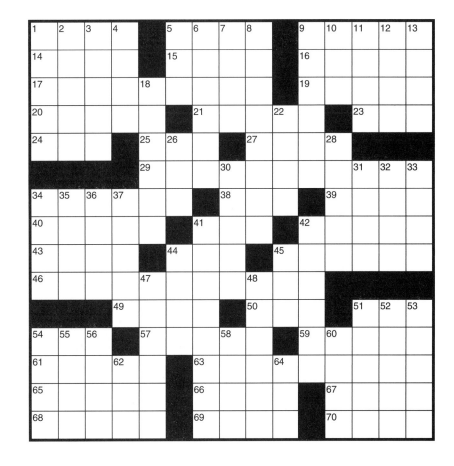

ACROSS

1 Spielberg classic
5 "Sweater girl" Turner
9 How you get spam
14 Adidas competitor
15 By and by
16 One way to be in love
17 "The only way to keep your health is to eat what you don't want, drink what you don't like, and do what you'd rather not."
19 Einstein type
20 "...he had some cows, ___"
21 Sound of the South?
23 Cancún loc.
24 Camera type, initially
25 Director Spike
27 Prefix with stat
29 "Never go to a doctor whose office plants have died."
34 Out of the rain
38 ___ de plume
39 Bring home the bacon
40 Owned apartment
41 Cabinet dept.
42 Come forth
43 *On the Waterfront* director Kazan
44 Under the weather
45 Flu symptom
46 "A woman's dress should be like a barbed-wire fence: serving its purpose without obstructing the view."
49 "This round's ___"
50 Yale student
51 Computer's core, briefly
54 Road service org.
57 Havens
59 Ace, à la Nolan Ryan
61 Lands' End competitor
63 "To succeed with the opposite sex, tell her you're impotent. She can't wait to disprove it."
65 Stadium
66 Zenith

67 Art Deco designer
68 All set
69 Final or midterm, e.g.
70 Bloodhound's clue

DOWN

1 Inspector Dalgliesh's creator P. D. ___
2 To no ___ (in vain)
3 Electrician, at times
4 H. H. Munro's pen name
5 Postgraduate pursuit
6 Ancient head wreath
7 Film genre since the '40s
8 Wolverines' home
9 Logo
10 Scratch or dent
11 Inspector Dalgliesh's first name
12 Nastase of tennis

13 Mountain cat
18 City in Spain or Ohio
22 Call from a grammatical owl?
26 Prior to, in poetry
28 Overweight
30 ___-Saxon
31 Comfort
32 Actress Penélope
33 Proposer's prop
34 Uses a Zamboni
35 ___ contendere
36 Scissors sound
37 The Gem State
41 Night prowler
42 Six outs
44 Alpo rival
45 Salt, to Sartre
47 Sort of

48 Prepares for another battle
51 Swiss ___ (beet variety)
52 Little old Ford
53 Out-and-out
54 Not quite shut
55 Farm parcel
56 Neighborhood
58 Doily material
60 Sandwich cookie brand
62 Put a stop to
64 Up to now

ANSWER, PAGE 201

NUMEROLOGY

Just in case you don't have enough numbers in your life, here are some
more. See if you can choose the correct number to fill in the blanks.

17	**71**	**1,860**	**164,848**
25	**200**	**17,508**	**350,000**
50	**295**	**38,387**	**366,144**

1. At any given time, there are _____ people traveling in airplanes.

2. A person swallows _____ times during an average meal.

3. Kareem Abdul-Jabbar scored ____ points over his entire career.

4. A healthy slug can travel _____ yards a day.

5. A pelican can hold _____ pounds of fish in his beak.

6. In 2003, _____ people in Germany were arrested for "offensive gestures."

7. If the elevators were broken in the Empire State Building you'd have to climb
   _____ steps to get to the top.

8. As of 2004, Japan had _____ industrial robots at work.

9. There are _____ species of penguin.

10. About 100 people die every minute; the number of people who are born in the same
    time span is about _____.

11. The number of calories a person consumes during a one-hour phone call is _____.

12. There are _____ islands in the Indonesian archipelago.

ANSWER, PAGE 201

* * * * *

RELAX, ALREADY!

Within 12 hours, how long does it take the average American to feel relaxed on a vacation?

ANSWER, PAGE 201

MONSTERS, INC.

Look out, because we've hidden 48 of the scariest movie-monster names and titles in the Dracula-shaped grid below. Once you've found all of them, the leftover letters will reveal the ending of the 1958 movie *The Blob* and why that should worry us today.

```
I                                                           F
K                                                           R
S   T                                                   H   A
W   P                                                   R   N
O   G   E                                           E   E   K
Z   R   C   C                       Y   C           P   K   S   E
A   E   A   F   I               W   R   H   M           O   O   I   E   N
W   M   F   P   Z   E           E   O   I   I       E   E   L   N   T   S
E   L   R   T   T   A   S           C   L           H   I   I   N   G   A   T
K   I   E   E   N   O   S   D   N   H   D   D   F   R       T   R   S   O   E   K   B   E
I   N   H   P   P   P   R   E   D   A   T   O   R   P   M   F   R   A   D   E   M   O   N   I
M   S   T   E   I   P   D   S   E   D   I   T   E   A   O   A   B   S   T   T   O   N   A   N
H   E   A   D   E   V   I   L   T   O   H   W   N   M   C   N   N   W   O   R   E   G   M   T
T   H   E   F   L   Y   M   R   S   R   A   B   O   D   Y   S   N   A   T   C   H   E   R   S
H   R   L   P   O   Y   B   T   E   L   U   T   F   R   M   E   N   J   B   A   T   O   O   T
    R   C   K   E   O   S   T   W   H   N   H   T   A   M   S   K   E   L   E   T   O   N
M   O   R   L   O   C   K   E   A   T   S   H   C   U   S   E   N   I   A   N   E   D
    S   B   H   O   O   N   H   L   E   K   E   U   M   E   N   F   N   L   P   R
    I   G   O   R   T   P   T   L   D   A   C   L   S   N   A   I   T   R   A   M
        G   U   T   R   O   F   I   H   E   O   A   E   F   M   D   E   G   O
        N   G   S   L   O   Z   O   R   R   L   J   R   E   S   O   O
            B   T   H   D   U   F   N   A   E   E   L   N
            E   C   O   S           T   D   D   B
            R   T   G   E           L   Y   D   I
            G   I   N               H   Y   S
            E   W   I               R   K   I
            I   D   H               M   R   V
            S   E   T               W   U   N
            T   K                   E   I
            N   C                   G   A
            A   I                   E   R
        M   I   W                   R   N   G
```

ALIEN	FREAKS	MICHAEL MYERS	SERPENT
ANTS	FREDDY KRUEGER	MIKE WAZOWSKI	SKELETON
BASILISK	GHOSTS	MORLOCK	*SPECIES*
BLOB	*GODZILLA*	MR. HYDE	SPIDER
BODY SNATCHERS	GORT	*(THE) MUMMY*	*(THE) TERMINATOR*
CARRIE	*GREMLINS*	NORMAN BATES	*THE FLY*
CHILDREN OF THE	HAUNTED HOUSE	*PHANTOM OF THE*	*THE OMEN*
CORN	*(THE) INVISIBLE MAN*	*OPERA*	*(THE) THING*
DEMON	JACK THE RIPPER	*POLTERGEIST*	WICKED WITCH OF
DEVIL	*JAWS*	*PREDATOR*	THE WEST
DRACULA	*KING KONG*	RAPTORS	WOLF MAN
DRAGON	LEATHERFACE	ROBOTS	WORMS
FRANKENSTEIN	MARTIANS	*RODAN*	

ANSWER, PAGE 201

LOONEY LAWS: THE QUIZ

Oh, sure, it's illegal in Stockton, California, to wiggle while you dance; everybody knows that. But are you familiar with these other laws that are actually on the books?

1. In Jonesboro, Georgia, it is illegal to say the words...

   a. "oh, boy!"
   b. "William Sherman"
   c. "cheese grater"

2. In Carmel, California, you need a permit if you want to wear...

   a. a brown hat
   b. high-heeled shoes
   c. German lederhosen

3. Well, I never! In Chicago, it is against the law for...

   a. "grossly fat"
   b. "ill-smelling"
   c. "exceedingly ugly"

 ...people to appear in public.

4. In California, you are allowed to possess one...

   a. antique glockenspiel
   b. bear gallbladder
   c. recipe for meatloaf

 ...but not two.

5. In Salem, West Virginia, you could be in trouble with the law if you leave home without...

   a. locking your front door
   b. knowing where you're going
   c. informing your neighbors first

6. In Arizona, you are not allowed to let your donkey sleep in...

   a. a bathtub
   b. a tree
   c. the nude

7. The children of Mesquite, Texas, are legally prohibited from having...

   a. "magazines of a comic nature"
   b. "pets younger the child"
   c. "unusual haircuts"

8. Oh, sure, it's okay when cops do it! In Paulding, Ohio, it IS legal for a police officer to...

   a. bite a dog
   b. curse in church
   c. kiss strangers on the street

9. Six days a week, it's fine, but on Sunday in Detroit, a man is not allowed to...

   a. scowl at
   b. wink at
   c. tickle

 ...his wife.

10. If you're changing a light bulb in Victoria, Australia, then you're breaking the law unless...

   a. you wear protective goggles
   b. you're a licensed electrician
   c. you recycle the old bulb

ANSWER, PAGE 201

WILDE ABOUT OSCAR

Oscar Wilde has let plenty of the bon mots drop. And now it's your turn. Just drop the letters from each vertical column—but not necessarily in the order in which they appear— into the empty squares below them to spell out the three quotes, reading from left to right. Words may wrap around from one line to the next; black squares signify the spaces between words.

1.

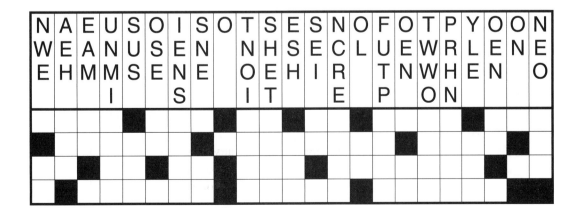

2.

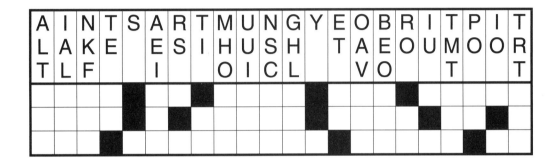

3.

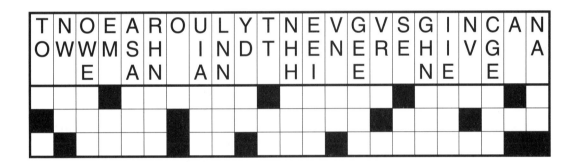

ANSWER, PAGE 201

CELEBRITY RUMORS

Being in the limelight brings all sorts of perks. But some of the nonperks are nasty rumors that celebrities sometimes have a hard time living down. Do you know which of these rumors are true and which are false?

1. Movie critic Gene Siskel, of TV's *Siskel & Ebert*, stipulated in his will that he wanted to be buried with his thumb pointing upward (the "thumbs up" sign being the seal of approval on the show).

2. Vanna White of *Wheel of Fortune* starred in a stage version of *The Diary of Anne Frank*. Her performance was so bad that when the Nazis came into the house, people in the audience stood up and shouted, "She's in the attic!"

3. Cher had her lowest pair of ribs surgically removed to make her waist look slimmer.

4. *Playboy* magazine founder Hugh Hefner used to place a number of small stars on the cover of his magazine to indicate how many times he'd slept with that month's cover girl. If he found her satisfactory, he placed them inside the "P" of the magazines masthead. If he was disappointed, he placed them next to the "P."

5. Iron Eyes Cody, the famous "crying Indian" of the "Keep America Beautiful" anti-littering ad campaign of the 1970s, was actually Italian.

6. Sigmund Freud wrote papers praising cocaine for two drug companies: Merck & Company and Parke, Davis & Company, who at the time were the leading makers of cocaine-based pharmaceuticals.

7 J. Edgar Hoover was a cross-dresser and, in fact, was once introduced at a party in New York as "Mary," wearing a wig, a black dress, lace stockings, and high heels.

8. Gazillionaire Bill Gates was christened William Henry Gates III, and now likes to be known officially as Bill Gates III. When the letters of the latter name are converted into ASCII, a standard computer code, they add up to 666, the traditional number of the Antichrist.

9. John Wayne didn't fight in World War II even though he was a healthy 34-year-old at the time of Pearl Harbor; instead he applied for a deferment for dependency reasons (he had four children at the time). He told his friends that he intended to enlist after he made one or two more movies, but he never did.

10. The Grateful Dead's Jerry Garcia played guitar with only nine fingers; the tenth finger had been chopped off by his older brother when he was a kid.

ANSWER, PAGE 202

THE QUOTABLE JOHN

We've taken three little-known but fascinating factoids we found in Uncle John readers and translated them into cryptograms by simple letter substitution.

    For instance, if we encoded UNCLE JOHN, he might end up looking like this: BRJAQ TLPR, where U = B, N = R, and so on. The letter substitutions remain constant throughout any one cryptogram, but they change from one cryptogram to the next. Here are some hints: A lot of words end in E, S, Y, R, and D; a single letter is usually an A or I; and look for words that begin with the same two-letter combination—those letters might stand for TH, as in THE, THAT, THEY, and so on. Proper nouns and capitalized terms are preceded by an asterisk (*).

"I" Am Not a Camera

UDF PESF "*IGAEI" DEX PG SFEPHPV. WGKPAFT *VFGTVF

*FEXUSEP FZRBEHPFA, "UDF BFUUFT *I DEX MFFP E

WELGTHUF JHUD SF. HU XFFSX E XUTGPV, HPOHXHLF XGTU

GW BFUUFT."

Something Completely Different

UJ NDXFJ, *ZYIJP *RPJEYI VUF YI FY QUJT JEUJ DJ GYKQM

YIQP UJJXUGJ U GKQJ NYQQYVDIL, VEDGE ZTUIJ,

UGGYXMDIL JY JET *RPJEYIF, "DIFYZIDUGF,

DIJTQQTGJKUQF, UIM SKXLQUXF."

When in Rome

IRLUNI LDLQTNT EP *QPSLC IPRTYNQI GPQ HQLUNQJ YC

HLEERN DNQN ACPDC LI "LTTYKEI." NUNCEFLRRJ, EVN

ENQS KLSN EP SNLC L MNQIPC DVP DLI L IRLUN EP

LCJEVYCZ.

ANSWER, PAGE 202

I LOVE A PARADE

And who doesn't? Use the clues scattered here and there to figure out
when these parades first started, then put them in chronological order.

Chinese New Year Parade – San Francisco
The Chinese New Year celebration can be traced back almost into prehistory, but this version is a lot
more recent, having been started by the Chinatown Chamber of Commerce in the same year that *Flower
Drum Song* hit Broadway. Held in early February, the parade features Gum Lung, a 200-foot long
dragon, drawn through the streets by 100 members of White Crane, a San Francisco martial arts group.

St. Patrick's Day Parade – New York City
Given the rather "fluid" nature of the postparade celebrations—and to the possibly inferior record-
keeping of pre-independence America—confusion over the exact date the first parade was held is no
surprise. But we can make an educated guess based on the first year that a military unit led the parade.

The Rose Parade – Pasadena
The first parade was mounted to show off the warmth and fertility of Southern California, but it wasn't
until 1902 that the organizers thought of tagging on a football game. Michigan trounced Stanford (49-0)
that year, to the embarrassment of the Californians. It would be another 16 years before they tried
football again.

Mardi Gras Parade – New Orleans
Mardi Gras came to New Orleans in 1743, celebrated with costume balls by the well-to-do and chaotic
street revelry by the lesser mortals. It wasn't until nearly a century later that the parade brought some
order—but not all that much—to the chaos.

The First Ticker-Tape Parade – New York City
The Wall Street area was the perfect route for victory parades because of the instant decorations it
produced: tons and tons of ticker tape. The first official parade of its kind was a spur-of-the-moment
affair celebrating the dedication of the Statue of Liberty.

The Mummers Parade – Philadelphia
The Swedes and the English brought the New Year's mummer tradition to the U.S. In it, groups of men
(no women allowed!) went house to house presenting costume plays in hopes of some reward: money or
some kind of seasonal treat. By the turn of the new 20th century the tradition evolved into a parade.

Santa Claus Parade – Toronto
Eaton's department store started their annual Santa Claus Parade (featuring one float) to attract
customers. But the thousands of onlookers took their Christmas shopping to a rival store because, with
Santa installed on the premises, Eaton's was too crowded. The store continued the parade anyway, for
more than 75 years, until retiring from the parade biz in the 1980s.

Macy's Thanksgiving Day Parade – New York City
The first-generation immigrants who worked at Macy's wanted to celebrate their new American
holiday—Thanksgiving—with the kind of festivals they loved and left in Europe. So they dressed up as
clowns and sheiks and knights and cowboys, and borrowed 25 live animals from the Central Park Zoo.
The first parade drew 250,000 onlookers. The big balloons appeared a little later, in 1927.

ANSWER, PAGE 202

YOU'RE INVITED TO A POTTY

Actually, we've got 38 potties, all of them synonymous with
"bathroom." See if you can fit them into the grid, crossword-style.

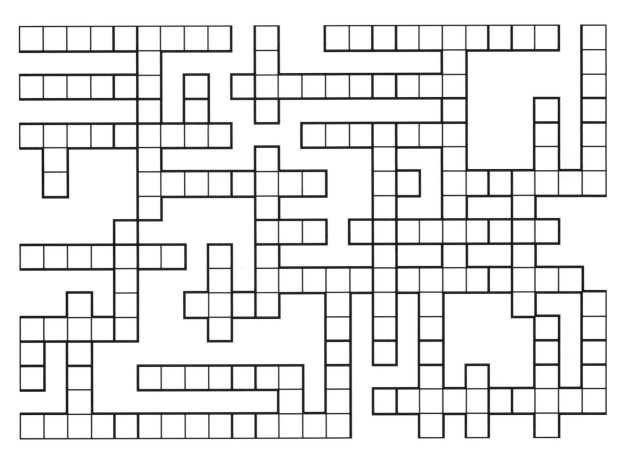

2-letter word
WC

3-letter words
Bog
Can
Lav
Loo
Pan
Pot

4-letter words
Bank
Head
Jane
John

5-letter words
Biffy
Gents'
Privy
Toidy

6-letter words
Kermit
Ladies'
Wizzer

7-letter words
Crapper
Flusher
Leakery
Library

Out back
Pissoir
Pit stop
Showers

8-letter words
Outhouse
Restroom

9-letter words
Cloakroom
Litter box
Necessary

10-letter words
Chamber pot
Honey wagon
Porta-Potty
Powder room

11-letter word
Water closet

14-letter words
Comfort station
Porcelain altar

ANSWER, PAGE 203

R.I.P.

The engravings on gravestones don't have to be all that grave.

ACROSS

1 "Leaving on ___ Plane"
5 Part of a public lecture, maybe
10 Heats in the microwave
14 Evan ___, senator from Indiana
15 Mohican of fiction
16 Nicollette's *Desperate Housewives* role
17 Pulitzer-winning screenwriter James ___
18 Como's home
19 Longtime Georgia pol Sam
20 **Mel Blanc's epitaph**
23 Turn frigid
25 1.5 volt battery
26 Casual Friday castoff
27 **With 49 Across, Frank Sinatra's epitaph**
31 Some still-life objects
33 Match maker?
34 Mad as a wet ___
35 Opposite of 35 Down
36 **Sonny Bono's epitaph**
42 Long in the tooth
43 U.S.S., in the U.K.
44 Rapper Mos ___
46 Stage, moonwise
49 **See 27 Across**
52 "You've got mail" co.
53 Bio. or chem.
55 ___ Penh, Cambodia
56 **George Burns and Gracie Allen's epitaph**
61 From ___ (all-inclusive)
62 Unattached
63 Grown-up eft
66 Graham, the Galloping Gourmet
67 Bob Dylan's "___ Believe You"
68 1997 Fonda title role
69 Notion
70 Early PC interface
71 Multiscreen cinema suffix

DOWN

1 Former hoopsters' org.
2 Crying ___ (nonstop tears)
3 Some canines
4 Boston's nickname
5 Go cold turkey
6 Aardvark's lunch
7 Pac-10 overseer
8 TV premiere of 4/2/78
9 Sanctuaries, old-style
10 Stoic of ancient Greece
11 Most attendees of R-rated films
12 Little digit
13 It's wise to come to them
21 Gorilla
22 Green Bay star Brett
23 Part of T.G.I.F.
24 David's longtime co-anchor
28 Molt
29 Tokyo ceremony
30 Words before money or bag
32 Loser to D.D.E.
35 Opposite of 35 Across
37 Dawn goddess
38 Made holy, biblically
39 Heathrow Airport clock setting (abbr.)
40 Rosie who was on daytime TV
41 Animated lost fish
45 Not neut. or masc.
46 New York's governor
47 Was owlish?
48 Popular vote winner of 2000
49 Turns over the podium
50 ___-Locka, Florida
51 Exercise for passing the bar?
54 *The Chosen* author Potok
57 Pound the poet
58 Crucifix
59 The "A" in A.D.
60 Figures out
64 Teensy
65 John Ritter's dad

ANSWER, PAGE 202

WOULD YOU RATHER LIVE IN...

In *Uncle John's Slightly Irregular Bathroom Reader*, we coupled the names of real American towns like Can Do, North Dakota, with Defeated, Tennessee. Unscramble the letters to figure out where you'd rather live.

1. _ _ _, Mississippi, or _ _ _ _, Mississippi
   UNS   NOMO

2. _ _ _, West Virginia, or _ _ _ _ _, Alabama
   ARW   AECEP

3. _ _ _ _, Kansas, or _ _ _ _, Oklahoma
   CORK   LORL

4. _ _ _ _, Virginia, or _ _ _ _, Tennessee
   ETUD   LOOS

5. _ _ _ _, Hawaii, or _ _ _ _ _ _, Kentucky
   AAPP   EMIMUM

6. _ _ _ _ _, Louisiana, or _ _ _ _, Georgia
   TASTR   TOPS

7. _ _ _ _ _ _ _ _, Oklahoma, or _ _ _, Oklahoma
   GARTISHT   YAG

8. _ _ _ _ _ _, Oregon, or _ _ _ _ _ _ _, Indiana
   GRIBON   UPTARER

9. _ _ _ _ _ _ _ _ _, Ohio, or _ _ _ _ _, Ohio
   VELID   WONT   GLANE

10. _ _ _ _ _ _, Kentucky, or _ _ _ _ _ _ _, Kentucky
    BRITLYE   TESCUJI

11. _ _ _ _ _ _ _, California, or _ _ _ _, Michigan
    SAPIREDA   LEHL

12. _ _ _ _ _ _ _ _ _ _, Montana, or _ _ _ _ _ _, Montana
    RUGHYN   REOSH   LERFLU

ANSWER, PAGE 203

IT'S LIKE...A SIMILE

A simile is a figure of speech in which two dissimilar elements are compared using the words "like" or "as." Match the front end of each simile (1-10) to the back end that seems most appropriate (a-j).

_____ 1. "Alimony is like…
_____ 2. "Dressing a pool player in a tuxedo is like….
_____ 3. "Eating responsibly at McDonald's is like…
_____ 4. "Giving money and power to government is like…
_____ 5. "Hubert Humphrey talks so fast that listening to him is like…
_____ 6. "Naming a national forest after Ronald Reagan is like…
_____ 7. "Sex at 90 is like…
_____ 8. "Trying to get the presidency to work is like…
_____ 9. "Trying to sneak a fastball past Hank Aaron is like…
_____ 10. "Writing about music is like…

a. buying oats for a dead horse."
b. dancing about architecture."
c. giving whiskey and car keys to teenage boys."
d. going to a strip club for the iced tea."
e. naming a day-care center after W. C. Fields."
f. playing pool with a rope."
g. putting whipped cream on a hot dog."
h. trying to read *Playboy* with your wife turning the pages."
i. trying to sew buttons on a custard pie."
j. trying to sneak the sunrise past a rooster."

ANSWER, PAGE 203

* * * * *

UNCLE OSCAR'S BIG NIGHT #1

We've taken some Academy Award-winning actors and actresses and the movies they won Oscars for (which were also Best Picture winners) and mixed them up in two ways. First, we scrambled the letters in all the names and titles. Then we mixed up the order of the columns. The numbers that follow each anagram reflect the number of letters in the names; for example, Jamie Foxx would be (5 4). Can you unscramble the names and titles and match them up again?

The Stars	**The Films**
1. NO JADE FAN (4 5)	a. INTENT PIG HEADPHONE (2 8 3 5)
2. BLACK LAGER (5 5)	b. PEACHTREE HAS LINT (6 2 3 5)
3. HE LENT HUN (5 4)	c. TREK NOW (7)
4. CHEF RIP NET (5 5)	d. GOAD EGOTIST ASS (2 4 2 2 4)
5. IF LADS YELL (5 5)	e. GO HIM, CONE ME (6 4)

ANSWER, PAGE 203

DEPP PERCEPTION

Directions: The grid contains a quotation that reads from left to right. The words in it wrap around to the next line; the black squares signify the spaces between the words.

Start by answering as many of the clues as you can. Write your answers on the numbered dashes, then transfer the letters to the correspondingly numbered squares in the puzzle grid.

As an extra-added bonus (or a tool to use if you get stuck), if you read the first letters of the words in the word list in sequence, you'll find an acrostic—a hidden message about the subject of the quotation.

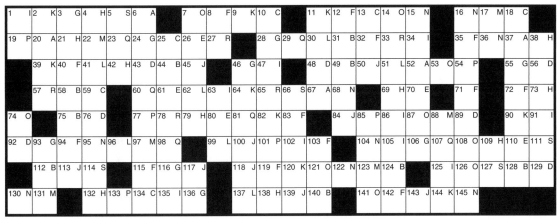

A. America's Cup racer

‾6‾ ‾67‾ ‾37‾ ‾20‾ ‾52‾

B. NCAA football champs of 2002 (2 wds.)

‾44‾ ‾58‾ ‾49‾ ‾75‾ ‾124‾ ‾31‾ ‾112‾ ‾128‾ ‾140‾

C. Underdogs seek them

‾134‾ ‾10‾ ‾13‾ ‾59‾ ‾25‾ ‾18‾

D. Imitations; petty thefts

‾43‾ ‾92‾ ‾48‾ ‾129‾ ‾76‾ ‾56‾ ‾89‾

E. Large African antelope

‾26‾ ‾80‾ ‾61‾ ‾70‾ ‾110‾

F. Doris Day movie musical of 1957 (3 wds.)

‾115‾ ‾103‾ ‾142‾ ‾40‾ ‾12‾ ‾35‾ ‾32‾ ‾72‾ ‾71‾
‾83‾ ‾94‾ ‾119‾ ‾8‾

G. Great director who never won an Oscar

‾116‾ ‾46‾ ‾93‾ ‾106‾ ‾3‾ ‾24‾ ‾55‾ ‾28‾ ‾136‾

H. Author of *Devil in the White City* (2 wds.)

‾138‾ ‾42‾ ‾73‾ ‾38‾ ‾79‾ ‾21‾ ‾109‾ ‾132‾ ‾69‾ ‾4‾

I. Legal order to refrain

‾105‾ ‾135‾ ‾1‾ ‾91‾ ‾47‾ ‾125‾ ‾102‾ ‾63‾ ‾86‾ ‾34‾

J. Commuter's daily purchase

‾113‾ ‾117‾ ‾45‾ ‾84‾ ‾139‾ ‾118‾ ‾143‾ ‾100‾ ‾50‾

K. "Square" star of kids' TV

‾39‾ ‾9‾ ‾2‾ ‾82‾ ‾90‾ ‾144‾ ‾11‾ ‾120‾ ‾64‾

L. Deviled eggs garnish

‾30‾ ‾51‾ ‾137‾ ‾62‾ ‾96‾ ‾99‾ ‾41‾

M. Do a Hartford or Allstate task

‾17‾ ‾131‾ ‾97‾ ‾123‾ ‾22‾ ‾88‾

N. Oscar-winning director of *A Beautiful Mind* (2 wds.)

‾95‾ ‾130‾ ‾68‾ ‾16‾ ‾122‾ ‾145‾ ‾36‾ ‾104‾ ‾15‾

O. Colin Farrell title role of 2004

‾108‾ ‾141‾ ‾14‾ ‾74‾ ‾126‾ ‾87‾ ‾7‾ ‾53‾ ‾121‾

P. Bridge players often collect these

‾85‾ ‾77‾ ‾101‾ ‾19‾ ‾133‾ ‾54‾

Q. Ulysses' home town

‾81‾ ‾98‾ ‾107‾ ‾29‾ ‾60‾ ‾23‾

R. Once around, to Alan Shepard

‾78‾ ‾27‾ ‾65‾ ‾33‾ ‾57‾

S. Techie types

‾5‾ ‾66‾ ‾127‾ ‾114‾ ‾111‾

ANSWER, PAGE 203

THE CAT'S PAJAMAS

Some lingo from the Roaring Twenties—like "killjoy" and "nifty"—has survived the decades, but lots of other slangy terms need a bit of reviving. We've hidden 32 slang terms in all in the grid below, which is shaped like a fig leaf (the '20s name for a one-piece bathing suit). When you've circled all the list items in the grid, the leftover letters will reveal a few more examples of 1920s lingo. See the answer section for definitions.

```
            O S N C                   E I S N
          A D H I R T       Y       W H I H L B
        E M E E A D N S       F     R O M T E R I M
          E F B R B U T T O N S H I N I N G
            A F M R A L A E R I F L K
          C H O I C E B I T O F C A L I C O T O
        T I B G M T E V E A S I H O K I L L J O Y
      A R L L P A A E S S C H R Y D D A D R A G U S
    O O L E T E R R W T T O E E R N W O D E P I P I S
    A I A Y E C T A O U E R P E T T I N G P A N T R Y
  N B F G K A W N     P I N E X M A     N J W H J O F S
  P E N A T I K       R L S M T I D     S O A A L O O
  T A C N S Y         D U R H D I C S R     E C C S O S
    E S T W           E N A R I N N H G       L K L G
                    A S E H E T G R U E I
                  U B G P C D G U H L T R B
                  E B U I U D G I G H Y E Y
                  P A N T H E R S W E A T S
                  E M I T R E H T A F T
                  I S T H M Z E E I B A
                  C K S E E R N A T
                    O F E A C
                    A R R
                    B
```

BEARCAT	DOG JOCK	OLIVER TWIST
BIG SIX	FACE STRETCHER	PANTHER SWEAT
BILLBOARD	FATHER TIME	PETTING PANTRY
BREEZER	FIG LEAF	PIPE DOWN
BRILLO	FIRE ALARM	PRUNE PIT
BUTT ME	FIRE EXTINGUISHER	SHEBA
BUTTON SHINING	GOOFY	SHEIK
CAKE-EATER	HIGH HAT	SUGAR DADDY
CHARLIE	JACK	SWANKY
CHOICE BIT OF CALICO	KILLJOY	TEN MINUTES
CORN SHREDDER	NIFTY	

ANSWER, PAGE 204

FRANKENSTEIN'S GREAT-AUNT TILLIE

Don't laugh. It was a real movie, released in 1983. And it did very well at the box office. (Now, that's *not* real.) But what of these other monstrosities? Can you tell the real movies from the fakes?

Frankenstein Meets the Space Monster (1965)
A simple story. NASA builds a robot named Frank and sends it into space, where it meets a space monster and goes berserk.

Jesse James Meets Frankenstein's Daughter (1966)
Frankenstein's granddaughter, Maria, tries to capture Jesse James and his sidekick to turn them into monsters.

Frankenstein General Hospital (1988)
Frankenstein's 12th grandson tries his experiments in the basement of a modern hospital.

My Brother, Frankenstein (1985)
The doctor's younger, jealous brother is exiled to the Island of the Undead where—between zombie attacks—he sets about trying to build a better monster than his brother's.

Frankenstein Created Woman (1967)
Baron Frankenstein installs the soul of a recently executed—but innocent—man in the body of a young woman named Christina, after which Christina starts to kill the people whose false accusations led to the man's execution.

Frankenstein Island (1981)
Frankenstein's great-great-grandaughter, Sheila, is living on a remote island among a tribe of bikini-clad warrior women descended from aliens when a group of balloonists lands on the island.

Frankenstein's Castle of Freaks (1974)
Using his "Electric Accumulator," Count Frankenstein (played by Rossano Brazzi) brings back Goliath the Caveman, Kreegin the Hunchback, and Ook the Neanderthal Man.

Frankenstein of the Future (1984)
The monster highjacks his creator's time machine and goes far into the future, where he meets mutants, robots, and "people" just like himself.

The Erotic Adventures of Frankenstein (1972)
A Spanish-French concoction in which Dr. Frankenstein is attacked by a naked vulture woman who tears him to shreds. While investigating the death, Frankenstein's daughter, Vera, is captured by the evil Cagliostro the Wizard and is forced to undergo the erotic adventures alluded to in the title.

Frankenstein on Campus (1970)
A college student plots to turn his fellow students into monsters. *Creature Features Movie Guide* said of it: "If you can sit through this tripe, go to the head of the class."

ANSWER, PAGE 203

GIVE 'EM HELL, HARRY

Harry S Truman was famous for saying, "The buck stops here." Here are some other things Harry said. The letter-substitution code changes from one quote to the next.

ALL THE PRESIDENT IS

1. UCC HLY EWYKNSYVH NK NK U DCPWNMNYS EJOCNZ

WYCUHNPVK TUV ALP KEYVSK LNK HNTY MCUHHYWNVD,

XNKKNVD, UVS XNZXN VD EYPECY HP DYH HLYT HP SP ALUH

HLYR UWY KJEEPKYS HP SP UVRAUR.

A PESSIMIST IS

2. H BCWWFPFWY FW QRC UTQ PHOCW ZFLLFVJGYFCW QL

TFW QBBQAYJRFYFCW HRZ HR QBYFPFWY FW QRC UTQ

PHOCW QBBQAYJRFYFCW QL TFW ZFLLFVJGYFCW.

A POLITICIAN IS

3. I GATYSYWYIQ YC I RIQ MPA XQOJVCSIQOC DABJVQRJQS. I

CSISJCRIQ YC I GATYSYWYIQ MPA'C EJJQ OJIO KAV KYKSJJQ

LJIVC.

THREE THINGS CAN RUIN A MAN

4. OMKXX OMQBHW VYB KZQB Y EYB—ESBXC, RSIXK, YBJ

ISEXB. *Q BXTXK MYJ YBC ESBXC, *Q BXTXK IYBOXJ RSIXK,

YBJ OMX SBAC ISEYB QB EC AQDX QW ZR YO OMX MSZWX

KQHMO BSI.

ANSWER, PAGE 204

DOUBLE TIME

In which we present a familiar story, crossword-style.

ACROSS

1 Be a part of
6 Sick person's refuge
9 "The game's ___!"
14 Louisiana bowlful
15 Lennon's wife
16 African mammal most dangerous to humans
17 Shipments to the smeltery
18 Lawn ornament with a cone-shaped hat
20 Committed perjury
21 Where a famous tale begins
23 Carson's replacement
24 College org.
25 Keeps after annoyingly
27 Knock out, in a way
30 Ones assembled in the tale
35 Like half the letters in "knight"
37 Design sunk below the surface
38 Improbable, as chances
39 DDE's predecessor
40 "___ it the truth!"
41 Warrior famous for his heel
44 Meal
46 Where the tale ends
48 *"In excelsis ___"*
49 Being, in Latin
50 Notable periods
52 Former German capital
55 Tale revealed by assembling puzzle answers of this length
60 Aid in crime
61 Instrument for Ravi Shankar
62 "...___ saw Elba"
63 Sits on a 59 Down after baking
65 Rug rat
66 Brightest star in Orion
67 African exporter of black tea
68 Half of a donkey imitation
69 Grassy mound

DOWN

1 Wide-eyed
2 Doctor's goal
3 Govt. agents
4 *Peer Gynt* playwright
5 Admonishment to a dog
6 Dwarf tree
7 *The Dukes of Hazzard* spin-off
8 Not recessive, as a gene
9 Depressing sound?
10 Plays a much-needed role
11 Floyd the barber cut his hair
12 Ready for business
13 Heading on a list
18 A beanstalk led to his home
19 Glorify
22 Digitize artwork
26 HS cume
27 State that borders Tibet
28 "Roger" follower in radio talk
29 Nobel Peace Prize winner Root
31 ___ payment (skip one month)

32 Work featuring 41 Across
33 Step 2 on a shampoo bottle
34 ___ voce (in an undertone)
36 Notably
39 Enclosed, in legalese
42 Superiors of sgts.
43 Endures
44 Less common
45 Coup d'___
47 Empathize
51 Oktoberfest "klinker"
52 Upright chair part
53 Duck portrayer in *Peter and the Wolf*
54 Gas for signs
56 Plains Indian
57 Thus
58 Film holder
59 Part of a window
64 Arg.'s locale
66 *The Jungle Book* author, initially

ANSWER, PAGE 205

RHYMES WITH TICKLES

...and prickles. Some memorable insults from Don Rickles, a.k.a. "The King of Zings."

1.

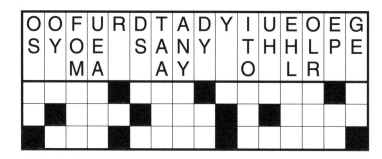

2.

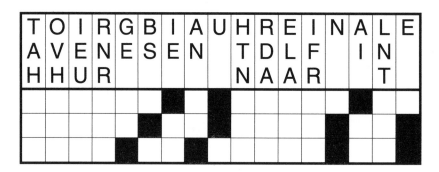

3.

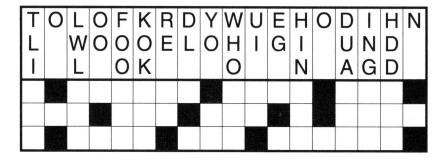

ANSWER, PAGE 203

* * * * *

A KISS IS JUST A KISS?

What do they call a French kiss in France?

    a. A French kiss
    b. An English kiss
    c. It doesn't have a name, silly.

ANSWER, PAGE 203

FILL IN THE LIMERICKS

More of Uncle John's favorite forms of wordplay, presented in puzzle-book style.
Fill in the blanks (one for each missing letter) to complete these classics.

1. A daring young lady of Guam
   Observed, "The Pacific's so __ __ __ __,
   I'll swim out for a lark,"
   But she met a large __ __ __ __ __ __ —
   Let us now sing the Twenty-third __ __ __ __ __.

2. An accident really uncanny
   Occurred to my elderly __ __ __ __ __ __;
   She sat down in a chair
   While her false teeth were __ __ __ __ __
   And bit herself right in the __ __ __ __ __.

3. A sea serpent saw a big tanker,
   Bit a hole in her side and
      then __ __ __ __ __ __ __.
   It swallowed the crew
   In a minute or __ __ __,
   And then picked its teeth with
      the __ __ __ __ __ __.

4. There was an old monk in Siberia
   Whose existence grew
      gradually __ __ __ __ __ __ __
   Till he broke from his cell
   With an ear-piercing __ __ __ __
   And eloped with the
      Mother __ __ __ __ __ __ __.

5. An opera star named Mariah
   Who tried to sing higher and __ __ __ __ __ __
   Hit such a high note
   That it stuck in her __ __ __ __ __ __.
   Now she sings with the heavenly __ __ __ __ __.

6. An oyster from Kalamazoo
   Told a friend he was feeling quite __ __ __ __.
   "For," he said, "as a rule
   When the weather turns __ __ __ __
   I invariably get in a __ __ __ __."

7. A nervous young girl named Camille
   Once went up in a big Ferris __ __ __ __ __.
   But when halfway around
   She looked down at the __ __ __ __ __ __
   And it cost her her five-dollar __ __ __ __.

8. As they fished his new plane from the sea,
   The inventor just chortled with __ __ __ __.
   "I shall build," and he laughed,
   "A submarine __ __ __ __ __
   And perhaps it will fly. We shall __ __ __."

9. There was a young cutie named Florence
   Who for kissing professed
      great __ __ __ __ __ __ __ __ __ __.
   But once she'd been kissed
   And found what she'd __ __ __ __ __ __,
   She cried till the tears came
      in __ __ __ __ __ __ __.

10. A hapless young gent named McBride
    Fell into an outhouse and __ __ __ __.
    His unfortunate brother
    Fell into __ __ __ __ __ __ __
    And now they're
       in-turd __ __ __ __-__ __-__ __ __.

ANSWER, PAGE 205

RED ALL OVER

STOP! Danger! Oh, and good luck. Those are just a few of the things the ever-popular color red symbolizes in various cultures. See if you can fit all 34 shades of red into the grid, crossword-style.

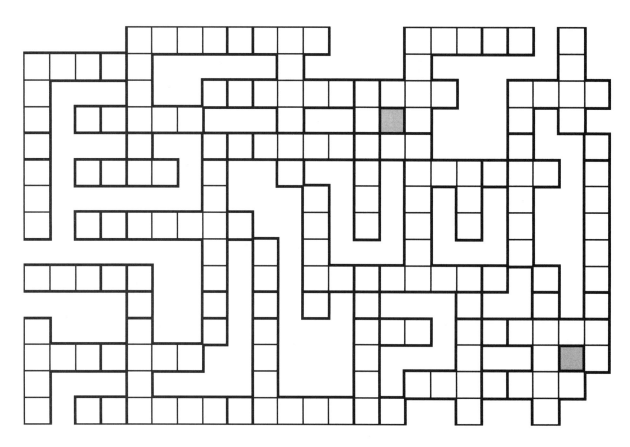

3-letter words
Bay
Red

4-letter words
Beet
Pink
Rose
Wine

5-letter words
Brick
Coral
Mauve
Poppy
Umber

6-letter words
Auburn
Cerise
Claret
Garnet
Maroon
Rufous
Sienna
Titian
Tomato

7-letter words
Carmine
Fuchsia
Magenta
Oxblood
Paprika
Scarlet

8-letter words
Cinnabar
Cramoisy
Pimiento

9-letter words
Cranberry
Vermilion

10-letter words
Candy-apple
Fire-engine

13-letter word
Lustie-gallant

ANSWER, PAGE 205

CRAZY EIGHTS

It's said that good things come in threes, but we think they come in eights. First, circle all 39 words and phrases in the eight-sided grid below (COLUMBIA is doing double duty as a college and a river; it appears in the grid just once). When you've found them all, the leftover letters will reveal another category and its eight members in chronological order.

President

```
            C O L U M B I A
          P R A E S N I W D E
        N T C E L I Z A B E T H
      P P R I N C E T O N A S U S
      E S O F R H O E M D W C V I T R
    N G S I W O D R A V R A H Y N O Y I
    N M S A P L E C U C A R T R S E M W A J
    S E I H A B R R G O I U E N T M A R Y O
    G T O S R E N J B L G E R F O M T F E A
    I R U O S S I M Y O R S S T R O O N M N
    A D W S L I I S F R A O K N R M E U O I
    R N O N E R S W O A E T I W A I S K T E
    L I G L Y I A S C D L L I H C R U H C
    O L O P A R M H I Q E N N N R Y Y U C H
      A L G S T E E B P R R G R G I T A S
      F O R N L L T Y P N L E R T N T
        A M A C K E N Z I E Y E I L
        Y O N R A C N D W L P I
          L S D A V I D O S L
            N T E U Q O R C
```

Vegetables in V-8 Juice	Kids in *Eight Is Enough*	Ivy League Colleges	Defunct Olympic Sports	Longest Rivers in North America
BEETS	DAVID	BROWN	CROQUET	CHURCHILL
CARROTS	ELIZABETH	COLUMBIA	GOLF	COLORADO
CELERY	JOANIE	CORNELL	LACROSSE	COLUMBIA
LETTUCE	MARY	DARTMOUTH	POLO	MACKENZIE
PARSLEY	NANCY	HARVARD	POWER	MISSISSIPPI
SPINACH	NICHOLAS	PENN	BOATING	MISSOURI
TOMATOES	SUSAN	PRINCETON	RUGBY	RIO GRANDE
WATERCRESS	TOMMY	YALE	TUG-OF-WAR	YUKON
			WATERSKIING	

ANSWER, PAGE 205

THEY ALMOST GOT THE ROLE

Some movie roles are so closely associated with particular
actors that it's hard to imagine they weren't the first choice.

ACROSS

1 Energizes (with "up")
5 Audacity
10 Somewhat
14 *E pluribus* ___
15 Kind of cuisine
16 Green stone
17 He lost the role of Forrest Gump to Tom Hanks because he was still considered a comic actor
19 Points of no return?
20 Football linemen (abbr.)
21 Org. for Agassi
22 Pan Am rival
24 Bowler or boater
25 Conjures up
28 Raison d'___
30 Trackman Lewis
31 He had already filmed several scenes as Marty McFly in *Back to the Future* but was fired when Michael J. Fox decided to do it
35 Wrigley Field's wall cover
37 Get a table for one
38 "___ no questions..."
41 Cause of some '60s trips
42 ___ blanche
43 Short hit to the green
45 Do moguls
46 He turned down the chance to play the Pinball Wizard in *Tommy* because Elton John convinced him that he'd look ridiculous in the garish costumes
48 CD component?
52 Will be, to Doris Day
53 Circus Hall of Fame city
55 Cave dweller
57 Mos. and mos.
59 Actor Kilmer
60 Rimsky-Korsakov's *Le Coq* ___
61 Prefix with distant or lateral
63 He was the first choice to play Batman but decided against it because he didn't think he could be an action star
66 Clump of hair
67 Edit
68 Change for a five
69 Ump's call
70 Turns down
71 Fourposters, e.g.

DOWN

1 Part of CPA
2 2001 movie about British code breakers
3 Astronomical flasher
4 Abbr. on a shirt label, maybe
5 East Indian relish
6 1966 Paul Newman title role
7 Fr., Ger., Ital., etc.
8 *"L'___, c'est moi"*
9 Gulf vacation spot
10 1977 double-platinum Steely Dan album
11 Guy who believes in "better dead than wed"
12 Light bulb, in comics
13 Word with acid or road
18 ___ tai
23 Snipe at
26 Quick look
27 Afternoon naps
29 Tums alternative
32 Bounder
33 Explosive letters
34 Alphabet ender
36 Church anteroom
38 From left to right (abbr.)
39 "___ 'nuff!"
40 Child's play
41 Underhanded
44 Listen, in olden days
45 Wisps of hair
47 Gorge
49 Common antiseptic
50 High, and not on life
51 Pet
54 Having a high pH (abbr.)
55 Goes to the $2 window
56 Pale bluish-green
58 Big rig
62 Brooklyn trailer?
64 Irritate
65 High tennis shot

ANSWER, PAGE 206

ALABAMA KLEENEX

A lot of places have slang terms named after them. Take, for instance, the "Chicago violin," a.k.a. the Thompson submachine gun. See if you can match these other names (1-10) with their definitions (a-j).

_____ 1. Alabama Kleenex

_____ 2. Arizona nightingale

_____ 3. Arkansas wedding cake

_____ 4. Boston strawberries

_____ 5. Colorado Kool-Aid

_____ 6. Full Cleveland

_____ 7. Michigan bankroll

_____ 8. Missouri featherbed

_____ 9. Tennessee toothpick

_____ 10. West Virginia coleslaw

a. a '70s-style leisure outfit: loud pants and shirt, white belt, white loafers

b. a big wad of small-denomination bills with a big bill on the outside

c. a burro

d. baked beans

e. chewing tobacco

f. Coors beer

g. cornbread

h. a raccoon bone

i. a straw mattress

j. toilet paper

ANSWER, PAGE 205

* * * * *

ALL YOU NEED IS LOVE...

The Beatles' "All You Need Is Love" was recorded on the 1967 BBC special *Our World* and televised via worldwide satellite link-up. Now let's see if you can link up JOHN to PAUL in six steps by changing one letter at a time to form a new word, and then do the same from NEED to LOVE in six steps. (Warning: you may have to use—how shall we say?—a "bathroom word" to get through the latter in the proposed six steps, but if you'd rather not use it, you can do it in seven.)

JOHN

_____

_____

_____

_____

_____

PAUL

NEED

_____

_____

_____

_____

_____

LOVE

ANSWER, PAGE 206

CREATURE FEATURE

Directions for solving are on page 13.

A. 1956-84 TV soap/mystery series (4 wds.)

$\overline{145}$ $\overline{65}$ $\overline{11}$ $\overline{183}$ $\overline{152}$ $\overline{157}$ $\overline{57}$ $\overline{45}$ $\overline{72}$ $\overline{166}$ $\overline{115}$
$\overline{187}$ $\overline{95}$ $\overline{141}$

B. Defenders of beliefs or ideas

$\overline{122}$ $\overline{119}$ $\overline{158}$ $\overline{135}$ $\overline{18}$ $\overline{113}$ $\overline{53}$ $\overline{76}$ $\overline{84}$ $\overline{43}$

C. Classic building toy since 1916 (2 wds.)

$\overline{159}$ $\overline{146}$ $\overline{41}$ $\overline{132}$ $\overline{92}$ $\overline{49}$ $\overline{7}$ $\overline{154}$ $\overline{111}$ $\overline{186}$ $\overline{97}$

D. Star of *The Matrix* trilogy (2 wds.)

$\overline{182}$ $\overline{131}$ $\overline{6}$ $\overline{93}$ $\overline{99}$ $\overline{5}$ $\overline{155}$ $\overline{91}$ $\overline{27}$ $\overline{38}$ $\overline{81}$

E. Writer/star of TV's *Punk'd* (2 wds.)

$\overline{32}$ $\overline{106}$ $\overline{56}$ $\overline{3}$ $\overline{36}$ $\overline{116}$ $\overline{13}$ $\overline{161}$ $\overline{64}$ $\overline{107}$
$\overline{25}$ $\overline{136}$ $\overline{46}$

F. Burl Ives' *Cat on a Hot Tin Roof* role (2 wds.)

$\overline{79}$ $\overline{105}$ $\overline{70}$ $\overline{156}$ $\overline{126}$ $\overline{61}$ $\overline{101}$ $\overline{167}$

G. Confidential, to a politician (hyph.)

$\overline{4}$ $\overline{138}$ $\overline{44}$ $\overline{148}$ $\overline{77}$ $\overline{153}$ $\overline{169}$ $\overline{40}$ $\overline{30}$ $\overline{59}$ $\overline{179}$ $\overline{83}$

H. Becoming apparent

$\overline{112}$ $\overline{69}$ $\overline{63}$ $\overline{190}$ $\overline{58}$ $\overline{21}$ $\overline{133}$ $\overline{100}$ $\overline{47}$

I. *Angels in America* playwright (2 wds.)

$\overline{42}$ $\overline{151}$ $\overline{33}$ $\overline{188}$ $\overline{178}$ $\overline{118}$ $\overline{15}$ $\overline{114}$ $\overline{54}$ $\overline{139}$ $\overline{17}$

J. Ancient Mesoamerican people on the Gulf of Mexico

$\overline{98}$ $\overline{127}$ $\overline{171}$ $\overline{96}$ $\overline{140}$ $\overline{129}$

K. Slowest of wit

$\overline{23}$ $\overline{29}$ $\overline{75}$ $\overline{52}$ $\overline{66}$ $\overline{10}$ $\overline{55}$

L. Fits together harmoniously

$\overline{8}$ $\overline{102}$ $\overline{87}$ $\overline{82}$ $\overline{109}$ $\overline{120}$ $\overline{20}$ $\overline{128}$ $\overline{149}$

M. Show embarrassment, perhaps

$\overline{110}$ $\overline{165}$ $\overline{50}$ $\overline{88}$ $\overline{12}$

N. De Koven song popular at weddings (3 wds.)

$\overline{180}$ $\overline{121}$ $\overline{175}$ $\overline{60}$ $\overline{173}$ $\overline{150}$ $\overline{68}$ $\overline{142}$ $\overline{22}$ $\overline{35}$ $\overline{172}$

O. Available to anyone who really wants it (3 wds.)

$\overline{176}$ $\overline{191}$ $\overline{168}$ $\overline{28}$ $\overline{184}$ $\overline{117}$ $\overline{124}$ $\overline{1}$ $\overline{164}$ $\overline{71}$

P. Prima ballerina who danced for Balanchine (2 wds.)

$\overline{130}$ $\overline{170}$ $\overline{94}$ $\overline{67}$ $\overline{89}$ $\overline{2}$ $\overline{14}$ $\overline{80}$ $\overline{162}$
$\overline{181}$ $\overline{125}$ $\overline{144}$ $\overline{73}$ $\overline{34}$ $\overline{26}$

Q. Signs of an economic downturn

$\overline{74}$ $\overline{143}$ $\overline{9}$ $\overline{62}$ $\overline{137}$ $\overline{103}$ $\overline{163}$

R. Mystery/romance author Janet

$\overline{78}$ $\overline{37}$ $\overline{134}$ $\overline{177}$ $\overline{48}$ $\overline{19}$ $\overline{123}$ $\overline{90}$ $\overline{85}$

S. Heroine created by the above (2 wds.)

$\overline{147}$ $\overline{24}$ $\overline{86}$ $\overline{16}$ $\overline{104}$ $\overline{108}$ $\overline{174}$ $\overline{185}$ $\overline{31}$
$\overline{189}$ $\overline{160}$ $\overline{51}$ $\overline{39}$

ANSWER, PAGE 206

DUMB JOCKS

Sports figures aren't always the most articulate people. Maybe they should just keep their mouths shut. Nah…then there'd be no room for their feet. The letter-substitution code remains the same for all the quotes.

Don King: EQHK QX IOK YFKNI *QKCLZDEKE LT IOK JQFVC ONRK

WKKT WDLVI WU *CQTNVC *IFDHZ.

George Steinbrenner: *CNRLC *PQTK LE LT N PVNEE WU OLHEKVX

JLIO IOFKK QF XQDF QIOKF ZVNUKFE.

Joe Theismann: OK'VV INAK UQDF OKNC QXX NI IOK WVLTA QX N

ONI.

Broadcaster Jerry Coleman: TKGI DZ LE *XKFTNTCQ *YQTMNVKM, JOQ

LET'I ZVNULTY IQTLYOI.

Basketball coach Jack Kraft: IONI JNE IOK TNLV IONI WFQAK IOK

PQXXLT'E WNPA.

Outfielder Mike Greenwell: *L'H N XQDF-JOKKV-CFLRK-ZLPADZ IUZK

QX YDU, NTC EQ LE HU JLXK.

Baseball Manager Danny Ozark: KRKT *TNZQVKQT ONC OLE *JNIKFYNIK.

Pitcher Larry Anderson: LX N YDU LE N YQQC XNEIWNVV OLIIKF,

CQKE IONI HKNT *L EOQDVC IOFQJ OLH N WNC XNEIWNVV?

ANSWER, PAGE 206

* * * * *

IS IT HOT IN HERE?

What is the only U.S. state that has never recorded a temperature below 0°F?

ANSWER, PAGE 205

I DON'T GET IT

That's okay, you're not supposed to. But if you insist, here's what you've got to do: For each set below, rearrange the location of the second line (known loosely as the "punch line") so that it matches the correct first line. You'll know you've got it right if you hear yourself groan.

1. **Q:** Why can't a bicycle stand alone?
   A: Fruit flies like a banana.

2. **Q:** What's the definition of a will?
   A: A jab well done.

3. **Q:** Time flies like an arrow…
   A: A case of wife or death.

4. **Q:** What's the definition of acupuncture?
   A: Always use condiments.

5. **Q:** In democracy it's your vote that counts.
   A: But she broke it off.

6. **Q:** Did you hear about the man who fell into an upholstery machine?
   A: You've seen a mall.

7. **Q:** She had a boyfriend with a wooden leg.
   A: He's fully recovered.

8. **Q:** When you've seen one shopping center…
   A: In feudalism it's your count that votes.

9. **Q:** Practice safe eating.
   A: Because it is two-tired.

10. **Q:** What's the definition of a shotgun wedding?
    A: A dead giveaway.

ANSWER, PAGE 207

* * * * *

INCENTIVE TO WIN?

True or false: At the end of every New York Yankees home game, the P.A. system plays the song "New York, New York": the Frank Sinatra version if they win…and the Liza Minnelli version if they lose.

ANSWER, PAGE 205

THE SUSPENSE IS KILLING ME!

We've hidden the name of a famous person and six of his works in this puzzle. See if you can find them all before this book blows up.

ACROSS

1 Name on a range
6 Part of a full house
10 Shipment to a brewery
14 Gathering at chez Stein, e.g.
15 Julie's *East of Eden* role
16 Pennsylvania city
17 Musical Joplin
18 Doubt
20 Something worthless may be for this
22 Under control
23 Ex-Cubs slugger
24 Size at Thom McAn
25 Tide alternative
26 Small application
28 Wild excitement
31 ___ Schwarz
34 Community of plant and animal life
37 Heaven, in *Field of Dreams*
39 He said "Drama is life with the dull bits cut out"
43 Good spot to chill
44 Craters of the Moon National Monument site
45 Pasture sound
46 Lunatic
49 Acct. accrual
51 Choker in the jungle
52 Eminent start?
54 "I Ain't Marchin' Anymore" singer
58 "Enough already!"
61 It can prevent that sinking feeling
63 Infamous
65 Sonata movement, perhaps
66 Power group
67 Iditarod destination
68 *Dead Souls* writer
69 Folding money
70 A ton
71 ___ Mountain, Georgia

DOWN

1 Some profs.
2 Studly
3 Fugard drama *A Lesson From* ___
4 "Pretty nice!"
5 Prefix with lock or knock
6 ___ deux
7 Grounds for divorce
8 Org. that gets many unhappy returns
9 Swashbuckler's weapon
10 Car doc
11 *"Un bel di"* is one
12 Figure on England's shield
13 Be predisposed
19 As to
21 Bridge declaration, perhaps
27 Justice Fortas
28 Greek salad topping
29 Go like blazes
30 Community ctr.
31 Sols' neighbors
32 Crooked
33 Does in
35 Ted Turner's birthplace
36 Central
38 Wanted poster abbr.
40 Ed Sullivan's orchestra leader
41 Powwow participant
42 Sweetie
47 Coconut fiber
48 What bigots do a lot of
50 As well
52 Downright
53 Gets up
55 Michael Crichton novel set in Africa
56 Wore
57 Pinched
58 *Market Week* airer
59 Green-skinned girl in *Star Wars*
60 Western Indians
62 Work units
64 Tic-tac-toe win

BANANARAMA

Everything you always wanted to know about bananas, but were too busy to ask.

1. Americans eat an average of (75, 110, 376) bananas a year per person.

2. The (banana split, banana milkshake, Banana Bag brand of multivitamins) was invented in 1904 by Dr. David Strickler, a drugstore pharmacist in Latrobe, Pennsylvania.

3. Technically, the banana is (a vegetable, a berry, a legume).

4. A banana has about (75, 110, 376) calories.

5. The banana has been Fruit of the Month (more than any other fruit, second only to apples, never).

6. The song, "Yes, We Have No Bananas" was an enormous hit in 1923. True or false: The popularity of the song spurred a new dance craze: dancing the Charleston on banana peel-covered floors.

7. The hugely popular Chiquita Bananas advertising jingle, created in 1944, was once played on the radio (75, 110, 376) times in one day.

ANSWER, PAGE 208

* * * * *

AND MUDDY WATERS?

Small crostic puzzles are solved just like the big ones (directions on page 13) but the first letter of the fill-in words **do not** spell out a hidden message.

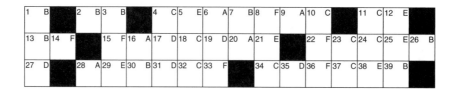

A. Gets lighter

　—　—　—　—　—
　16　20　6　9　28

B. Part of Newfoundland, or a dog

　—　—　—　—　—　—　—　—
　26　1　2　30　13　7　3　39

C. Personal slight one might have to suffer

　—　—　—　—　—　—　—　—　—
　11　32　4　18　34　24　23　37　10

D. She won the Nobel Prize for both Physics and Chemistry

　—　—　—　—　—
　19　35　17　31　27

E. Slugger Barry Bonds's team

　—　—　—　—　—　—
　25　5　38　21　29　12

F. Send up smoke, perhaps

　—　—　—　—　—　—
　22　36　33　14　15　8

HO, HO, HO!

Chances are it isn't Christmas—or even December—but we've made out a list anyway. Fill in the blanks of the 28 Christmas songs with the missing words or phrases (the number of blanks indicates the number of words that you're looking for). After you've found them all in the grid reading across, down, and diagonally, the leftover letters will reveal a Christmas fact that's pure Uncle John. If you need help filling in the blanks, a list of the missing words is included on the answer page.

```
                        E
                    Y   E   M
                A   E   R   N   N
            R   M   A   T   O   Y   H
        H   S   E   R   A   E   L   C   I
    S   T   T   H   E   N   L   O   G   R   I
        E   I   D   A   E
        A   L   E   P   N   M   N
    M   S   H   T   T   S   I   W   W
    Y   A   D   T   L   H   T   F   E   O   I
W   O   N   D   E   R   L   A   N   D   R   N   N
K   J   B   G   M   B   N   I   C   H   O   L   A   S   E
    E   S   D   T   E   H   U   G   R
    N   R   L   H   S   A   R   N   S   I   F
W   A   R   F   L   L   N   I   G   H   T   H   O
A   E   O   U   A   L   S   S   S   B   O   R   N   W
I   H   W   L   S   S   S   A   N   T   A   C   L   A   U   S   T
                    N   W   M
                    A   O   A
                    P   T   S
                    R   I   L
```

All I Want for Christmas Is My ___ ___ ___

Angels From the Realm of ___

Angels We Have Heard on ___

Away in a ___

Deck the ___

Do You Hear What I ___?

The First ___

Frosty the ___ ___

God Rest Ye Merry, ___

Good King ___

Hark! The Herald Angels ___

Have Yourself a Merry Little ___

I Heard the Bells on Christmas ___

I Saw Mommy Kissing ___ ___

I Saw Three ___

It Came Upon the Midnight ___

It's the Most Wonderful Time of the ___

Jingle ___

Jolly Old Saint ___

Joy to the ___

The Little Drummer ___

O Come, All Ye ___

O Little Town of ___

Rocking Around the Christmas ___

Rudolph the Red-Nosed ___

Santa Claus Is Coming to ___

Silent ___

Winter ___

ANSWER, PAGE 207

THAT'S DR. PRESIDENT TO YOU, BUDDY!

A few facts, both naughty and nice, about some of the men who've inhabited the White House.

ACROSS

1 Stomach upsetter
5 Months, to Mohawks
10 Popular sneakers
14 Shoot up
15 Schoolyard retort
16 "Acoustic Soul" singer India.___
17 Sunday song
18 Raison ___
19 Come down with
20 The only president who earned a Ph.D.
23 Fuss
25 "Balderdash!"
26 Connect
27 The first president to use a telephone in the White House
32 Place to remember
33 Drew's *50 First Dates* costar
34 Let out, in a way
35 Title role for Arnold
37 Pierre's st.
41 Start of a seasonal tune title
42 Musical's orchestration
43 The only president who turned his entire salary over to charity
47 Take the podium
49 Loser to DDE
50 Canal zone?
51 The only president arrested for speeding on a Washington street
56 Unfit for polite society
57 Biting nails, maybe
58 Old West lawman
61 List-ending abbr.
62 Surname of a seasonal visitor
63 Pill bottle
64 Fast-food chicken stop, affectionately
65 Sleepy co-worker
66 *Sesame Street*'s ticklish one

DOWN

1 Smoker's litter
2 Acting reluctant, but not, really
3 Helen Reddy's 1972 hit
4 Bond foe
5 Critter to steer clear of
6 Code of silence
7 Aware of
8 Scand. land
9 Be hot and bothered
10 *The Prophet* author Gibran
11 Wiped out
12 Remnant on a golf course
13 Evil start?
21 Approximately
22 List entry
23 Open slightly
24 Ex-Senator Bumpers of Arkansas
28 CPR provider
29 Vacation's purpose, briefly
30 Agcy. concerned with meds
31 Holm who played Bilbo Baggins
35 Ernie Banks, notably
36 Corrida cry
37 Sgt., e.g.
38 Fit together nicely
39 Sphere of expertise
40 Either star of *Tea and Sympathy*, 1956
41 Big, clumsy boats
42 Slammin' Sammy
43 Time of glory
44 Kindergarten equipment
45 Tries to come home on an out
46 Unorthodox opinion
47 More certain
48 Disney dog
52 Cut glass?
53 Ward on TV
54 Ginger cookie
55 Actress Campbell
59 One of the flock
60 Mideast org.

ANSWER, PAGE 208

LUCKY AT CARDS...

You bought the potato chips and the beer, but there's one thing you forgot. This handy-dandy list of superstitions that's sure to change your luck. And we mean that in a good way. But first you'll have to figure out which of the following will bring you the good kind of luck or the other.

	Good	Bad
1. Being dealt the four of clubs, especially in the first hand	____	____
2. Blowing or spitting on the cards	____	____
3. Dropping a black ace on the floor	____	____
4. If you're a man, playing in a room where there's a woman present unless she's playing with you, and vice versa if you're a woman	____	____
5. Lending another player money during a game	____	____
6. Letting anyone put their foot on the rung of your chair	____	____
7. Picking up your cards before they've all been dealt	____	____
8. Playing cards:		
a. in a room with a dog in it	____	____
b. on a bare table	____	____
c. with a cross-eyed person	____	____
9. Seeing a hunchback on your way to the game	____	____
10. Singing or whistling during a game	____	____
11. Sitting on a handkerchief	____	____
12. Sitting with your legs crossed	____	____
13. Wearing a pin in your lapel	____	____
14. Wearing an article of dirty clothing	____	____

ANSWER, PAGE 208

* * * * *

THE EYE HAS IT

How did the term "private eye" come about?

a. In the Civil War, soldiers who spied on enemy positions were called the "eyes of the army," or simply "eyes." (The new term replaced spy, which many recruits felt was derogatory.) When private detectives began operating in the 1880s (and mostly doing surveillance work), it seemed natural to call them "private eyes."

b. When Allan Pinkerton formed the Pinkerton National Detective Agency, he chose a large open eye as his logo (along with the motto "We Never Sleep"). Detectives have been known as "private eyes" ever since.

c. The original term was "private I," where "I" stood for investigator. But many listeners misinterpreted it as "private eye"—including newspaper men, who officialized the incorrect spelling in print.

ANSWER, PAGE 206

PROVERBIAL WISDOM

You know that "a stitch in time saves nine," but there are countless other proverbs that you may never have heard of. We've taken some of our favorites from other countries and translated them by simple letter substitution code. In this particular puzzle, **the letter substitution stays constant throughout the whole list**. For further instructions see page 7.

China: VYA UOTACV SMN SC XAVVAF VYOM VYA XACV WAWQFE.

Germany: TAV EQDF YAOI WA WQFA VYOM O PDMMAT VQ EQDF CVQWOBY.

Niger: YQTI O VFDA PFSAMI HSVY XQVY YOMIC.

Zimbabwe: SP EQD BOM HOTN EQD BOM IOMBA. SP EQD BOM VOTN EQD BOM CSMR.

Spain: IQM'V RSKA WA OIKSBA, RSKA WA WQMAE.

Greece: ISCVFDCV VYA OIKSBA QP VYA SMVAFACVAI.

Japan: POTT CAKAM VSWAC, CVOMI DU ASRYV.

Wales: XA YQMQFOXTA EQDFCATP SP EQD HOMV VQ OCCQBSOVA HSVY YQMQFOXTA UAQUTA.

France: SP QMTE VYA EQDMR NMAH; SP QMTE VYA QTI BQDTI.

Italy: VYA XACV HOE VQ RAV UFOSCA SC VQ ISA.

ANSWER, PAGE 208

* * * * *

CAPITAL IDEA!

Piece of cake, armchair traveler! Just find the capital cities lurking in these words and phrases.

1. FROM EAST TO WEST
2. CZECHOSLOVAKIA
3. RUBBERNECKER
4. OPPORTUNIST
5. MENTAL IMAGE
6. ANCHOR STEAM ALE

ANSWER, PAGE 208

MIX-UP AT THE HONKY-TONK

When it comes to country songs, Uncle John naturally tends toward sentiments like "If I Can't Be Number One in Your Life, Then Number Two on You." We've taken ten other country song titles and removed two key words from each one. Can you put the 20 removed words back in their proper places?

BANISTER	BOTTLE	GOD	GOODBYE
GREYHOUND	KIDS	KISS	LETTER
LOBOTOMY	ME	MINE	NOTHIN'
OVER	RACKET	RING	SHAFT
SPLINTER	TONGUE	UGLY	YUCK

1. "Get Your _____ Outta My Mouth 'Cause I'm Kissing You _____"
2. "I Would Have Wrote You a _____, But I Couldn't Spell _____!"
3. "I'd Rather Have a _____ in Front of Me Than a Frontal _____"
4. "She Got the Gold _____ and I Got the _____"
5. "Tennis Must Be Your _____ 'Cause Love Means _____ to You"
6. "Thank _____ and _____ She's Gone"
7. "When the Phone Don't _____, Baby, You'll Know It's_____"
8. "We Used to Just _____ on the Lips But Now It's All _____"
9. "You Were Only a _____ As I Slid Down the _____ of Life"
10. "You're the Reason Our _____ Are So _____"

ANSWER, PAGE 209

* * * * *

HOLD ON TO YOUR HAT!

The letters of ten U.S. states are scrambled below, followed by the number of tornadoes they're visited with in an average year. Once you've unscrambled all the names, you'll know what states to avoid during twister season.

1.	ESAXT	124	_____
2.	HAKMALOO	52	_____
3.	ASANKS	47	_____
4.	DRIFOLA	46	_____
5.	KANBARES	37	_____
6.	AIWO	31	_____
7.	SILONILI	26	_____
8.	SIMIROSU	26	_____
9.	DORCOLAO	25	_____
10.	NAUSILAIO	25	_____

ANSWER, PAGE 209

THEY NEVER WON A GRAMMY

What do Diana Ross and the Beach Boys have in common? Not much, you would think. But in fact they're among the ranks of music legends who never took home a Grammy. Here are four more....

ACROSS

1 Basics
5 Item on a to-do list
9 Go for ___ (drive around)
14 Cotton bundle
15 Prefix with plasm
16 Anne Stiller, née ___
17 Actor Morales
18 A certain glow
19 Computer chip company
20 Hard-rock group that never won a Grammy
23 Medicare org.
24 One, in Italian
25 Lampoon
27 Classified information
31 Figure at Delphi
34 Different
35 Press
38 Open-handed blow
39 Sch. Woody Allen attended for a semester
40 When things don't go very well
43 Wall St. opening
44 Gremlins, at one time
46 Bryce Canyon locale
47 Like windows
49 Gather up the loot
51 Luau strings
53 Word with tiger or Lancer
56 Pitching stat
57 Personal datum
59 Guitarist who never won a Grammy
64 Suit material
66 Similar
67 Nod off
68 Threesome on a triceratops
69 Love, in tennis
70 A party to
71 Giza's land
72 First place?
73 Zilch

DOWN

1 Genesis son
2 Military fort
3 Wearing (with "in")
4 Search partner
5 Whistler on the range
6 "...___ of kindness yet"
7 Throat problem
8 Cute "bear"
9 Mozart's *Mass in* ___
10 Mem. of Congress
11 Country singer who never won a Grammy
12 Makes angry
13 *The Lion King* love interest
21 *Calendario* starter
22 Dry humor
26 Court figures, briefly
27 Sub's "ears"
28 Earliest forms of a word
29 Singer/songwriter/ guitarist who never won a Grammy
30 Ready flour for a recipe
32 Jacket flap
33 Lyric poem
36 Vitamin bottle abbr.
37 Diamond Head's island
41 Mushrooms and molds
42 Reject
45 Call, in poker
48 *Arabian Nights* hero
50 For laughs
52 Excited about
54 Impress mightily
55 Was partial to
57 Queens stadium
58 Soc. studies study
60 Take on
61 Columnist Barrett
62 Crocodile shirt company
63 TV's Warrior Princess
65 Econ. concern

ANSWER, PAGE 209

WOULD WE LIE TO YOU?

You bet we would! In this quiz, we explain the origins of some phrases that you may have wondered about. The only trouble is, we're offering too many explanations. Can you find the one true answer in each set?

1. Why does "not up to snuff" mean below standard?
   a. The use of finely-powdered tobacco, or snuff, was once nearly universal in England. Connoisseurs prided themselves on being able to judge the quality of snuff—and amateurs at tobacco-judging were scorned as being "not up to snuff."
   b. Originally, to call something "not up to snuff" was to say, literally, that it stank. The term was first applied to butchers' meat in 18th century America, which was often of dubious quality. Savvy customers would smell the meat before buying it, to make sure it wasn't rotten.
   c. "Up to snuff" is actually a mistaken derivation of the Middle English phrase *aptus enough*, which simply means "smart enough."

2. When people are sent to prison, why do we say they've been "sent up the river?"
   a. This phrase refers to the ancient Roman practice of sewing convicted criminals up in a sack (often with live animals also inside the sack, such as a dog, rooster, and/or viper) and tossing the sack into a river.
   b. After the mid-Atlantic states became free states, many slaves were illegally shipped southward on the Mississippi, or "sold down the river." Southerners caught engaging in this trade were consequently "sent up the river" (to a free state) to be sentenced.
   c. The phrase refers to New York landmarks: the river is the Hudson, and the prison is Sing Sing, which is upriver from the Big Apple. The phrase started out as a New York thing but like so many other New York things soon spread all over the country.

3. Getting married is referred to as "tying the knot." What knot are we talking about?
   a. The knot on the girdle worn by ancient Roman brides. Actually, it wasn't just one knot—the girdle was traditionally tied together with hundreds of knots, which the new husband had the responsibility of untying. (Given the inducement, he presumably found a way.)
   b. It refers to a symbolic piece of tied ribbon displayed on the church wall at old English weddings. If this "love knot" fell to the ground during the ceremony, the idea was that your marriage wouldn't last.
   c. Actually, the phrase is purely symbolic; it's not referring to a literal knot. The use of the knot as a symbol for marriage dates back to at least 300 B.C., when the poet Qu Yuan used it in his "Songs of Chu."

4. To fail miserably is to "lay an egg." Why?
   a. In a scathing review of an 1898 production of Chekhov's "The Seagull," George Bernard Shaw claimed that the actress playing Nina (the symbolic "seagull" of the title) "squawked her lines as if in the process of laying an egg." The phrase soon came to be applied to any poor performance.
   b. The phrase comes from the British sport of cricket. To lay an egg means to score no runs, and thus put a zero (or "goose egg") on the scoreboard.
   c. The phrase originally appeared in an Al Capp cartoon. A suspect running away from Fearless Fosdick drops a jewel he's stolen, prompting Fosdick to say, "He didn't just chicken out, he laid an egg!"

5. If you're blissfully happy, you're said to be "happy as a clam." Why are clams so happy?
   a. The idea is that clams, encased snugly inside their shells, are completely unaffected by the worries of the outside world.
   b. The original phrase was "happy as a clam at high tide." Clams would be happy at high tide because clam diggers can't dig them. The phrase was later shortened for convenience.
   c. It's a polite alteration of the phrase "happy as a Clem," with "Clem" being old British slang for an Aussie. As you might suspect, it was meant as a slur; the stereotypical Clem's "happiness" was really obliviousness (or, alternately, drunkenness).

ANSWER, PAGE 209

BAD HAIR DAYS

We've all had them: Michael Jackson's hair caught fire during a commercial, and Bill Clinton was (falsely) accused of tying up an airport runway for 56 minutes while he got an expensive haircut. We've collected a number of other hair-raising experiences, with a couple of ponytails—er, *phony* tales—among them. Can you spot the fake hair pieces?

THE ORIGINAL BAD HAIR DAY
According to a 1991 interview with comedian Garry Shandling, *Us* magazine referred to him as having complained about a "bad hair day" when he had said no such thing. A month after that, the phrase appeared in the *Los Angeles Times*, then in the *Toronto Star* (describing Robert De Niro), and then... everywhere. Garry Shandling, bad hair day pioneer!

THE WAR OF THE WHISKERS
King Louis VII of France married Eleanor of Aquitaine in 1137. Shortly thereafter, he shaved his beard, which shocked Eleanor: she found him ugly when she could see his face. Louis refused to grow the beard back, so she left him and married King Henry II of England. Louis refused to return Aquitaine, which he had gained when he married Eleanor, and Henry declared war. The "War of the Whiskers" lasted—get this—301 years.

CUT DOWN
In 1957, Mafia leader Albert Anastasia had fallen asleep in his chair while having his hair cut in a New York barbershop when two gunmen walked up to him and opened fire. Anastasia jumped up and tried to retaliate, but it was too late. He collapsed on the barbershop floor and died.

MODEL BEHAVIOR
In 1973, catalog model Jacques Cannard was doing quite well, in large part because of his luxurious mane of curly blonde hair. But his girlfriend Lorette eventually got sick of his preening and decided to play a prank on him. One night, after Jacques had passed out after a heavy evening of drinking, she slipped a "bald cap" over his head, making it look as if he'd lost all his precious hair. In the morning, when he looked at himself in the mirror, he screamed, just as Lorette had expected. What she didn't expect: The shock was so great that most of his hair turned gray, thus ruining his career. And the relationship.

CHÈVRE AND A HAIRCUT, TWO BITS
In 1993, a 31-year-old Dutch vagrant named Hans Hoffman robbed a bank of $15,000, telling the teller that he needed the money for a haircut and a piece of cheese. A few hours later, he walked into a police department, surrendered, and handed over the cash he'd stolen, which was all present and accounted for...minus the cost of a haircut and a piece of cheese.

COMING OUT AHEAD
The Borgias of Italy were well known for their ruthlessness, which extended into every corner of their lives. At a dinner ball, Lucrezia Borgia watched jealously as another woman was garnering great praise for her elaborate hairdo. Borgia sent her brother Cesare to engage the lady in a private talk. After the conversation, the woman went into a back room and returned to the party with a simple, unadorned hairdo. The other lady guests took the hint and from then on wore their hair in styles that wouldn't compete with Lucrezia's.

HAIR DIE
A 16th-century Austrian man named Hans Steingeger was well-known for having the longest beard in the world. Unfortunately, this proved to be his undoing. One day in September 1567, he was climbing the stairs to a council chamber in Austria and tripped on his own beard. This wasn't, alas, just a close shave; he fell down the stairs and died.

ANSWER, PAGE 209

WHAT'S YOUR SIGN?

Some say that people who believe in astrology are full of bull. We'd say that this bull is full of astrology. There are 36 words associated with astrology hidden in the Taurus-shaped grid below. You may know that the 12 zodiac signs are constellations, but did you know that the sun actually moves through those constellations plus one other? After you've found all the words in the grid, the leftover letters will tell you more about it.

```
O G R I V
        O                                    T       H
      L E                              E           A
      L                                V           R
      U                          I S T P H A C
      B                        R C S S S Q I H
        I R T R            G O A T E U I O E
      P E R C H A R T E I I R E P I A C R G R
      S N T T G N M H W N P I S R R C O S U N A
      Y L L N H E O D L I B R A I I S   O I A P
      C F I S H D H I O M N I U C C F   U P T
      H S N O I T A L L E T S N O C
      I S U I R A T T I G A S P R R
    R C S W A T E R B E A R E R N A C
    E E H   U A         S L T   B I H
    C E     R         S A         R
    N       T         C         E R
    A P     H E       S N   T B
    C E     A R       E R
```

AIR
AQUARIUS
ARCHER
ARIES
BIRTH DATE
BULL
CANCER
CAPRICORN
CHART
CONSTELLATIONS
CRAB
CUSP

EARTH
FIRE
FISH
GEMINI
GOAT
HOROSCOPE
HOUSE
LEO
LIBRA
LION
PISCES
PSYCHIC

RAM
RISING
SAGITTARIUS
SCALES
SCORPIO
SIGN
TAURUS
TWINS
VIRGIN
VIRGO
WATER
WATER-BEARER

ANSWER, PAGE 209

QUOTATIONARY

Familiar words defined in brand new ways. The letter substitution code remains the same throughout.

Animal: FJOYECMTK MTHYTEYG SQ BXZTEF EJ OJHY FYYGF ZVJWTG.

Camel: Z CJVFY GYFMKTYG SQ UJOOMEEYY.

Comedy: Z NWTTQ AZQ JN SYMTK FYVMJWF.

Cheese: OMXR ECZE QJW UCYA.

Gossip: ACYT QJW CYZV FJOYECMTK QJW XMRY ZSJWE FJOYJTY QJW GJT'E.

Guilt: ECY KMNE ECZE RYYBF JT KMHMTK.

Laughter: ECY FCJVEYFE GMFEZTUY SYEAYYT EAJ BYJBXY.

Playboy: Z OZT ACJ SYXMYHYF MT AMTY, AJOYT, ZTG FJ XJTK.

Stock market: Z AYZBJT ECZE GYFEVJQF BYJBXY SWE XYZHYF SWMXGMTKF FEMXX FEZTGMTK.

Sweater: Z KZVOYTE AJVT SQ Z UCMXG ACYT CMF OJECYV NYYXF UCMXXQ.

Tact: ECY ZSMXMEQ EJ GYFUVMSY JECYVF ZF ECYQ FYY ECYOFYXHYF.

ANSWER, PAGE 210

CIRCULAR REASONING

Sometimes we just get tired of the same old squares.

ACROSS

1 Rather stick-in-the-mud
6 Circles in a box
10 Circle in a rite
12 Hay bundles
13 It might be set for 7:00 a.m.
15 Media for Rembrandt
16 Hors d'oeuvres holder
17 The A in B.A.
18 Drug that's dropped
21 It gives people gas in Canada
23 Ending for many pastas
24 Circles cut out of 6 Across
26 Cardinals, on the scoreboard
27 Yale mascot Handsome ___
28 Land on the Nile
29 "___ just my Bill..."
30 What a chick first pecks at
31 Nuts' tool kit partners
32 Quite a lode
33 Bombay wrap
35 Gov. Pataki's bailiwick
36 *Wheel of Fortune* chance
37 Island off the Scottish coast
39 Cowboy's coil
40 "___ fast!" ("Take it easy!")
42 Pajama cover-ups
43 Circle in a workshop
47 Circle in a roll
48 Clinch the deal

DOWN

1 Beer, slangily
2 ___ Friday's (popular eatery)
3 Philip of *Kung Fu*

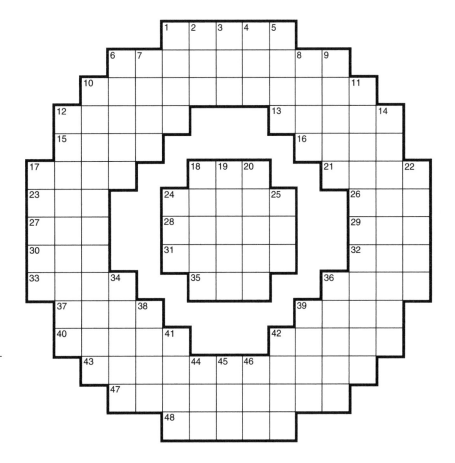

4 Verb suffix
5 ___ mater (brain membrane)
6 Many PCs
7 Praiseful verses
8 Pinball no-no
9 It's a trap
10 Crowded spot at the doctor's office
11 It can jump 20 times its body length
12 Like one who's gotten religion
14 Solving ends them
17 Presidential assistants
18 Enter a user name and password
19 In a foxy manner

20 Sects. at Macy's
22 Mary-Kate or Ashley
24 Lang. spoken in Israel
25 Peter, Paul, and Mary (abbr.)
34 Pentium chip maker
36 Not under the influence
38 Sparkling Italian wine
39 Architect Ludwig Mies van der ___
41 Klutzes
42 Invitation request
44 Jackie's sister
45 Opposite of ENE
46 Junior Olympics Games org.

YEAH, WRIGHT

Comic Steven Wright wows his fans with his own brand of existential humor.
Take, for example, "I was a subliminal advertising executive…but only for a second."

1.

2.

3.

ANSWER, PAGE 210

TOM SWIFTIES

You remember Tom Swift, boy hero? Well, he's returned to our pages for another round of painfully silly wordplay. Finish each sentence (1-10) with the word (a-j) that makes the most appropriate pun.

a. absentmindedly   c. crankily   e. dryly   g. glowingly   i. periodically
b. crabbily   d. cryptically   f. fruitlessly   h. half-heartedly   j. recklessly

_____ 1. "But I don't know how to start a Model-T Ford," Tom said…
_____ 2. "I can't help thinking about the people who aren't here," Tom said…
_____ 3. "I'll have a martini, minus the vermouth," Tom said…
_____ 4. "I'm waiting for my magazine to arrive," Tom said…
_____ 5. "I've never had a car accident," Tom said….
_____ 6. "My grandfather's buried over there," Tom said…
_____ 7. "The doctors removed my left ventricle," Tom said…
_____ 8. "This seafood platter doesn't taste fresh to me," Tom said…
_____ 9. "Three Mile Island? I used to live there," Tom said…
_____ 10. "Yes, we have no bananas," Tom said…

ANSWER, PAGE 210

* * * * *

THAT SINKING FEELING

Small crostic puzzles are solved just like the big ones (directions on page 13) but the first letters of the fill-in words **do not** spell out a hidden message.

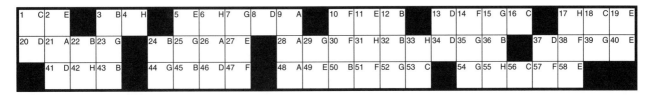

A. Turns the TV sound off
__ __ __ __ __
48 26 9 21 28

B. Realm of Yale et al. (2 wds.)
__ __ __ __ __ __ __ __ __
32 45 24 50 22 3 36 12 43

C. European city famous for its shroud
__ __ __ __ __
16 18 56 1 53

D. Golf course figures
__ __ __ __ __ __ __
20 41 37 13 34 46 8

E. West Pointers, after graduation
__ __ __ __ __ __ __ __
11 5 2 49 19 58 27 40

F. Kings, queens, dukes, etc.
__ __ __ __ __ __ __
47 14 10 38 57 51 30

G. Wild melee
__ __ __ __ __ __ __ __ __ __
23 44 15 35 39 54 7 25 52 29

H. Tried hard to achieve a goal
__ __ __ __ __ __ __
17 4 42 6 33 55 31

ANSWER, PAGE 210

FINAL NOTICE

A "politically incorrect" comment from Bill Maher, host of the former show of that name.

ACROSS

1 Part of a massage treatment
8 1985 Chevy Chase comedy
14 In the annals
16 Home of the Ramblers
17 **Start of a quip by Bill Maher**
19 Signal for a Vatican vote
20 Swear to
21 Winds down
22 Renovated a bathroom, maybe
25 Turkey seasoning
29 Paneled room
30 Soldier's pendant
35 **Part 2 of the quip**
37 Sunny, sandy stretch
38 Candy bar fillings
39 CN Tower locale
41 Ram in the zodiac
42 **Part 3 of the quip**
43 Cut off some more
45 Boston Bruins legend
46 Bluegrass banjoist Scruggs
47 Gives an answer
50 Vaulted church area
54 Android aboard the *Enterprise*
55 Listing on a mechanic's repair bill
60 **End of the quip**
63 Like "adult" books
64 Approach
65 Removes wiretaps
66 Fizzy drink

DOWN

1 Nerdy *Friends* character
2 U.S. motto word
3 Vivacity
4 At one's ___ and call
5 More treacherous, as a road
6 Silently agree
7 Increases
8 Proceeded smoothly
9 CNN host Dobbs
10 Brontë heroine
11 "Lonesome ___" (Ricky Nelson hit)
12 Dressed
13 *Airplane!* actor Robert
15 Louganis' talent
18 Roman sun god or Norse sun goddess
23 Do newspaper work
24 Guitar played on one's lap
25 Submarine detector
26 Prior to, in olden days
27 Astronaut's outfit
28 Rarin' to go
31 Sparkly stone
32 Tucker of country music
33 Role taker
34 Grave-robbing beast
36 Arafat of the P.L.O.
39 "Little Earthquakes" artist
40 Shrek, for one
42 Temple builder of ancient Mexico
44 Corpsmen
48 Golf hole posting
49 Was a double agent
50 Got 100 on
51 Use a fruit knife
52 High-hat type
53 "___, brute?"
56 Water color?
57 Longtime Kentucky coach Adolph
58 Jackson Five member
59 "___ the presses!"
61 Bo tree's fruit
62 Comedian Philips

ANSWER, PAGE 210

PERFECT 10 #1

The ten statements on this page are almost perfect, except that their numbers have been switched around. As a solving aid, we'll tell you that the numbers have been switched in pairs—i.e., if the number 1 should replace the 10, the 10 should also replace the 1. (That's just an example, of course.) Can you restore the perfect 10?

Worldwide, the average woman is **1** inch shorter than the average man.
The Danube River flows through **2** European countries.
A full moon is **3** times brighter than a half-moon.
There are **4** holes in a Ritz cracker.
A human eyeball weighs **5** ounces.
A "Big Band" is any band with **6** or more musicians.
A regulation hole in golf is no less than **7** inches deep.
Giant sequoia bark can be **8** feet thick.
According to criminal law, **9** people are necessary for a disturbance to be called a riot.
The average yawn lasts **10** seconds.

ANSWER, PAGE 211

* * * * *

DON'T LEAVE EARTH WITHOUT IT

Small crostic puzzles are solved just like the big ones (directions on page 13)
but the first letters of the fill-in words **do not** spell out a hidden message.

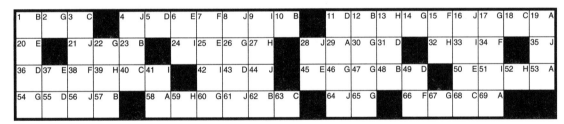

A. It follows "bell" and precedes "ball"

    ___ ___ ___ ___ ___
    58 53 19 29 69

B. Professional who'll likely fill you in

    ___ ___ ___ ___ ___ ___ ___
    57 62 10 1   12 23 48

C. Put the needle to

    ___ ___ ___ ___ ___
    68 40 18 63 3

D. Coin-op business

    ___ ___ ___ ___ ___ ___ ___
    5   55 36 43 11 31 49

E. Inform

    ___ ___ ___ ___ ___ ___
    37 25 50 6   45 20

F. Comic strip kid adopted by Uncle Ted

    ___ ___ ___ ___ ___
    66 34 7   38 15

G. Dapper Dan type (2 wds.)

    ___ ___ ___ ___ ___ ___ ___ ___ ___
    47 22 54 2   46 65 17 60 26

    ___ ___ ___
    67 14 30

H. Professional who'll likely put the needle to you

    ___ ___ ___ ___ ___ ___
    27 52 13 32 59 39

I. Follow, à la Kinsey Millhone

    ___ ___ ___ ___ ___ ___
    24 51 42 41 9   33

J. Honor bestowed on Paul McCartney and Elton John

    ___ ___ ___ ___ ___ ___ ___ ___ ___ ___
    4   56 61 8   35 64 21 16 28 44

ANSWER, PAGE 211

YOU BET YOUR SWEET PATOOTIE!

The grid below contains 23 slangy words and phrases from the 1930s, among them "thumber," '30s lingo for a hitchhiker, which is why the grid is shaped like a hand with outstretched thumb. So take things in hand and start by circling all the hidden lingo in the grid. When you're done, the uncircled letters will reveal one more phrase from the '30s and its definition. See the answer section for definitions.

```
                                                      T G R
                          H T A                     T S A O N
                   A D     S H H                  E S B F F O
              R R    C N I K U P E              L G K M F
              I E    K E Y Y M P R M          M E L O N
              E N F A I E S B R E S A      T L I D O
         S      R F M R I H E P L R E G Y M O Y
         G H    S B A F E O R L G T E D O C I E
         V L Y B A R N B U R N E R N T K O E
           I A M T A E T T S O R A A N T O T
              C M A C P A I R P C F T V O E O
              N P O K S I N C M L F T M E E
                 A U U I N G S I I I A N Y L
                 T R S R N H I L P C F N G
                    S I L B G T S J A R F
                    A P L O N G O T T
                       E P A Y O I O R E
                       B L B I N R Z A R
                       R D E L T N U R G E
```

ACKAMARACKUS	GRUNTLED	SKY-SHOUTING
BALLS-UP	INFANTICIPATE	SLIM
BARNBURNER	MELON	SPLIFF
CANDY LEGS	MILK BAR	SUPERETTE
CLIP JOINT	MODOCK	THE MAGOO
GAFF	PEN-FRIEND	THUMBER
GLAMOUR BOY	RIPPLE	TRAFFICATOR
GRAVEL	SHY-MAKING	

ANSWER, PAGE 211

FLUBBED HEADLINES

Uncle John scours the papers every day, hoping to find unintentionally silly headlines like MONTANA TRADED TO KANSAS CITY or MISSOURI WOMAN BIG WINNER AT HOG SHOW. We've taken ten equally goofy headlines and encrypted them using a simple letter-substitution code. To give you a head start, we've partially decoded the first one.

On this page, the letter substitution remains constant throughout the whole list. For further instructions and hints on how to solve, see page 7.

HILLARY CLINTON
1. *WBHHMJP *UHBTKCT CT QRHXMJR

2. IBHL YJBTLRJN MJR KGJTBTE KC SCQYRJ

3. IMT NWCCKN TRBEWZCJ QBKW IMUWRKR

4. JRKBJRY SJBRNK KC IMJJP *NSJBTENKRRT

5. YRXRTYMTK'N NSRRUW RTYN BT HCTE NRTKRTUR

6. TBTRKRRT XRRK ZJCLRT BT SCHR AMGHK

7. HMJER UWGJUW SHMTN UCHHMSNR

8. CXXBUBMH: CTHP JMBT QBHH UGJR YJCGEWK

9. ZJBKMBT BTUWRN EJGYEBTEHP KCQMJYN IRKJBU

NPNKRI

10. CHY NUWCCH SBHHMJN MJR JRSHMURY ZP MHGITB

ANSWER, PAGE 212

GEEKSPEAK

It's not too late to get hip to 21st century jive. Match the trendy terminology (1-10) with its definition (a-j).

_____ 1. Ant farms

_____ 2. Anus envy

_____ 3. Batmobiling

_____ 4. Begathon

_____ 5. Body Nazis

_____ 6. Deboning

_____ 7. Height technology

_____ 8. Meatspace

_____ 9. Prairie dogging

_____ 10. Um friend

a. A common condition among fans of Howard Stern or Rush Limbaugh who try to imitate their heroes.

b. A sexual relationship of dubious standing.

c. A TV or radio fund-raiser.

d. Computer-geek for "ladder."

e. Computer-geek for the physical world (as opposed to cyberspace); also known as the carbon community or RW (Real World).

f. Giant multiscreen movie complexes found in shopping malls.

g. Hardcore fitness fanatics who look down on anyone who doesn't exercise obsessively.

h. Putting up protective emotional shields just as a relationship enters an intimate, vulnerable stage.

i. The act of removing subscription cards and perfume ads from a magazine before reading it.

j. When someone raises a commotion in a cube farm, and everyone else's heads pop over the walls to get a look.

ANSWER, PAGE 212

* * * * *

WHAT'S SO FUNNY?

When you make someone laugh, why do we say you've put them in stitches?

a. Because they've "split their sides" laughing. The origin traces back to a Grimm fairy tale: a talking bean (!) splits its sides laughing, and must be stitched back up.

b. It comes from *stich*, a Greek word for a line of poetry. For traveling poets and singers, the most reliable way to keep the audience happy was to keep them well-supplied with stiches.

c. It comes from *stice*, an Old English word that means "to sting." When you put someone in stitches, you make them laugh so hard that it hurts.

ANSWER, PAGE 212

PLEASE PASS THE CORN

It's our favorite vegetable...

ACROSS

1 Ending for land or sea
6 Colt sound
10 Get-out-of-jail money
14 *Atlantic City* director Malle
15 Herman Melville novel
16 To be, to Henri
17 "Coffee ___ ?"
18 Street kid
19 "This thing weighs ___!"
20 Man's complaint to his physician
23 Bigger than big
24 Arthur C. Clarke's talking computer
25 Like old city streets
26 Former White House spokesman Fleischer
27 "___ about that?!"
28 Trident, say
29 Alas, in Austria
30 Mob
32 Apple pie maker's implement
34 With 53 Across, the physician's casual reply
39 With "Nickel," a cable network for kids
40 Improvise
42 SAT takers
45 Giant great Mel
46 Cranberry-growing site
48 *Cinco* minus *cuatro*
49 Official nose count
51 Novelist Levin
52 City near Phoenix
53 See 34 Across
56 Wild party
57 Apple product
58 Plumlike fruits
60 To ___ (just right)
61 Hamlet is one
62 Private response?
63 Quasimodo's Big Marie
64 "Omigosh!"
65 Bridge bid, briefly

DOWN

1 Road warning
2 Waled fabric
3 Old-fashioned helicopter
4 Get a ___ of the action
5 Actor Morales
6 Carpentry tool
7 Boy in a Menotti opera
8 Roulette bet, at Monte Carlo
9 "Who'da thunk it!"
10 Birdlike features
11 The Scourge of God
12 Like O. Henry stories
13 Geometric measure
21 Unit of electrical conductance
22 It's on Rover's collar
23 "So there!"
27 Lasted
28 Statehouse VIP
31 Twosome
32 Soup container
33 Curtain holder
35 Allow to deteriorate
36 Sexy
37 Prude
38 Brainiac
41 Fluffy scarf
42 Sacred Egyptian beetle
43 Tell
44 Whine pathetically
46 Prepared, as for a shock
47 Morsel in a feedbag
50 Romance writer Danielle
51 Bucky the Beaver's brand of toothpaste
52 Honeydew, e.g.
54 Online publication, for short
55 "Ignorance ___ excuse"
59 No-more-seats sign

ANSWER, PAGE 212

CELEBRITY SUPERSTITIONS

Can you tell the real superstitions from the one we made up just to aggravate you?

Luciano Pavarotti won't sing a note until he finds a bent nail onstage. If he can't spot one onstage, he searches the wings until he finds one.

Queen Elizabeth considers it bad luck to accept scissors as a gift, so she insists on making a token payment for the scissors she's given to cut ribbons at official openings.

Babe Ruth always stepped on first base when he came in from his right field position.

Winston Churchill thought it was unlucky to travel on Fridays. He tried to arrange his schedule so he could "stay put" on that day.

Bill Clinton believes that 13 is his lucky number. He once ordered Air Force One to slow down so it would arrive in Moscow just after midnight on the 13th instead of the 12th.

Cornelius Vanderbilt had the legs of his bed placed in dishes of salt to ward off attacks from evil spirits.

Michael Jordan always wore his North Carolina shorts under his Bulls uniform.

ANSWER, PAGE 212

* * * * *

THAT HEAVY TRUNK, TOO

Small crostic puzzles are solved just like the big ones (directions on page 13)
but the first letters of the fill-in words **do not** spell out a hidden message.

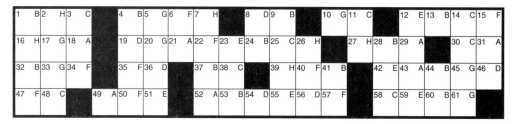

A. Roman god of the sea

‾‾ ‾‾ ‾‾ ‾‾ ‾‾ ‾‾ ‾‾
18 21 52 49 43 29 31

B. Demonstrably loving

‾‾ ‾‾ ‾‾ ‾‾ ‾‾ ‾‾ ‾‾ ‾‾ ‾‾ ‾‾ ‾‾
28 9 13 41 60 1 32 53 44 24 37 4

C. Famous far and wide

‾‾ ‾‾ ‾‾ ‾‾ ‾‾ ‾‾ ‾‾ ‾‾
14 58 25 38 30 11 3 48

D. Came down in buckets

‾‾ ‾‾ ‾‾ ‾‾ ‾‾ ‾‾
36 8 54 46 19 56

E. Mia's title role in a 1986 Woody Allen movie

‾‾ ‾‾ ‾‾ ‾‾ ‾‾ ‾‾
23 12 55 51 59 42

F. Symbol of the 1964 New York World's Fair

‾‾ ‾‾ ‾‾ ‾‾ ‾‾ ‾‾ ‾‾ ‾‾ ‾‾
35 40 15 57 22 34 47 6 50

G. Purest knight of the Round Table

‾‾ ‾‾ ‾‾ ‾‾ ‾‾ ‾‾ ‾‾
33 17 20 5 61 10 45

H. Put the kibosh on

‾‾ ‾‾ ‾‾ ‾‾ ‾‾ ‾‾
7 16 39 26 27 2

ANSWER, PAGE 212

CHICKEN À LA RING

Directions for solving are on page 13.

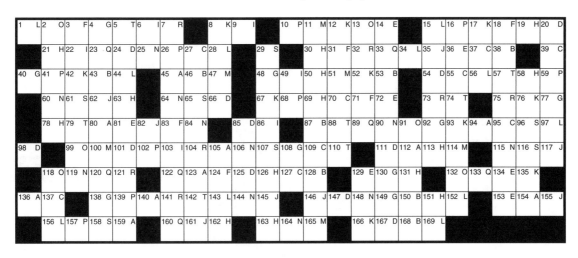

1 L	2 O	3 F	4 G	5 T	6 I	7 R		8 K	9 I		10 P	11 M	12 K	13 O	14 E		15 L	16 P	17 K	18 F	19 H	20 D
	21 H	22 I	23 Q	24 D	25 N	26 P	27 C	28 L		29 S		30 H	31 F	32 R	33 Q	34 L	35 J	36 E	37 C	38 B		39 C
40 G	41 P	42 K	43 B	44 L		45 A	46 B	47 M		48 G	49 I	50 H	51 M	52 K	53 B		54 D	55 C	56 L	57 T	58 H	59 P
	60 N	61 S	62 J	63 H		64 N	65 S	66 D		67 K	68 P	69 H	70 C	71 F	72 E		73 R	74 T		75 R	76 K	77 G
	78 H	79 T	80 A	81 E	82 J	83 F	84 N		85 D	86 I		87 B	88 T	89 Q	90 N	91 O	92 G	93 K	94 A	95 C	96 S	97 L
98 D		99 O	100 M	101 D	102 P	103 I	104 R	105 A	106 N	107 S	108 G	109 C	110 T		111 H	112 A	113 H	114 M		115 N	116 S	117 J
	118 O	119 N	120 Q	121 R		122 Q	123 A	124 F	125 D	126 H	127 C	128 B		129 E	130 G	131 H		132 O	133 Q	134 E	135 K
136 A	137 C		138 G	139 P	140 A	141 R	142 T	143 L	144 N	145 J		146 J	147 D	148 N	149 G	150 B	151 H	152 L		153 E	154 A	155 J
	156 L	157 P	158 S	159 A		160 Q	161 J	162 H		163 H	164 N	165 M		166 K	167 D	168 B	169 L				

A. Stephen King chiller set in a hotel (2 wds.)

$\overline{45}$ $\overline{136}$ $\overline{159}$ $\overline{80}$ $\overline{112}$ $\overline{94}$ $\overline{140}$ $\overline{154}$ $\overline{123}$ $\overline{105}$

B. Came to pass

$\overline{46}$ $\overline{168}$ $\overline{87}$ $\overline{150}$ $\overline{43}$ $\overline{53}$ $\overline{38}$ $\overline{128}$

C. Rhetorical gift

$\overline{137}$ $\overline{55}$ $\overline{95}$ $\overline{70}$ $\overline{37}$ $\overline{27}$ $\overline{109}$ $\overline{39}$ $\overline{127}$

D. Far from belles of the ball

$\overline{167}$ $\overline{20}$ $\overline{98}$ $\overline{24}$ $\overline{54}$ $\overline{101}$ $\overline{85}$ $\overline{111}$ $\overline{125}$
$\overline{147}$ $\overline{66}$

E. Secretly (3 wds.)

$\overline{14}$ $\overline{134}$ $\overline{81}$ $\overline{153}$ $\overline{72}$ $\overline{36}$ $\overline{129}$

F. Good name

$\overline{83}$ $\overline{18}$ $\overline{3}$ $\overline{71}$ $\overline{124}$ $\overline{31}$

G. Nautically neat

$\overline{48}$ $\overline{4}$ $\overline{108}$ $\overline{138}$ $\overline{92}$ $\overline{130}$ $\overline{40}$ $\overline{149}$ $\overline{77}$

H. Intensive questioning by the cops (3 wds.)

$\overline{63}$ $\overline{78}$ $\overline{131}$ $\overline{30}$ $\overline{58}$ $\overline{69}$ $\overline{126}$ $\overline{50}$ $\overline{162}$
$\overline{113}$ $\overline{19}$ $\overline{163}$ $\overline{21}$ $\overline{151}$

I. Deaden, as sounds

$\overline{22}$ $\overline{49}$ $\overline{86}$ $\overline{103}$ $\overline{9}$ $\overline{6}$

J. Tonsils' neighbors

$\overline{62}$ $\overline{145}$ $\overline{117}$ $\overline{161}$ $\overline{82}$ $\overline{35}$ $\overline{146}$ $\overline{155}$

K. Chekhov drama about an aging actress (2 wds.)

$\overline{17}$ $\overline{76}$ $\overline{52}$ $\overline{93}$ $\overline{8}$ $\overline{166}$ $\overline{135}$ $\overline{67}$ $\overline{42}$ $\overline{12}$

L. Winner of tennis' 2003 U.S. Open (2 wds.)

$\overline{97}$ $\overline{34}$ $\overline{44}$ $\overline{169}$ $\overline{1}$ $\overline{15}$ $\overline{152}$ $\overline{28}$ $\overline{56}$
$\overline{156}$ $\overline{143}$

M. Chaperone for a señorita

$\overline{51}$ $\overline{100}$ $\overline{47}$ $\overline{165}$ $\overline{114}$ $\overline{11}$

N. Remote (hyph.)

$\overline{25}$ $\overline{119}$ $\overline{60}$ $\overline{148}$ $\overline{90}$ $\overline{115}$ $\overline{106}$ $\overline{144}$ $\overline{64}$
$\overline{164}$ $\overline{84}$

O. Disorderly crowd of people

$\overline{132}$ $\overline{2}$ $\overline{118}$ $\overline{99}$ $\overline{13}$ $\overline{91}$

P. Courage worthy of a medal

$\overline{10}$ $\overline{157}$ $\overline{41}$ $\overline{102}$ $\overline{139}$ $\overline{68}$ $\overline{59}$ $\overline{16}$ $\overline{26}$

Q. Hamlet's ill-fated sweetheart

$\overline{89}$ $\overline{23}$ $\overline{33}$ $\overline{122}$ $\overline{120}$ $\overline{133}$ $\overline{160}$

R. Unlawful

$\overline{73}$ $\overline{121}$ $\overline{7}$ $\overline{141}$ $\overline{32}$ $\overline{104}$ $\overline{75}$

S. Volatile petroleum-based solvent

$\overline{96}$ $\overline{65}$ $\overline{158}$ $\overline{116}$ $\overline{107}$ $\overline{61}$ $\overline{29}$

T. Lending elegance to

$\overline{57}$ $\overline{88}$ $\overline{5}$ $\overline{142}$ $\overline{79}$ $\overline{74}$ $\overline{110}$

ANSWER, PAGE 213

HONEST ABE

A bit of folksy wisdom from Abe Lincoln. It may sound corny—but it's true.

ACROSS

1 Treat at Chili's
5 Kids' guessing game
9 Is a good dog, maybe
14 Actor Gold of TV's *Stacked*
15 Dutch filmmaker van Gogh
16 Greek letter after rho
17 Start of a quote by Abraham Lincoln
20 Silents vamp Bara
21 French or Dutch fixture
22 *Camino* ___
23 13 Down is one
25 Ear prefix
27 One billion years, in astronomy
28 Mayberry matriarch
32 Part 2 of the quote
36 Logan Airport code
37 NASA lander
38 Between *printemps* and *automne*
39 Part 3 of the quote
46 "Sweet" barbershop quartet girl
47 Kay ___, first woman governor of Nebraska
48 *C.S.I.* evidence
49 Minor of a major, maybe
54 Modern treasure chest
57 Caffeinated nut
59 Town in Tuscany
60 End of the quote
63 It comes before blanche
64 Class for four-year-olds, briefly
65 Lou Grant's ex-wife
66 Building add-on
67 Withered
68 *Your Erroneous Zones* author Wayne ___

DOWN

1 Carnival setups
2 Waikiki welcome
3 Cupid's antlered sleighmate
4 Losing, in a way
5 Addams family cousin
6 Casts off
7 1990s third party candidate
8 Canadian national park near Banff
9 Dallas-to-San Antonio dir.
10 *Pulp Fiction* star
11 Grippe symptom
12 Hit by the Village People
13 Comic Mort
18 Hawaiian pondfield plants
19 "Are you in ___?" (dealer's question)
24 Gershwin's *Concerto* ___
26 Boomer's initials?
28 "Oh dear!"
29 Telly network, familiarly, with "the"
30 Illustrator born Romain de Tirtoff
31 Wide shoe measure
32 How gazpacho is served
33 "Even ___ speak"
34 Country singer DeLange
35 "You don't say!"
36 Sheepish remark?
40 Just right, spaghetti-wise
41 The other half of yang
42 Very, very curvy
43 Popular tattoo
44 Sexy rendezvous
45 Ran circles around
49 Woodard of *Beauty Shop*
50 Worker on autumn leaves
51 Sounding like a flute
52 *That Old Ace in the Hole* writer Proulx
53 Stun gun
54 Humane Society partner (abbr.)
55 Actor Rickman
56 *Charlotte's Web* girl
58 "Clumsy me!"
61 John Ritter's dad
62 Mamie's mate

ANSWER, PAGE 212

TWO LADIES IN A SHOE STORE

Among some cardplayers, a queen is a "lady" and three pair are a "shoe store." See if you can fill in the blanks next to the 24 nicknames below with the correct groupings of cards. "A" stands for ace, "K" for king, "Q" for queen, and "J" for jack.

A-A	K-K	Q-J	9-8	5-10	4-4
A-K-4-7	K-Q	Q-9	9-5	5-7	3-9
A-J	K-J	J-J-5-5	8-8	5-5-5	2-4
A-2-3	K-9	10-10-10	7-7	4-5	2-2-2

1. ABC: ___-___-___

2. Ajax: ___-___

3. American Airlines: ___-___

4. Assault Rifle: ___-___-___-___

5. Mongrel: ___-___

6. Cowboys: ___-___

7. Dolly Parton: ___-___

8. Fred & Ethel: ___-___

9. Heinz: ___-___

10. Hockey Sticks: ___-___

11. Huey, Dewey, and Louie: ___-___-___

12. Jack Benny: ___-___

13. Jackson Five: ___-___-___-___

14. Jesse James: ___-___

15. Kojak: ___-___

16. Lucy & Ricky: ___-___

17. Lumberman's Hand: ___-___

18. Oldsmobile: ___-___

19. Quinine: ___-___

20. Sail Boats: ___-___

21. Snowmen: ___-___

22. Thirty Miles: ___-___-___

23. Washington Monument: ___-___-___

24. Woolworth: ___-___

ANSWER, PAGE 213

* * * * *

WHO'S THE BOSS?

Which of the following people, places, and things **aren't** owned by Rupert Murdoch?

The Los Angeles Dodgers
The New York Post
The Times (London)
TV Guide
Twentieth-Century Fox
Madison Square Garden
Fox News Channel
Verizon Communications

ANSWER, PAGE 213

LISTOGRAMS

The two lists of related words and phrases have been translated by simple letter substitution code. The code remains constant within each list, but changes from one list to the next. Here's a tip: Start by thinking of answers that might fit the category, then see if there are any words in the list that have the same letter pattern.

5 Greatest American Generals

ZFRCZF GMDDRP

YKBZOD FBQFPORKFC

YRAZUMQ EMIMCDOAC

IRUBP GRKFUU

ZFRCZF KMQOBPZDRP

The 5 Most Germ-Ridden Places at Work

KGAWD

SDTVJAK

EBJDI UAQWJBCW

NCFIAEBOD SAAI

VDPLABIS

ANSWER, PAGE 213

* * * * *

THE NEW ECONOMY

Small crostic puzzles are solved just like the big ones (directions on page 13)
but the first letters of the fill-in words **do not** spell out a hidden message.

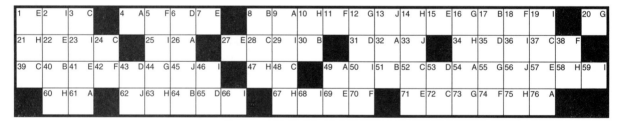

A. "Bread" and "bred," for example

<u> </u> <u> </u> <u> </u> <u> </u> <u> </u> <u> </u> <u> </u> <u> </u>
32 49 4 54 76 61 9 26

B. Throw trash out the car window, e.g.

<u> </u> <u> </u> <u> </u> <u> </u> <u> </u> <u> </u>
64 17 30 51 8 40

C. Brainiacs

<u> </u> <u> </u> <u> </u> <u> </u> <u> </u> <u> </u> <u> </u> <u> </u>
3 52 24 28 72 37 39 48

D. What Clue C's have aplenty

<u> </u> <u> </u> <u> </u> <u> </u> <u> </u> <u> </u>
6 65 35 53 31 43

E. Part of M.I.T.

<u> </u> <u> </u> <u> </u> <u> </u> <u> </u> <u> </u> <u> </u> <u> </u> <u> </u>
22 71 15 7 57 1 69 27 41

F. Amaretto ingredients

<u> </u> <u> </u> <u> </u> <u> </u> <u> </u> <u> </u> <u> </u>
11 70 74 5 18 38 42

G. Hand-arm connectors

<u> </u> <u> </u> <u> </u> <u> </u> <u> </u> <u> </u>
73 12 44 16 20 55

H. Toads or frogs

<u> </u> <u> </u> <u> </u> <u> </u> <u> </u> <u> </u> <u> </u> <u> </u> <u> </u> <u> </u>
75 60 67 21 63 10 47 14 58 34

I. Nitrous oxide, in the vernacular (2 wds.)

<u> </u> <u> </u> <u> </u> <u> </u> <u> </u> <u> </u> <u> </u> <u> </u> <u> </u> <u> </u> <u> </u>
36 68 50 19 2 25 23 46 59 29 66

J. Spore producers

<u> </u> <u> </u> <u> </u> <u> </u> <u> </u>
62 33 13 45 56

ANSWER, PAGE 213

LOOK BOTH WAYS

You probably know that a palindrome is a word or phrase that reads exactly the same either forward or backward. With that in mind, we've put together a puzzle that will have you going in all directions. First take a look at the grid—which is shaped like a cartoon detonator box of TNT—then circle all 40 entries. When you're done, the leftover letters will reveal three more palindromic phrases.

```
            B O R R T A N G Y G N A T O
            P A R T Y B O O B Y T R A P
                    W D
                    S E
                    I L
                    R I
                    A V
                    W E
        W B I R D R I B A R A C E C A R O S
        M L W A S I T A R A T I S A W R H W
        S A R O B N O R I D L V W E F E W A
        T O P S P O T C S A P I I N D O W P
        E C Y S T N K R W R O C O I I R O F
        P E O O D N A A O E O D D N R I L O
        O L B G O N Y B N V E E I D O D F R
        N O A T N O A I F I H A D A H I F I
        N T N U T U K A F L S N T M T D L A
        O S A N N O D I N E N O T M I D O P
        P S N A O P E U X D Y O L I N I W A
        E T A N D D M E N O S E A T P D R I
        T O B U G E S L T G V P E I T I S R
        S L O T T O M A D E E D A M O T T O
        N E Y E V I L O L I V E O M R A A F
        H C S E E S H S T A C K C A T S P P
        L O N E L Y T Y L E N O L D A R P A
        N A M E N O O N E M A N O N S E A W
        T L E S E N I L E F E L I N E S T S
        L E P U L L U P P U L L U P G R A M
```

A TOYOTA
BAR CRAB
BIRD RIB
CIVIC
DAMMIT, I'M MAD
DEIFIED
DON'T NOD
EVIL OLIVE
GNU DUNG
GO DELIVER A DARE,
   VILE DOG
HE DID, EH
I DID, DID I
IF I HAD A HI-FI

KAYAK
L.A. OCELOTS STOLE COAL
LEVEL
LION OIL
LONELY TYLENOL
MAPS, DNA, AND SPAM
NAME NO ONE MAN
NOW, SIR, A WAR IS WON
OTTO MADE ED A MOTTO
PARTY BOOBY TRAP
PEEP
PULL UP, PULL UP
RACE CAR
SENILE FELINES

SEXES
STACK CATS
STEP ON NO PETS
SWAP FOR I A PAIR
   OF PAWS
TANGY GNAT
TAP PAT
TIP IT
TOP SPOT
TUNA NUT
WAS IT A RAT I SAW
WE FEW
WOLF FLOW
YO, BANANA BOY

ANSWER, PAGE 214

WELL, I NEVER!

Lucky you. You've never been this insulted in your life. Decode the following cryptograms to hear what a first-class insult sounds like in the hands of trained professionals. **The letter substitution remains constant throughout.** For further instructions and hints on how to solve, see page 7.

Billy Wilder: ZTO CLEY *ELS *QTQC'K YLX ITX GOKUA.

Golda Meir: PTS'H DY COGDMY. ZTO'XY STH HCLH QXYLH.

George Bernard Shaw: KCY CLP MTKH HCY LXH TI ATSEYXKLHUTS,

DOH STH, OSITXHOSLHYMZ, HCY VTFYX TI KVYYAC.

Milton Berle: *U'G TMP? FCYS ZTO FYXY ZTOSQ, HCY *PYLP

*KYL FLK TSMZ KUAB!

Samuel Johnson: ZTOX GLSOKAXUVH UK DTHC QTTP LSP

TXUQUSLM; DOH HCY VLXH HCLH UK QTTP UK STH

TXUQUSLM, LSP HCY VLXH HCLH UK TXUQUSLM UK STH

QTTP.

Redd Foxx: KCY FLK KT OQMZ HCLH TSY HUGY KCY HXUYP

HT YSHYX LS OQMZ ATSHYKH. HCYZ HTMP CYX, "KTXXZ,

ST VXTIYKKUTSLMK LMMTFYP."

ANSWER, PAGE 213

* * * * *

CAUGHT IN THE MIDDLE

You won't be if you can match these middle names (1-6) with some well-known folks (a-f).

1. Bonaventure   a. Walt Disney
2. Elias   b. Actor Jim Carrey
3. Ernst   c. Actor Spencer Tracy
4. Eugene   d. Polar explorer Richard E. Byrd
5. Evelyn   e. Donald Duck
6. Fauntleroy   f. Author John Steinbeck

ANSWER, PAGE 214

FROM A TO Z

...and everything in between.

ACROSS

1 **Start of a sentence using the entire alphabet**
4 Inscribed with acid
10 Old money in Milan
14 ___ *vobiscum* (blessing from the Pope)
15 Ravel piece heard in *10*
16 Red sky at sunset, it's said
17 "___ 'em, Rover!"
18 **Sentence, part 2**
20 Prot. or Cath., e.g.
22 Basks by the pool
23 "___ we meet again"
24 Nectar flavor
26 Diplomatic emissary
27 Big babies at the zoo
28 Chinese ideal
30 Coup d'__
31 Caper
32 Clunky suit
34 Golfer Ernie
35 **Sentence, part 3**
38 Letters on an ambulance
41 Mission, or cottonwood tree that grows around it
42 Texas folklore figure ___ Bill
46 Photos
48 Dada artist Jean
49 Aplenty
50 Sign of progress
52 Snoop's "window"
53 Marketing link between products
54 Lodge letters
56 Dockworkers' org.
57 **Sentence, part 4**
60 Prov. neighboring Quebec
62 Lioness' lack
63 Attacked by a bear
64 Health and Human Services agcy.
65 Massachusetts' motto starter
66 Sucrose and fructose
67 **End of the sentence**

DOWN

1 Uses bathroom rolls in a prank, for short
2 Beehive fallout?
3 Sample text from a book
4 Fade away
5 Some trunks
6 What influential ones wield
7 Cut down
8 Shore birds
9 Two, in Toledo
10 Second-rate singer's milieu
11 Copy
12 Carnegie Hall performance
13 Short socks
19 "___ Sera, Sera"
21 Fat, to a doctor
24 "So that's it!"
25 Après-ski quaff
26 Tricky airplane maneuver
28 Melania Knauss' last name as of 2005
29 Bullets, briefly
32 Slightly open
33 Honor an IOU
36 Saran rival
37 Home to India's Mughal Palace
38 Perfect example
39 Cousin of a sport-utility vehicle
40 They let in breezes but not flies
43 Calm down
44 Epcot Center's locale
45 "Got it?"
47 Evening party
49 Old coot
51 Little hill builder
52 Fuzzy Qantas mascot
54 Boyfriend
55 Drain stopper
58 ___ *Pinafore*
59 NFL pickups
61 Tariff

ANSWER, PAGE 214

HARD AS NAILS

Have you ever noticed that almost everything in a hardware store is like—*hard*? Except for, like, tarps and stuff? What an amazing coincidence! While we're busy mulling that over, put all 46 items in the grid, crossword-style.

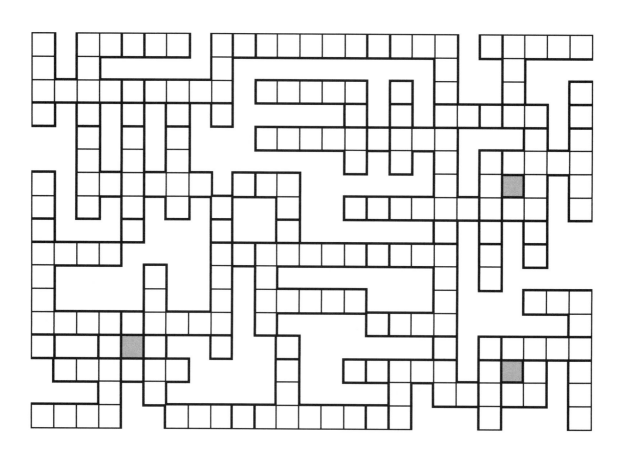

3-letter words
Axe
Mop
Nut
Saw

4-letter words
File
Hook
Keys
Knob
Lath
Lock
Pick
Pipe

Rope
Tarp
Vise
Wire

5-letter words
Caulk
Chain
Drill
Grout
Hinge
Nails
Paint
Plane
Spade
Tacks

6-letter words
Chisel
Pallet
Pliers
Screws
Shovel
Trowel
Wrench

7-letter words
Plywood
Spackle
Washers

8-letter words
Concrete
Tool belt

9-letter words
Drop cloth
Lawn mower
Sandpaper
Yardstick

11-letter words
Screwdriver
Tape measure
Wheelbarrow

16-letter word
Weatherstripping

ANSWER, PAGE 214

YOU'RE (NOT) THE TOPS

A number of top-three lists are presented below, but there's a hitch: They all contain four items.
Can you determine which item in each list doesn't belong among the top three?

1. The top three surgeries performed in the U.S.:
   a. Biopsy
   b. Angioplasty
   c. Hysterectomy
   d. Cesarean section

2. The top three items shoplifted from supermarkets:
   a. Candy
   b. Cigarettes
   c. Beauty aids
   d. Batteries

3. The three most talkative pet birds:
   a. Mynah
   b. Parakeet
   c. Cockatoo
   d. African gray parrot

4. The three best-selling soups in America:
   a. Chicken noodle
   b. Vegetable beef
   c. Cream of mushroom
   d. Tomato

5. The three most common dreams:
   a. Falling
   b. Being chased
   c. Being attacked
   d. Being naked in public

6. The three most popular Easter egg colors:
   a. Pink
   b. Purple
   c. Blue
   d. Orange

7. The three most common names for Popes:
   a. John
   b. Gregory
   c. Leo
   d. Benedict

8. The top three causes of home accidents:
   a. Power tools
   b. Glass doors
   c. Cutlery
   d. Stairs

9. The top three things that men lie about on dates:
   a. Willingness to commit
   b. Interest in more than sex
   c. Current relationship status
   d. Income

10. The three most common elements in the universe:
    a. Hydrogen
    b. Nitrogen
    c. Oxygen
    d. Helium

ANSWER, PAGE 214

* * * * *

COLORFUL QUESTION

What does the word "khaki" means in Hindi?

    a. Light yellowish brown
    b. Dusty
    c. "The color of a misbegotten dog's rear end"

ANSWER, PAGE 214

FLOWER POWER

Did you know that the word "orchid" comes from the Greek for "testicle" because that's what the plant's root tubers look like? Uh-huh. Here's a few more garden-variety factoids.

ACROSS

1 *Sturm und* ___ (storm and stress)
6 Japanese soup noodle
10 Somewhat
14 Kitchen tearjerker?
15 1 and 66, e.g.
16 Usual ballad topic
17 Also called grenadines, the official flowers of Mother's Day since 1907
19 Poker player's announcement
20 Where there was no room at the inn
22 Sixth-day creation
23 Word before "the ramparts" in "The Star-Spangled Banner"
25 Black, Yellow, or Red
26 Water or gas, e.g.
28 Stuck in ___
30 ___'acte
32 John Coltrane's instruments
33 Seafood patty
35 Phone syst. for the deaf
36 Flower adopted as the imperial crest when it first appeared in Japan in the eighth century
40 Halloween's mo.
41 Hot peppers
43 Pashmina garment
46 1993 Mariah Carey hit
47 River with Blue and White branches
48 Clothing brand with a scribbled logo
50 Join the marathon
52 Praiseful verse
53 Little devil
54 "Say what?"
57 Myanmar's neighbor
59 Flower whose name came from the ancient Greeks, who thought it looked like a dolphin
62 Self-images
63 "___ Want for Christmas"
64 Very, in music
65 Antitoxins
66 Sue of *Lolita*
67 Spoils, with "on"

DOWN

1 Elmer Fudd, to Bugs
2 Genetic initials
3 Photo touch-up tool
4 Number of times Chicago has won the World Series in the past 80 years
5 Tiny biters
6 Ceylon, now
7 Midwestern Indian
8 Film that saved MGM from bankruptcy
9 Something of value
10 Frazier opponent
11 Old-time westerns actor
12 Make like Amelia Earhart
13 Place for a Grand Slam Breakfast
18 Where Marco Polo traveled
21 ___ *Rogers' Neighborhood*
23 Bumbler
24 Monty Python member Idle
27 Non-expert
29 Loses on purpose
31 On edge
34 Recurring periodically
35 Finished
37 Edible turtle
38 Supporter of the North, in 1863
39 It makes blue cheese blue
42 Call, in poker
43 Friendly expressions
44 Tribute
45 ___ as a church mouse
46 Far from beautiful
49 Relating to form
51 Water nymph
55 Cockney's greeting
56 Not ___ many words
58 FICA funds it
60 Abu Dhabi's federation (abbr.)
61 Prefix meaning "badly"

ANSWER, PAGE 215

INSIDE HOLLYWOOD

Let's see if you've got what it takes to make it big in Hollywood; all you have to do is identify the movies we're talking about. This is how it works: the first clue, in column A, is a telling detail or memorable plot element; the second (column B) is a quote from the film; and the third (column C) is a bit of extra information about the film. Give yourself three points if you recognize the movie in question from just the first clue, two points if it takes two clues, and one if you need all three. Then add up your points and see where you fall amidst the Hollywood hierarchy.

COLUMN A

1. After Quint crushes his beer can in his hand, Matt Hooper squashes his paper cup.

2. The male lead is seen reading Stephen King's *Misery*, which would be the director's next film.

3. Dinner at Mom's with a body stashed in the trunk of the car outside.

4. It's 1927, and Don Lockwood and Lina Lamont are the darlings of silent movies.

5. Former coal miner Charles Bronson brought expertise to a few key sequences.

6. A 15-year-old boy is hired to tour with an up-and-coming rock band.

7. Jerry Lundegaard promises the kidnappers a car and $40,000.

8. One of the near-idiots mentioned at right impersonates a general.

9. The movie opens with two characters called Honey Bunny and Pumpkin.

10. A kiss on the beach.

COLUMN B

1. "I'm not gonna waste my time arguing with a man who's lining up to be a hot lunch."

2. "I'll have what she's having."

3. "How am I funny, like a clown? What is so funny about me?…Tell me. Tell me what's funny."

4. "I'd rather kiss a tarantula."

5. "You're crazy…Two hundred and fifty guys just walkin' down the road, just like that?"

6. "And you can tell *Rolling Stone* magazine that my last words were…I'm on drugs!"

7. "And I guess that was your accomplice in the wood-chipper."

8. "You've got one religious maniac, one malignant dwarf, two near-idiots, and the rest I don't even want to think about."

9. "Now I wanna dance, I wanna win. I want that trophy, so dance good."

10. "I'm a private no-class dogface. The way most civilians look at that, that's two steps up from nothin'."

COLUMN C

1. The movie went on to become a classic of its kind and the first movie to reach the coveted $100 million mark.

2. The lady customer just quoted is the director's real-life mother.

3. The director's mother played Joe Pesci's mother in the movie.

4. The star had a 103-degree fever when he danced to the title song.

5. James Clavell (*Shogun, Taipan*) wrote the screenplay.

6. Brad Pitt was slated to star, but admitted, "I just don't get it enough to do it."

7. None of the scenes are actually shot in the town this movie made famous.

8. John Wayne and Jack Palance were offered the lead role, but turned it down.

9. Daniel Day-Lewis wanted the lead but the director chose John Travolta.

10. The acting Oscar Frank Sinatra won revived his near-dead career.

ANSWER, PAGE 215

MARRIED-GO-ROUND

Some people are so cynical about the sacred institution of marriage!

1. Fred Flintstone

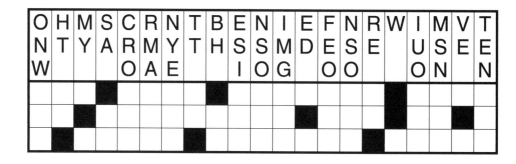

2. Adela Rogers St. Johns

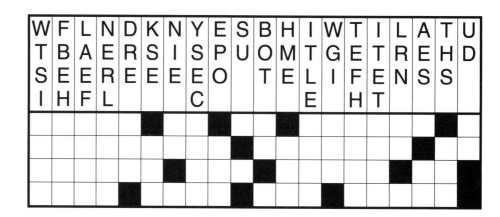

3. Paul Hornung

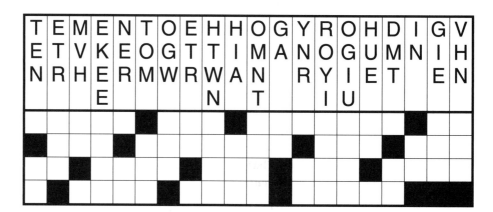

ANSWER, PAGE 215

FRUIT SALAD

Uncle John's collection of lists is legendary, and includes the list of five songs about fruit below. The cherry-shaped grid—a tribute to Neil Diamond's "Cherry Cherry"—is hiding all 31 of the capitalized items on the lists. Once you've found them in the grid, the leftover letters will reveal a message that begins, "7 Things Invented …"

```
                    B  S
                       A
                       L
                          E
                          M
                          O
                          U
           Y  C  W        A  Y  N  N  A        D  I  A
        B  A  N  A  N  A  B  O  A  T  S  O  N  G  R  H  N  S  F
        A  R  E  T  O  H  R  E  S  P  R  C  N  E  O  O  E  W  A
     G  M  L  A  T  O  Y  A  O  B  L  H  E  V  N  O  L  R  A  M  I
     N  L  L  I  H  Y  R  R  E  B  E  U  L  B  L  L  Y  A  E  I  P
     O  T  T  A  A  I  J  C  N  R  A  I  T  R  I  O  W  N  J  N  E
     S  H  L  W  L  E  R  A  R  R  S  P  L  V  W  L  A  D  E  E  U
     N  G  D  E  A  U  S  Y  N  T  A  I  R  O  L  C  T  Y  R  G  Q
     O  I  A  D  C  S  C  A  L  E  N  E  O  A  R  N  E  B  M  A  I
     M  R  M  I  C  H  A  E  L  G  T  D  R  K  E  I  R  B  A  E  L
     E  A  F  S  E  L  P  P  A  N  E  E  R  G  E  L  T  T  I  L  B
     L  I  G  R  U  W  A  S  E  N  T  I  H  R  I  K  N  K  N  G  O
     X  M  R  E  A  N  C  C  S  A  H  B  I  O  N  N  C  E  E  B  E
        Y  L  V  E  G  L  T  L  C  T  B  R  V  I  A  C  U  T  E
           C  I  R  F  A  I  R  V  I  E  W  E  J  R  A  U  N
           G  R  E  K  U  R  G  Z  I  R  P  P  E  F  S  R  A
              N  E  Q  D  F  L  H  O  G  H  T  A  E  D  H
                 E  C  N  E  L  I  T  S  E  P  O  R  N
                    I  S  O  S  C  E  L  E  S
```

9 Jackson Siblings

MICHAEL
JANET
LATOYA
REBBIE
MARLON
RANDY
TITO
JACKIE
JERMAINE

4 Horsemen of the Apocalypse

WAR
DEATH
PESTILENCE
FAMINE

7 Types of Triangles

EQUILATERAL
ISOSCELES
SCALENE
RIGHT
ACUTE
OBTUSE
OBLIQUE

6 Things That Can Kill Dracula

SUNLIGHT
GARLIC
CRUCIFIX
HOLY WATER
WOODEN STAKE
SILVER

9 Most Common U.S. Street Names

FAIRVIEW
MIDWAY
OAK GROVE
FRANKLIN
RIVERSIDE
CENTERVILLE
MOUNT PLEASANT
LIBERTY
SALEM

5 Songs About Fruit

BANANA BOAT SONG
 (Harry Belafonte)
BLUEBERRY HILL
 (Fats Domino)
CHERRY CHERRY
 (Neil Diamond)
LEMON SONG
 (Led Zeppelin)
LITTLE GREEN
 APPLES (O. C. Smith)

ANSWER, PAGE 215

SHARK ATTACKS PUZZLE EXPERTS

That was an actual headline that scared the devil out of a lot of our friends, until we realized that... oh, "attacks" is a noun and "puzzle" is a verb there, not the reverse. Whew! In a similar vein, we present a few other headlines that are either misleading or just plain goofy. Can you finish the actual headlines (1-12) below by matching each with its proper ending (a-l)?

a. A SON
b. BAD WEATHER
c. BELTED
d. COMMUNAL DUMP
e. COOKIE
f. DIRTY TOILETS
g. GAS IN SPACECRAFT
h. MORE BEARS
i. NOT DEAD
j. RADIO PLAY
k. SCRORES
l. SEAWORTHY

1. ASTRONAUT TAKES BLAME FOR ___

2. CALIFORNIA GOVERNOR MAKES STAND ON ___

3. CRITICS SAY SUNKEN SHIPS NOT ___

4. ECUADOREAN PRESIDENT DECLARES HE'S ___

5. MOORPARK RESIDENTS ENJOY A ___

6. NUDE SCENE DONE TASTEFULLY IN ___

7. REASON FOR MORE BEAR SIGHTINGS: ___

8. SAFETY EXPERTS SAY SCHOOL BUS PASSENGERS SHOULD BE ___

9. STORM DELAYED BY ___

10. SUMMER SCHOOLS BOOST ___

11. THANKS TO PRESIDENT CLINTON, STAFF SGT. FRUER NOW HAS ___

12. WOMAN NOT INJURED BY ___

ANSWER, PAGE 216

* * * * *

UNCLE OSCAR'S BIG NIGHT #2

More scrambled Oscar-winning stars and the Oscar-winning films
they won for. For complete directions on how to solve, see page 12.

The Stars

1. MEREST REPLY (5 6)
2. OH! OH! SKINNY PANT! (7 7)
3. FRY HAD NONE (5 5)
4. JOHN LACKS COIN (4 9)
5. SHIRK ANY LAW (6 5)

The Films

a. LONDON DOG PEN (2 6 4)
b. AID ILL BOB NORMALLY (7 6 4)
c. LATCH HIM TO FEEBLENESS (3 7 2 3 5)
d. HI! HE SPIES COCO (7 6)
e. WE COO OUR FLOCKS' SEVENTEENTH (3 4 4 3 7 4)

ANSWER, PAGE 215

TWISTED TITLES

A quadriplex of movies you'll never get to see, because we made them up by altering each title a wee bit.

ACROSS

1 Shoe's EEE, for one
6 Thick slice
10 Mr. Hulot portrayer
14 Quite amazed
15 1970 Kinks hit
16 Actor McGregor
17 Bigwig
18 A party to
19 Nick's TV time
20 With "A," an all-star World War II movie about a hungry couch potato?
23 Beg
25 Rap sheet notation
26 Harrison Ford thriller about the DAR?
30 Computer key
31 Joker
32 Part of the birth process
36 Environment subj.
38 Fancy window treatments
40 Inside shot?
41 Arctic or Antarctic
43 Novelists Van Lustbader and Ambler
45 Corvallis sch.
46 Nicole Kidman movie set in an Alaskan oilfield?
49 *Remington* ___ (Pierce Brosnan TV series)
52 Laundry batches
53 Foreign biopic about Pinocchio?
57 Start the bidding
58 Estate document
59 Sedates, slangily
63 Fast time
64 Military no-show
65 Blake of ragtime fame
66 The Bee Gees, e.g.
67 Mouths off
68 Governor's realm

DOWN

1 Preakness wager
2 Concert ending?
3 Smidgen
4 Special ticket for a Broadway show
5 Like the laws of Moses
6 Went down by luge
7 Shelley of *Cheers*
8 Lotion ingredient
9 Diminutive, as a rooster
10 One of a jazz combo
11 "The farmer takes ___..."
12 Farewells, in Falmouth
13 Like krypton
21 Movie superstars
22 Pitcher Hershiser
23 Washington city
24 Gen.'s subordinate
26 Sound from the hatchery
27 Provided some road service
28 Grumpy was one
29 Gram prefix
33 Extensive
34 Desert relief
35 Former mile record-holder Jim
37 Attack
39 Rower's boat
42 Massage, in a way
44 Naps
47 Flexibility
48 Lay a glove on, in baseball
49 Young salmon
50 Lab worker who classifies blood
51 Kate Nelligan title role
54 Sony competitor
55 Hardly gourmet cooking
56 "___ fair in love..."
60 Jazz org.
61 Do-it-yourselfer's buy
62 Watch

ANSWER, PAGE 216

IT'S ALL YOUR FAULT

Directions for solving are on page 13.

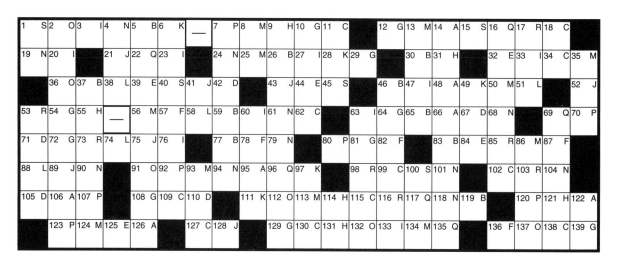

A. Professor's podium

$\overline{106}$ $\overline{66}$ $\overline{48}$ $\overline{122}$ $\overline{95}$ $\overline{14}$ $\overline{126}$

B. Jack Paar's autobiography—really! (4 wds.)

$\overline{77}$ $\overline{59}$ $\overline{30}$ $\overline{46}$ $\overline{119}$ $\overline{83}$ $\overline{26}$ $\overline{65}$ $\overline{37}$ $\overline{5}$

C. Pro boxer of 130 pounds

$\overline{130}$ $\overline{115}$ $\overline{62}$ $\overline{109}$ $\overline{11}$ $\overline{127}$ $\overline{138}$ $\overline{34}$ $\overline{102}$
$\overline{99}$ $\overline{18}$

D. Grocery item sold in cakes

$\overline{42}$ $\overline{110}$ $\overline{105}$ $\overline{67}$ $\overline{71}$

E. Senator Lott of Mississippi

$\overline{84}$ $\overline{44}$ $\overline{125}$ $\overline{39}$ $\overline{32}$

F. Mammal that feeds on abalone

$\overline{57}$ $\overline{136}$ $\overline{78}$ $\overline{82}$ $\overline{87}$

G. Staple of sci-fi alien invasion flicks (2 wds.)

$\overline{139}$ $\overline{64}$ $\overline{108}$ $\overline{10}$ $\overline{129}$ $\overline{54}$ $\overline{29}$ $\overline{81}$ $\overline{72}$ $\overline{12}$

H. Made a fencing attack

$\overline{114}$ $\overline{121}$ $\overline{31}$ $\overline{9}$ $\overline{131}$ $\overline{55}$

I. Live (3 wds.)

$\overline{60}$ $\overline{3}$ $\overline{133}$ $\overline{63}$ $\overline{23}$ $\overline{20}$ $\overline{27}$ $\overline{47}$ $\overline{76}$ $\overline{33}$

J. Star of three self-named prime time sitcoms

$\overline{75}$ $\overline{128}$ $\overline{89}$ $\overline{52}$ $\overline{43}$ $\overline{41}$ $\overline{21}$

K. Kind of larceny

$\overline{111}$ $\overline{49}$ $\overline{28}$ $\overline{97}$ $\overline{6}$

L. Total; complete

$\overline{38}$ $\overline{51}$ $\overline{88}$ $\overline{74}$ $\overline{58}$

M. Former name of Vanuatu (2 wds.)

$\overline{50}$ $\overline{86}$ $\overline{56}$ $\overline{124}$ $\overline{134}$ $\overline{113}$ $\overline{93}$ $\overline{8}$ $\overline{25}$
$\overline{13}$ $\overline{35}$

N. Nickname for Alabama (2 wds.)

$\overline{94}$ $\overline{90}$ $\overline{104}$ $\overline{101}$ $\overline{19}$ $\overline{61}$ $\overline{79}$ $\overline{68}$ $\overline{24}$
$\overline{118}$ $\overline{4}$

O. Small glitch in the proceedings

$\overline{137}$ $\overline{2}$ $\overline{36}$ $\overline{132}$ $\overline{112}$ $\overline{91}$

P. #1 advice from the Beatles in 1970 (3 wds.)

$\overline{107}$ $\overline{7}$ $\overline{123}$ $\overline{70}$ $\overline{80}$ $\overline{120}$ $\overline{92}$

Q. Crept forward slowly

$\overline{117}$ $\overline{96}$ $\overline{69}$ $\overline{22}$ $\overline{16}$ $\overline{135}$

R. Mississippi port on the Mississippi

$\overline{17}$ $\overline{53}$ $\overline{98}$ $\overline{116}$ $\overline{85}$ $\overline{103}$ $\overline{73}$

S. Play the part of

$\overline{45}$ $\overline{1}$ $\overline{100}$ $\overline{15}$ $\overline{40}$

ANSWER, PAGE 216

THE LANGUAGE OF LOVE

"Dear Ms. Lonely Hearts … Sometimes when I see someone who's incredibly sexy, I try to talk to them but I get all tongue-tied and speechless. What should I do?" Signed, At a Loss for Words

"Dear At a Loss … You've got to to improve your vocabulary. And to that end, here's a list of forgotten words from the Victorian era that deal with the language of love. I've hidden 33 of them in the grid. After you've circled them all, the leftover letters will reveal the definitions of GANDERMOONER, CURTAIN-SERMON, and SMICK respectively." Signed, Ms. Lonely Hearts

```
                                                              F
                                                           U
              F  R  I  M              A  H  M  A        L
           N  W  H  E  O  C        H  A  A  A  S  S     Y
        E  S  O  K  T  N  H  E     R  L  N  L  W  M  P  E
        B  R  I  D  E  L  O  P  E     O  C  M  O  F  E  O  A  N
  D  Y  R  L  A  V  A  R  O  U  R  H  I  N  M  M  G  R  P  T  H
  E  F  L  E  S  H  S  H  A  M  B  L  E  S  R  A  F  M  Y  I  R
  S  T  O  G  R  A  N  D  G  O  R  E  N  T  E  R  B  A  T  H  E
  B  M  V  O  T  N  F  T  H  D  A  E  F  T  S  R  E  L  R  D  R
  H  E  E  I  L  S  A  W  I  E  S  F  D  E  N  O  E  S  A  H  F
     E  S  O  O  G  R  E  T  S  E  H  C  N  I  W  A  E  L  U
     S  H  P  V  G  D  H  I  T  Y  V  E  U  A  N  R  B  C  A
        I  I  A  R  R  C  T  Y  E  H  A  R  T  G  L  U  C
        P  E  L  W  Y  A  C  P  E  T  U  P  R  R  S  H  E
           G  I  V  L  V  D  I  H  N  D  D  U  E  A  N
           A  M  O  R  E  T  E  T  I  A  E  C  R  B  Y
              A  S  L  H  D  C  N  K  E  W  N  W  L
              U  M  C  I  E  I  S  H  E  F  I
           M  G  N  I  R  H  S  U  R  T  B  E
     B        A  H  C  T  E  M  I  S  B
  E     A           C  D  K  I  T  A  I
  M     T           E  T  B  O  F
  E  K  I           S  A  S
                    B
```

ACHARNE
AMORET
BABIES-IN-THE-EYES
BESPAWLED
BRIDELOPE
CHICHEVACHE
CLARTY-PAPS
CURTAIN-SERMON
DELUMBATE
ENTERBATHE
FAIRHEAD

FARDRY
FLESH-SHAMBLES
FRIKE
FRIM
FUCUS
FULYEAR
GANDERMOONER
GRANDGORE
GREADE
HALCH
HALF-MARROW

LAVOLT
LIBS
LOVESHIP
MODESTY-PIECE
MORMALS
MUSKIN
RAVALRY
RUSH RING
SMICK
STEWED PRUNE
WINCHESTER GOOSE

ANSWER, PAGE 217

WHAT'S THE WORD?

We use them all the time. We even know how to spell some of them.
But do we know where those strange-to-our-ears words got their start?

ACROSS

1 Thanksgiving veggies
5 Barter
9 Breakfast order
14 Cain's brother
15 Walt Kelly strip
16 Overhead
17 From the French meaning "to heat," it once referred to the "fireman" who stoked the fires on steamships and locomotives
19 Cotton-blend fiber
20 Arthur Hailey novel
21 Snake charmer
23 Put a word in
24 "Don't give up!"
25 Big Ten sch.
27 Designer Saint Laurent
29 It's from the French expression *"allez-fusil"* ("forward the musket!"), and became common in Ireland after French troops landed there in 1798
34 Like dives
37 Auto ID
38 Throw in a monkey wrench
39 TV's singing cowboy of the '50s
40 Shake up
41 "___ big deal"
42 Problem
43 Word with drop or point
44 Hits hard
45 A toy invented in 1817, its name is derived from three Greek words meaning "observer of beautiful forms"
48 Go postal
49 Role for Nicole in *Cold Mountain*
50 "Harper Valley ___"
53 Songwriters' org.
56 Marriott alternative
58 Like supermarket tabloids
60 Fragrance

62 Word derived from a roll of names that all feudal nobles and gentry had to sign as a token of allegiance
64 Sparkler in a crown
65 Tom-tom, e.g.
66 Skating jump
67 Proverb
68 The Abominable Snowman
69 Harp's kin

DOWN

1 Marine limo?
2 Detest
3 Substantive
4 Turn sharply
5 Letters on a Coppertone label
6 Wretched

7 *Casa* quaff
8 Cartoon legend
9 Cask
10 Kentucky Colonels' org.
11 Unconscious state
12 *Metamorphoses* poet
13 Basis for aid
18 She's not as good as she should be
22 Bjorn's Wimbledon rival
26 Furtive
28 Military raid
29 Popcorn orders
30 Declares
31 Unseat
32 Fan's mag
33 Time periods in Barcelona
34 It borders N. Dak.

35 ___ Park, in old Coney Island
36 List ender, for short
40 Art Fleming was its first host
41 Old Chevy
43 6/6/44
44 Ireland, "the auld ___"
46 We do it all the time
47 String material
50 Kind of vote
51 Bathroom contractor
52 Fred Astaire's sister
53 Western peninsula
54 TV's equine talker
55 *State Fair* state
57 Dunlop product
59 River to the Caspian
61 *Hurlyburly* star Ryan
63 Big year for Kubrick?

ANSWER, PAGE 216

DANGER! MAD SCIENTIST AT WORK

The most brilliant inventor of the 20th century—Nikola Tesla—died broke, friendless, and nuttier than a fruitcake. Herewith, some of his amazing accomplishments and peculiar obsessions.

1. *KDFCP QZBCJ RWZJBQD CTEUKYTYE SZCKF,
FRPWGF WBYYTYE PQWZFF KUD EWZBYJ, PYJ
EUZFKCM SCBD ECZVF TY KUD PTW. TY XPQK,
PCC KUZFD VTCJ-DMDJ ADY TY VUTKD QZPKF TY
*UZCCMVZZJ RTQKBWDF PWD SPFDJ ZY UTA.

2. JDP PYPQJCRQRJX OYEBDRKN ECWZKV *VC.
*OCEKLPKBJPRK'B QEBJYP? E VRCPQJ QWHX WO
CPEY-YROP QWKVRJRWKB RK *JPBYE'B YEU.
*OCEKLPKBJPRK AEB JDP ORCBJ WO FEKX
FWIRPB JW ZBP CPEY *JPBYE QWRYB JW NPJ
JDWBP APRCV ECQB WO ECJRORQREY YRNDJRKN.

3. AJ DZU Z WHZUUEW TYUJUUEFJ-WTPOGHUEFJ DAT
HTFJK OEVJTSU, NAJ KZCL, ZSK NAJ SGPYJC
NACJJ, ZSK DZU NJCCEREJK TR KECN, VJCPU,
ZSK CTGSK TYQJWNU, JUOJWEZHHX OJZCHU. AJ
UTPJNEPJU UEVSJK AEU HJNNJCU "*V.*E." RTC
*VCJZN *ESFJSNTC. TNAJC NAZS NAZN AJ DZU
RESJ.

ANSWER, PAGE 216

LET ME WRITE
SIGN—I SPEAK ENGLISH

When traveling in a foreign country, you might not be the only one who's having language problems. We've taken 6 signs, in somewhat broken English, that have been found in foreign countries. Your job is to put the words in the correct order so that they (almost) make sense. For example, the words DAILY OPEN RESTAUROOM when rearranged become RESTAUROOM OPEN DAILY.

On the grass in a Paris park:
A BE DO DOG NOT PLEASE

Outside a Hong Kong dress shop:
FITS HAVE LADIES UPSTAIRS

On a menu in Nepal:
BEAR COMPLIMENTARY GLASS OF OR WINE

In a Rome hotel room:
7 AUTO DIAL FROM GARBAGE PLEASE RETRIEVE THE TO YOUR

On a menu in China:
AND BLUBBER CHILDREN COLD IN SAUCE SEA SHREDDED SPICY

At a Seoul hotel desk:
BED CHOOSE KING KONG MARRIAGE NO OR REGRET SIZE SIZE TWIN WE

ANSWER, PAGE 217

* * * * *

IT SOUNDS WORSE THAN IT IS

Trust the medical establishment to make even the most minor ailment or symptom sound frightening. Can you match each ominous-sounding medical term (1-12) to its not-so-bad real meaning (a-l)?

____ 1. Bilateral perorbital hematoma	a. Black eye
____ 2. Epistaxisis	b. Burp
____ 3. Eructation	c. Dry skin
____ 4. Horripilation	d. Earache
____ 5. Otalgia	e. Goosebumps
____ 6. Pandiculation	f. Hiccup
____ 7. Punctuate pruritis	g. Ice cream headache
____ 8. Singultus	h. Itchy spot
____ 9. Spheno pulatine ganglio neuralgia	i. Nosebleed
____ 10. Sternutation	j. Sneeze
____ 11. Verruca vulgaris	k. Wart
____ 12. Xeroderma	l. Yawn

ANSWER, PAGE 217

PERFECT 10 #2

Here are 10 more *almost* perfect statements. Remember that the numbers have been switched in pairs: If the 2 should replace 10, the 10 should also replace the 2. Can you restore the 10 to perfection?

The first Apple computer in 1976 had **1** byte of RAM.
A married man is **2** times more likely to die during sex if his partner isn't his wife.
Etiquette experts claim you should hang up if no one answers your call after **3** rings.
After 84 days in Skylab, astronauts found they were **4** inches taller.
The average Briton brews about **5** pounds of tea a year.
One ton of iron can turn into **6** tons of rust.
In the average film, male actors utter **7** times as many profanities as female actors.
The element astatine accounts for about **8** ounces—total—of the Earth's crust.
Shirley Temple won an honorary Oscar in 1934, when she was only **9** years old.
The average Ph.D. candidate spends **10** years on his/her dissertation.

ANSWER, PAGE 218

* * * * *

GROUNDED FOREVER

Small crostic puzzles are solved just like the big ones (directions on page 13) but the first letters of the fill-in words **do not** spell out a hidden message.

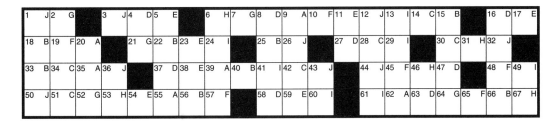

A. Terminus for the Chunnel

___ ___ ___ ___ ___ ___
9 39 20 62 55 35

B. Manager's starting pitchers, e.g.

___ ___ ___ ___ ___ ___ ___ ___
40 25 15 33 66 18 22 56

C. Come into bloom

___ ___ ___ ___ ___ ___
14 34 51 30 42 28

D. England's "Iron Lady"

___ ___ ___ ___ ___ ___ ___ ___
16 47 27 8 37 58 4 63

E. Geena Davis's Olympic sport

___ ___ ___ ___ ___ ___ ___
23 17 11 38 59 5 54

F. Best Picture of 1982

___ ___ ___ ___ ___ ___
57 19 65 48 10 45

G. Four-footed movie star

___ ___ ___ ___ ___
52 64 2 21 7

H. Elbow grease

___ ___ ___ ___ ___
67 6 53 31 46

I. Constant complaining

___ ___ ___ ___ ___ ___ ___
29 13 60 61 49 24 41

J. Large quarry for warm water anglers

___ ___ ___ ___ ___ ___ ___ ___ ___
32 44 36 12 43 26 1 50 3

ANSWER, PAGE 218

THE TEXICON

If you're planning a visit to the Lone Star State, you might want to study up on the language first. Just fill in the blanks with the words from the list below.

biggo	fixinta	hair yew	ite	putnear
binness	gace	idjit	jeet	sketty

1. A common greeting in Texas, as in "Mornin', darlin', _____ today?"

2. A dish served in an Italian restaurant, as in "Ahl have the meatballs and _____."

3. A question about a person's previous meal, as in "Hey, _____ yet? Ahm hungry."

4. Almost, as in "Ah was so tard ah _____ fell asleep."

5. Intending to, as in "Ahm _____ go to the movies."

6. Large or extreme, as in "He's nothin' but a _____ drunk."

7. Personal concern, as in "It's none-a yer goldam _____ where Ahm goin'!"

8. Someone who's not too sharp, as in "That boy's an _____!"

9. The next number in the sequence: "...four, fahve, six, seb'n, _____..."

10. What makes a car run, as in "Y'all got enough _____ in yer truck to git there?"

ANSWER, PAGE 218

* * * * *

A.K.A. HIS NIBS

Why is a pompous big shot known as a "high-mucky-muck?"

a. It comes from the Chinook phrase hayo makamak, which literally means "plenty to eat." In Native American culture, having lots of food was a sign of being rich and powerful.

b. It comes from "high MacAmac," an old English slur directed towards Scotsmen awarded titles in the English aristocracy. The name MacAmac is a joke on the Scottish tendency to prefix names with "Mac."

c. It's from Major Muckety-Muck, a self-important but ineffectual character from an Alan Ayckbourn play. The name was no doubt chosen because "muck" is British slang for something of no inherent worth.

ANSWER, PAGE 218

MISNOMERS

From Uncle John's exhaustive collection of things that are named for what they're not.

ACROSS

1 *Matilda* star Wilson
5 Compare
10 Franz's *"SNL"* partner
14 Prayer ender
15 Amazed
16 Head out
17 Misnamed pine tree
19 Friend in war
20 Bleeper
21 Broth brand
23 Drives the getaway car, e.g.
24 Put out on first
25 He held the world on his shoulders
29 Embellish, as a résumé
30 Scrape (out)
32 Cell phone purchase incentive
33 Weapon with a pin
36 Eurasian mountain range
37 Misnamed relative of spiders and scorpions
40 Prefix for physics
41 Shows the way
42 Goat-men
44 ___ X
45 ___ de deux (ballet set)
48 Mature
49 That girl
51 Concert, for example
53 Must
55 Come to light
56 ___ Velva
59 Misnamed Asian lake
61 Shirley Temple feature
62 Shorten, maybe
63 Pickle flavor
64 Word after muscle or dial
65 Inferno
66 Be fresh

DOWN

1 Zany
2 One-celled organism
3 Met up, as alumni
4 Uneasy feeling
5 Don't trust a guy like this
6 Org. that formerly policed the border
7 *The Trial* author Franz
8 Ex-Knick Patrick
9 Claudius' stepson
10 Misnamed condition of the esophagus
11 Guns n' Roses singer Rose
12 Zip
13 Miss Piggy's home?
18 Yankees, in the 2004 Series
22 Scottish explorer of the Arctic John ___
24 Nervous
26 Actress ___ Flynn Boyle
27 Run ___ (pay later)
28 Salt, to Sartre
31 Ships' backbones
32 Shortstop Pee Wee
33 Misnamed black sea creature
34 "Eureka!"
35 Ram maker
37 "I ___ you" ("Got it")
38 *Beetle Bailey* pooch
39 Show place?
40 Additive found in Chinese food
43 Genetic material
45 It's now called Iran
46 Anaheim team
47 Picks a pocket or two
49 Public bathroom feature
50 Garden plant
52 Sells
54 Replacement worker
55 The Emerald Isle
56 Play part
57 Status ___
58 Coffee container
60 Candy dispenser

ANSWER, PAGE 218

SHOW ME THE MONEY

One of the joys of traveling is (not) exchanging currency. For a small commission, we've listed 42 international currencies, old and new. Your job is to find their proper places in the grid. Feel free to visit the answer section if you're curious about what country is attached to each.

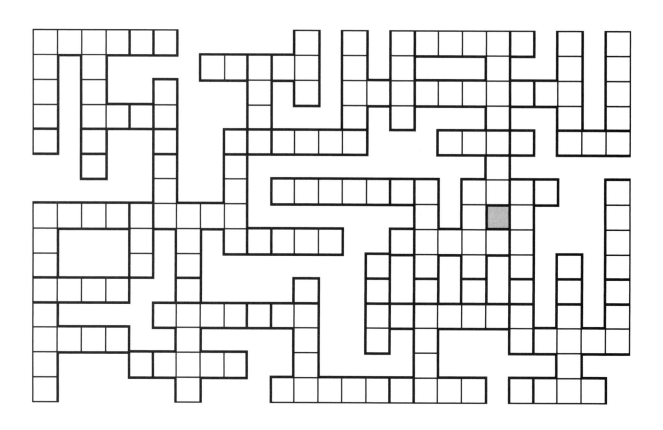

3-letter words
Lev
Won
Yen

4-letter words
Baht
Birr
Euro
Kina
Lira
Mark
Peso
Rand
Real

5-letter words
Colon
Franc
Krona
Litas
Pound
Riyal
Rupee
Sucre
Tolar
Zloty

6-letter words
Balboa
Dollar
Escudo

Florin
Markka
Peseta
Rouble
Shekel

7-letter words
Afghani
Bolivar
Drachma
Guilder
Quetzal
Ringgit

8-letter words
Ngultrum
Nuevo Sol

9-letter words
Lilangeni
New Kwanza
Schilling

10-letter word
Cordoba Oro

ANSWER, PAGE 219

SEX-CESS STORIES

Answering the question, "Is sex dirty?" Woody Allen said,
"Only if it's done right." Here are a few more opinions on the subject.

1. Billy Crystal

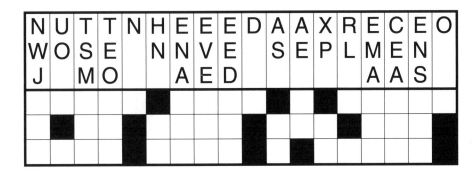

2. Joan Rivers

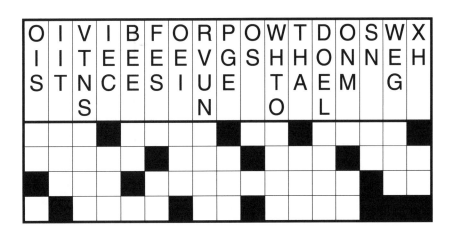

3. George Burns

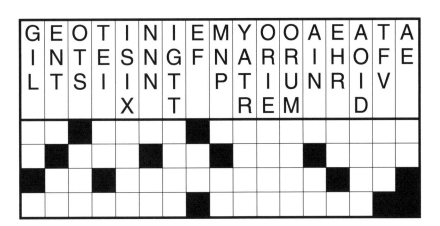

ANSWER, PAGE 218

HOMONYMICAL MARRIAGE

Whether you're in favor of it or not, two words that are spelled differently but sound alike make for a darn good puzzle.

ACROSS

1 Flatfoot's problem?
5 One of a famous ocean trio
10 Fish entrée choice
14 Ritz crackers rival
15 Deplete
16 Voracious
17 Blue-pencil
18 Poet non grata?
20 Place where devotees flock
22 Particle with a charge
23 Former *Cheers* actress
24 Earthenware pot
26 Past *due*?
27 Mister Ed, with laryngitis?
32 Not yet scheduled, for short
35 Holiday quaff
36 Oxlike antelope
37 Disallow
38 Take it on the lam
39 Printed again
41 Logical start?
42 Apt. amenity
43 In agreement
44 Grasp
46 NFL gains
47 Dessert served at The Happy Hunter?
49 End of many Web addresses
50 Latvian capital
51 First player covered in baseball?
54 I love, to Virgil
56 Apple pie order?
60 Quaint lodgings?
63 Mathematician Turing
64 Ballfield cover
65 Danger
66 Cosby/Culp TV series
67 Rice at Borders
68 Smart one
69 Computer input

DOWN

1 "I'm waiting…"
2 Tease
3 Fashionable
4 Third base, in baseball lingo
5 Saloon
6 Book before Jeremiah
7 Forum fiddler?
8 Go bad
9 Gibbon, for one
10 Mercury model
11 Picture frame shape
12 Old Italian dough
13 Whirlpool
19 Challenge
21 Furthermore
25 Space, especially in a plane
26 Tidal anomaly
27 Glad competitor
28 Gave the once-over
29 Golden ___ (seniors)
30 Shrek and kin
31 Genetic conduit
32 Fusses
33 Coffin stands
34 Building brick
37 Presentation enhancement
40 Rock impresario Brian
45 Marshes
47 Debatable
48 R-rated, perhaps
49 Brunch pancake
51 Old film canine
52 Epitome of grace
53 Gull relative
54 *The Clan of the Cave Bear* novelist Jean
55 Entangle
57 Rick's love
58 Kirk or Hook (abbr.)
59 "Sail Away" singer
61 Restoration location?
62 Benevolent order member

ANSWER, PAGE 219

I LOVE THE '80s!

Were you really paying attention during the Gimme Decade? Using a little knowledge
and a little logic, you should be able to fill in the correct year for each set of events.

198__
* Oliver North indicted for his role in the Iran-Contra scandal
* Table tennis is introduced as an Olympic sport
* Soviet army begins withdrawal from Afghanistan, opening the way for the Taliban to take over
* First smoking ban on U.S. flights goes into effect

198__
* Live Aid concert held in New York and London simultaneously
* Rock Hudson dies of AIDS
* Greenpeace's *Rainbow Warrior* is bombed by the French during a protest of nuclear testing.
* The number of Barbie dolls surpasses the U.S. population

198__
* 52 U.S. hostages are released from Iran on the day of Ronald Reagan's first inauguration
* Sandra Day O'Connor becomes first female Supreme Court Justice
* Prince Charles weds Lady Diana
* MTV debuts

198__
* The space shuttle *Challenger* explodes
* Martin Luther King Day becomes a U.S. holiday
* Soviet nuclear plant Chernobyl has a major meltdown
* Paul Simon's *Graceland* is Album of the Year

198__
* First permanent artificial heart transplant performed on Barney Clark
* Falklands War begins and ends
* *Late Night With David Letterman* debuts
* Prince William of England is born

198__
* *Exxon Valdez* crashes, causing worst oil spill in U.S. history
* President George Herbert Walker Bush is inaugurated president
* Chinese troops quash pro-democracy demonstration in Tiananmen Square
* Mikhail Gorbachev is named *Time* Person of the Year for the second time

198__
* Televangelist Jim Bakker resigns after sex scandal with secretary Jessica Hahn
* Stock market crashes on October 17—"Black Monday"
* Mikhail Gorbachev is named *Time* Person of the Year
* Hasbro takes away Mr. Potato Head's pipe, bowing to anti-smoking groups

198__
* The first CD is released: Bruce Springsteen's *Born in the U.S.A.*
* The Soviet Union organizes a revenge boycott of the Olympics in Los Angeles
* Indira Gandhi is assassinated
* Geraldine Ferraro is the first American woman nominated for vice president by a major political party

198__
* Mount St. Helens erupts
* The U.S. boycotts the summer Olympics in Moscow to protest the Soviet invasion of Afghanistan
* Sony introduces the Walkman; 3M introduces Post-It notes
* John Lennon is assassinated

198__
* Final episode of *M*A*S*H* airs
* U.S. invades Grenada
* Michael Jackson's *Thriller* becomes the best-selling album of all time
* Barney Clark dies 112 days after his groundbreaking surgery

ANSWER, PAGE 218

GET A JOB

The Dictionary of Occupation Titles is published by the U.S. Department of Labor, and lists some 25,000 real job titles both ordinary and peculiar. So if you're looking new career, consider the 21 occupations hidden in the grid below. (Yes, it's shaped like a rabbit, but that's because Easter Bunny is indeed a job title.) After you've circled all the jobs in the grid, the leftover letters will reveal five more job titles you may or may not want to add to your résumé.

```
        M M                           D R
    O U I G                       F O E O
    D C L D                       R O P U
    G K K B                       E R M H
    B B O O                       L E U M
    I O F T X                 B E G D E
    R S L T E                 L S G N L
      S I O G                 I I E A
      S M M G                 N H P E
    O E B S N I L E D L D C N B
      S U M I A N E N D H D I
      L F E I S L T R E O A A
      I A F L B U T A C O O E H Y
    R S K E L U B A K C S K H C N R
    S E E R E M B E R L E E Y M N E
  A S S R E R M R B E L E R R O U B F
  R E T O R T F O R K E R T I O B B S
  H F L I P P E R A C N O D P L R U A
  N T Y H O S E C K I E R D R Y E R R
  P I C K L E P U M P E R O T B T D C
  H M U T T O N P U N C H E R B S E C
  L O S I N G M L A I C H I N O A B E
    O P E R A L D E A D H E A D E R
      T O R E S S E R P M O S O B
        R E T A E B R U F R
```

BEAN DUMPER

BED RUBBER

BLIND HOOKER

BOLOGNA LACER

BOSOM PRESSER

BOTTOM BUFFER

BRAIN PICKER

DEAD HEADER

DOBBYLOOM CHAINPEGGER

EASTER BUNNY

EGG SMELLER

FUR BEATER

HEAD CHISELER

KIER DRYER

LAP CHECKER

MILK-OF-LIME SLAKER

MUCK BOSS

MUTTON PUNCHER

PICKLE PUMPER

RETORT FORKER

TOE PULLER

ANSWER, PAGE 220

IS DE WIDDLE FELLA HUNGWY?

Directions for solving are on page 13.

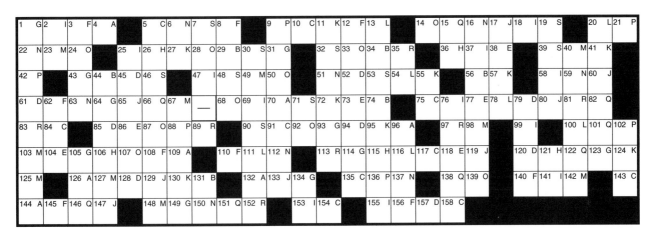

A. Punk rock pioneer and Stooges front man (2 wds.)

$\overline{144}\ \overline{109}\ \overline{96}\ \overline{4}\ \overline{126}\ \overline{70}\ \overline{132}$

B. Fodder preserved through fermentation

$\overline{131}\ \overline{56}\ \overline{34}\ \overline{44}\ \overline{74}\ \overline{29}$

C. Author of the Babar books (2 wds.)

$\overline{135}\ \overline{158}\ \overline{5}\ \overline{117}\ \overline{91}\ \overline{84}\ \overline{10}\ \overline{75}\ \overline{154}\ \overline{143}$

D. Naked (3 wds.)

$\overline{94}\ \overline{79}\ \overline{120}\ \overline{52}\ \overline{85}\ \overline{45}\ \overline{128}\ \overline{61}\ \overline{157}$

E. Persistently found fault

$\overline{73}\ \overline{86}\ \overline{104}\ \overline{77}\ \overline{118}\ \overline{38}$

F. Extremely close game (hyph.)

$\overline{108}\ \overline{62}\ \overline{140}\ \overline{12}\ \overline{3}\ \overline{156}\ \overline{110}\ \overline{8}\ \overline{145}$

G. Country music's Texas Troubadour (2 wds.)

$\overline{105}\ \overline{134}\ \overline{123}\ \overline{149}\ \overline{31}\ \overline{64}\ \overline{93}\ \overline{114}\ \overline{43}\ \overline{1}$

H. European mountain ash

$\overline{106}\ \overline{26}\ \overline{121}\ \overline{36}\ \overline{115}$

I. Director of *Nashville* and *Gosford Park* (2 wds.)

$\overline{69}\ \overline{153}\ \overline{47}\ \overline{18}\ \overline{76}\ \overline{141}\ \overline{99}\ \overline{155}\ \overline{58}$

$\overline{25}\ \overline{2}\ \overline{37}$

J. Kent Haruf's *Plainsong* sequel

$\overline{60}\ \overline{17}\ \overline{133}\ \overline{129}\ \overline{147}\ \overline{80}\ \overline{119}\ \overline{65}$

K. 1967 collection of Erma Bombeck humor (3 wds.)

$\overline{11}\ \overline{124}\ \overline{41}\ \overline{72}\ \overline{27}\ \overline{57}\ \overline{55}\ \overline{95}\ \overline{130}$

L. Wastes time

$\overline{20}\ \overline{78}\ \overline{111}\ \overline{116}\ \overline{54}\ \overline{13}\ \overline{100}$

M. Onetime steel-making hub in the Northeast

$\overline{125}\ \overline{40}\ \overline{49}\ \overline{23}\ \overline{103}\ \overline{142}\ \overline{67}\ \overline{127}\ \overline{148}\ \overline{98}$

N. Jaundiced in appearance

$\overline{137}\ \overline{150}\ \overline{6}\ \overline{16}\ \overline{112}\ \overline{51}\ \overline{22}\ \overline{63}\ \overline{59}$

O. Lassie's creator (2 wds.)

$\overline{50}\ \overline{87}\ \overline{33}\ \overline{14}\ \overline{24}\ \overline{139}\ \overline{107}\ \overline{68}\ \overline{28}\ \overline{92}$

P. Capital island of Kiribati

$\overline{88}\ \overline{136}\ \overline{21}\ \overline{102}\ \overline{9}\ \overline{42}$

Q. Blunders

$\overline{82}\ \overline{138}\ \overline{66}\ \overline{101}\ \overline{15}\ \overline{151}\ \overline{122}\ \overline{146}$

R. Wisconsin city on Lake Winnebago

$\overline{83}\ \overline{81}\ \overline{113}\ \overline{35}\ \overline{97}\ \overline{152}\ \overline{89}$

S. "If something can go wrong, it will" (2 wds.)

$\overline{32}\ \overline{7}\ \overline{30}\ \overline{90}\ \overline{39}\ \overline{46}\ \overline{19}\ \overline{48}\ \overline{53}\ \overline{71}$

ANSWER, PAGE 220

PARLEZ-VOUS DOUBLESPEAK?

Here's a batch of real-life euphemisms used in business and advertising. Can you unscramble the scrambled-up words and figure out exactly what they're trying so hard not to say?

1. "Portion controlled" __ __ __ __ __ __
   CLESID

2. "Form persuader" __ __ __ __ __ __
   DEGLRI

3. "Entropy control engineer" __ __ __ __ __ __ __
   NOTJIRA

4. "Clothing refresher" __ __ __ __ __ __ __ __ __
   YDR   NACLEER

5. "Facial-quality tissue" __ __ __ __ __ __ __ __ __ __ __
   OLTTIE   ARPEP

6. "Automotive internist" __ __ __ __ __ __ __ __ __ __ __
   ACR   NACCIHEM

7. "Interdental stimulator" __ __ __ __ __ __ __ __ __
   COPTKOTIH

8. "Career associate scanning professional" __ __ __ __ __ __ __ __ __ __ __ __ __
   UHKOCTEC   KELRC

9. "Animal control warden" __ __ __ __ __ __ __ __ __ __
   ROCTHEGADC

10. "Social expression products" __ __ __ __ __ __ __ __ __ __ __ __ __
    RIGGENTE   DASRC

11. "Interment excavation expert" __ __ __ __ __ __ __ __ __ __ __
    VIGEGRGADER

12. "Equity retreat" __ __ __ __ __ __ __ __ __ __ __ __ __
    CTKOS   REMKAT   SRHAC

13. "Media courier" __ __ __ __ __ __ __ __ __ __ __ __ __ __ __
    WARNSEPPE   VERIDEREL

14. "Service technician" __ __ __ __ __ __ __ __ __
    ARMIPRENA

ANSWER, PAGE 219

IN THE TRENCHES

"The screaming-meemies" is just one expression that was coined during World War I, referring to the high-pitched whine made by German artillery shells just before they exploded. No wonder the term came to mean a state of near-hysteria. Here are a few more Great War slang terms that you might hear every day.

ACROSS

1 Adv. math class
5 Shout from the sidelines on TV
10 Jewish month
14 Epps of *House*
15 Stars and Stripes land, for short
16 Big rig
17 Territory between the Allied and German trenches
19 Book ID#
20 TV host who's asked a lot of questions
21 Pedicure items
23 Sit back and enjoy
25 Biblical pronoun
26 "How about that?!"
27 Bit of mockery
30 Madison Avenue worker
33 Simpson trial judge
34 Busy as ___
36 Egg-dropping sounds
39 Leaving the trenches to attack the enemy's front line
42 Transgressor
43 Wishes it wasn't so
44 Roger Clemens stat
45 Where a single sleeps
47 Tennis score after deuce, maybe
48 Wall St. worker
50 ___-mo
51 Arab chieftain
54 Trigger for a werewolf
57 Feels like a rash
61 Links hazard
62 Acute stress syndrome resulting from exposure to constant bombardment by the enemy
64 Sounded
65 Rose-red dye
66 K-12, in education
67 ___-Seltzer
68 Actress Perez
69 Cheer (for)

DOWN

1 Abbr. at the bottom of a page
2 Cupid
3 Shiny fabric
4 Tarzan player Buster
5 Gets the corn ready
6 Aruba, e.g.
7 Castle border
8 Important
9 Hurried
10 The East
11 Appointed
12 Stroll along
13 Washer phase
18 Teachers' org.
22 Satyrs' companions
24 Chicken ___
27 Dances in Dublin
28 Yours, to Yvette
29 At ___ range (very close)
31 Big name in tractors
32 Bass, for one
34 Discrimination against seniors
35 Schlemiel
37 Singer Amos
38 Cable network, with "C-"
40 Compass dir.
41 Boorish
46 Blubber
47 *Kane and Abel* novelist
48 Actors' grp.
49 Living in the country
52 Winnie-the-Pooh's creator
53 The "I" in TGIF
55 Annika Sorenstam's org.
56 Kevin Costner movie role
58 Gram or graph starter
59 Mountain feedback
60 *SNL* bit
63 Caesar's card deck count?

ANSWER, PAGE 220

BACK TO THE TRENCHES

As you may know, World War I wasn't, as advertised, the war to end
all wars. More wartime slang, this time from World War II on.

ACROSS

1 Biblical verb ending
4 "___ de lune"
9 Computer shortcut
14 Miss Piggy, to herself
15 Discontinued Ford
16 Orangy-brown
17 Beer, in World War II
20 Ticklish Muppet
21 Put on
22 Big trouble, in the Korean War
27 Rose of Tralee, maybe
28 Buffy portrayer
29 ___ Kim of rap
31 Every last one
34 Made like Sonny Liston
36 Storage chest material
40 Area inside the 20-yard line
42 Installment of a soap
44 *People* subject
45 He played the Green Goblin in *Spider-Man*
47 ___-Mex cuisine
48 It comes before omega
50 Sheriff's gang
52 Bra specification
55 Courage inspired by 17 Across, in World War II
60 Lassoed
62 October birthstone
63 Gentle criticism of a subordinate, in the Vietnam War
68 Beer container
69 Amalfi's country
70 Rim dangler
71 Goat feature
72 Fix a shoelace
73 Prohibition proponent

DOWN

1 Place (a reporter) with the troops
2 *Confederacy of Dunces* author John Kennedy ___
3 Blackjack request
4 Pvt.'s superior
5 Tell it like it isn't
6 Plus
7 ___ *Garry Shandling's Show*
8 Like angry seas
9 A little less than 31 Across
10 Hero of the *Iliad*
11 Yao Ming's home
12 Doesn't own
13 They're good with milk
18 Lids
19 Buzz's moon buddy
23 Skewered entrées
24 Anemic one's lack
25 Reached your credit card limit, with "out"
26 Revolutionary Guevara
30 Least friendly
31 Bow shape
32 Martial arts expert Bruce
33 Bad cholesterol, for short
35 Clear the windshield
37 One-third of an ellipsis
38 Summer quaff
39 T. ___ (museum skeleton)
41 Airship of old
43 One of the Spice Girls
46 Kwik-E-Mart owner on *The Simpsons*
49 Storklike bird
51 One of the Ghostbusters
52 1929 event
53 Admit, slangily
54 Michigan's ___ Peninsula
56 Radio station sign
57 Flip over
58 Less wild
59 Stony gray
61 Cozy rooms
64 Western Indian
65 Victim of curiosity
66 Yalie
67 Beholder's feature?

ANSWER, PAGE 220

ELEPHANTS
PLEASE STAY IN YOUR CAR

A few selections from Uncle John's private stash of silly signs. Match
the place of business (1-10) with the sign we found displayed there (a-j).

_____ 1. At a convalescent home

_____ 2. At a drycleaner

_____ 3. At a McDonald's

_____ 4. In a department store

_____ 5. In a hospital maternity ward

_____ 6. In a safari park

_____ 7. In the offices of a loan company

_____ 8. Next to a traffic light

_____ 9. Outside a house

_____ 10. Outside a photographer's studio

a. 38 Years on the Same Spot

b. Ask About Our Plans for Owning Your Home

c. Bargain Basement Upstairs

d. Elephants Please Stay in Your Car

e. For Sale Buy Owner

f. For the Sick and Tired of the Episcopal Church

g. Have the Kids Shot for Dad From $24.95

h. No Children Allowed

i. Parking for Drive-Thru Service Only

j. This Light Never Turns Green

ANSWER, PAGE 221

* * * * *

MYSTERY PLATE

American G.I.'s tried to make their chow more palatable by renaming it, for instance, they
called hash "mystery plate" and canned milk "armored cow." The column on the left lists
the food; the right-hand column the nickname. As an added hint, the left-hand column is in
alphabetical order. So why don't we start with some beans, that staple of the G.I. diet? **The
letter substitution remains constant throughout the list.**

_B E A N S_

HREQP

HZREL

WGDDRR

WZEWIRZP

UZEVR QFNP

ECCFQSNSGQ

UFQ AELLSQU

HENNRZB EWSL

LGU HSPWFSNP

PXZEVQRY

ANSWER, PAGE 221

MORE SEX-CESS STORIES

Was the first time good for you, too? Let's do it again.

1. Rodney Dangerfield

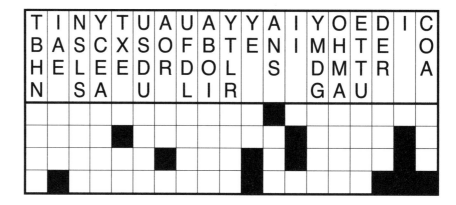

2. Sharon Stone

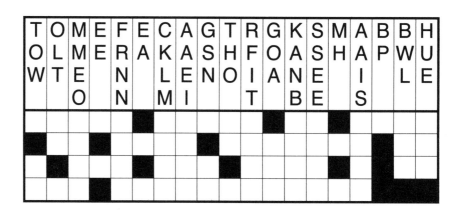

3. Steve Martin

ANSWER, PAGE 221

I FOUND IT ON eBAY

Some pretty wacky items have been auctioned off on eBay. Here's a list that was published in *Uncle John's Slightly Irregular Bathroom Reader* sans the items on the list that brought in no bids at all—turtle poop, dog hair, Bob Eubanks, and a perfectly good Assistant Manager. But check out our list, noting the opening bids, and then see if you can figure out what each item went for using the prices at the bottom of the page.

ITEM: Grandma—MUST SEE!!
DESCRIPTION: "We are so sure you will be happy with your grandma that we will throw in an extra pair of dentures. THAT'S NO TYPO! Warning: Grandma is known to spout profanity at times, and does get cranky if not given her medicine. (Medicine not included.)"
OPENING BID: $10.00   **WINNING BID**: _____

ITEM: The Meaning of Life
DESCRIPTION: "I have discovered the reason for our existence and will be happy to share this information with the highest bidder."
OPENING BID: $0.01   **WINNING BID**: _____

ITEM: Vial of Authentic *Melrose Place* TV Show Pool Water
DESCRIPTION: "Your favorite stars have swum and soaked in this pool for years. Now that the show is going to be gone forever you can still have a piece of history."
OPENING BID: $7.99   **WINNING BID**: _____

ITEM: One jar of air from Woodstock (the 1999 concert, not 1969)
DESCRIPTION: "I caught the air in the jar myself, it is real Woodstock air. So many came but how many thought to take some of the air with them? Get yours now."
OPENING BID: $9.99   **WINNING BID**: _____

ITEM: One package of 2 Krispy® Original Saltine Crackers
DESCRIPTION: "Seller reserves the right to eat this package of crackers at any time, and will replace said package with a suitable replacement."
OPENING BID: $0.01   **WINNING BID**: _____

ITEM: $1.00—One dollar!
DESCRIPTION: "One dollar bill, slightly used, ready for you to use! Works in most vending machines!"
OPENING BID: $.0.67 (Buyer pays 33¢ shipping & handling.)   **WINNING BID**: _____

ITEM: Justin Timberlake's French Toast
DESCRIPTION: "This is Justin's leftover French toast as eaten live on Z100 radio. You'll get his half-eaten French toast, the fork he used, and the plate…complete with extra syrup! Any bids over $1,000 will be verified by Z100 by phone for authenticity."
OPENING BID: $1.00   **WINNING BID**: _____

ITEM: My Dignity
DESCRIPTION: "Winning bidder will receive a piece of paper that says 'My Dignity' on it, with my signature. Warning: I may become a sad man after relinquishing my dignity."
OPENING BID: $2.00   **WINNING BID**: _____

$0.05	$3.26	$10.50	$1,000,300
$0.67	$7.99	$3,154	$9,999,999

ANSWER, PAGE 221

GRAVE HUMOR

Some tombstones' epitaphs tell you a bit about how a person lived. Others are a loving tribute from family members. And then ... there's this one.

ACROSS

1 Quarter moon, for example
6 Place for a soccer player's guard
10 Ham's father
14 Second showing
15 Sound on a phone line
16 Ticklish Muppet
17 Start of an anonymous epitaph
19 Stuff in a trap
20 Also-ran of 2000
21 Healing substances
23 Big house
27 Small amount
28 Uncommon sense
29 Trojan War hero
30 Word with duck or turkey
31 Carnival's setting
32 Rings of islands?
33 Drive in Los Angeles
34 Sylvester, to Tweety
35 Middle of the epitaph
39 Kind of service
41 Motherless calf
42 Hero of *The Phantom Tollbooth*
45 Give a massage to
46 Manipulative person
47 It's full of cells
49 The A of ETA (abbr.)
50 Animation fan's collectible
51 Space Needle's home
52 *Nixon* actor David
54 Digital camera's lack
55 Isaac's eldest son
56 End of the epitaph
62 Tanginess
63 Shade of green
64 Terpsichore is its Muse
65 Scarfs down
66 Ballooned
67 He resigned in 1973

DOWN

1 Debate position
2 Female octopus
3 Fly ball's path
4 Proceed with litigation
5 Mysterious thing
6 Belle of the Wild West
7 Sprinkler alternative
8 Bed-and-breakfast
9 Corporate profit figure
10 Jodie Foster movie
11 Classic 1830s novel
12 Affliction prevalent in soap operas
13 Hip place to go
18 Problems
22 Computer peripheral, e.g.
23 Actor Mineo
24 *Crouching Tiger, Hidden Dragon* director
25 "Paper Roses" singer
26 Fit together
27 *Good Morning America* rival
30 Display fear
33 Orion's brightest star
36 Bring out
37 Exotic facial adornment
38 Skip over
39 Big top feature
40 Huge land mass
43 Chat room chuckle
44 Word on a penny
47 Trapper's booty
48 Embassy Suites rival
51 Muscular strength
53 Makes funny faces
54 Part of a manicure set
57 Publicize
58 It may be running
59 Advice maven Landers
60 Road hazard
61 Heretofore unseen

ANSWER, PAGE 221

GAMES PEOPLE PLAY

It's your move. There are 57 games, including chess, hidden in the king and queen below. After you've found them all in the grid, the leftover letters will reveal a tip on how to change your luck at the table. And don't take all day about it, okay?

```
                                          T O
                                      B O A E
                    L T E E           U S R T
                    T E G E         E N H K A H
                R S E D B I         E C C O B C F T
                C I K I S H         Q U O I T S A E
                R H S R I U         E R N A W O F J
                T W E B R H         E C C A E P R D
                V O C F               S Y N A
                E G H A K T           O E U T C L
            R G B S N L E H         A G C S Y H V E
            L S A E D T U R       O T G A R Q I S U R
        E N Y C S Y O Q N S       U C N R I U S S R B
        U C C K R L H O E M       A A O T A E I O I I
        L C H G O A T R T A       C R J E H S I L N N
        C R A A H N B C T R       S E H C C T L I A G
        R I R M I D A B E B       S E A R L I O T M O
        U B A M N E F I L L       O R M O A O D A G T
        H B D O R R E A U E       T S O R C N E I N T
        I A E N D E C G O S       G P D M I S N R A E
        B G S A S K A N R N       N S D W S R A E H L
    P O K E R K J O K E R S W I L D M U I N A R C R O
    E E Z T H A Y O U J N S O R R Y M M U R K C O N K
    D I S T C S E N R O B E L L I M A N C A L A T H R
    E E T K R E T S I W T I M E Y L O P O N O M I S S
```

BACKGAMMON
BADMINTON
BILLIARDS
BINGO
BLACKJACK
BOCCE
BOGGLE
BRIDGE
BUNCO
CANASTA
CANDY LAND
CAREERS
CATCH
CHARADES
CHECKERS

CHESS
CLUE
CRANIUM
CRIBBAGE
CROQUET
DARTS
ECARTE
EUCHRE
FARO
FRISBEE
GIN RUMMY
HANGMAN
HORSESHOES
JACKS
JENGA

JOKERS WILD
KNOCK RUMMY
LIFE
MAH-JONGG
MANCALA
MARBLES
MILLE BORNES
MONOPOLY
MUSICAL CHAIRS
PACHISI
POKER
POOL
QUOITS
REVERSI
RING TOSS

ROOK
ROULETTE
SCRABBLE
SIMON
SKEET
SNOOKER
SOLITAIRE
SORRY
TWENTY
    QUESTIONS
TWISTER
WHIST
YAHTZEE

ANSWER, PAGE 221

DANCELY POPULATED

In Rio de Janeiro it's illegal to dance the samba in a tunnel. That's from Uncle John's bottomless collection of Looney Laws. But we hasten to add that it's perfectly legal to take the samba in the list below and put it, along with the 43 other dances, in the grid, crossword-style.

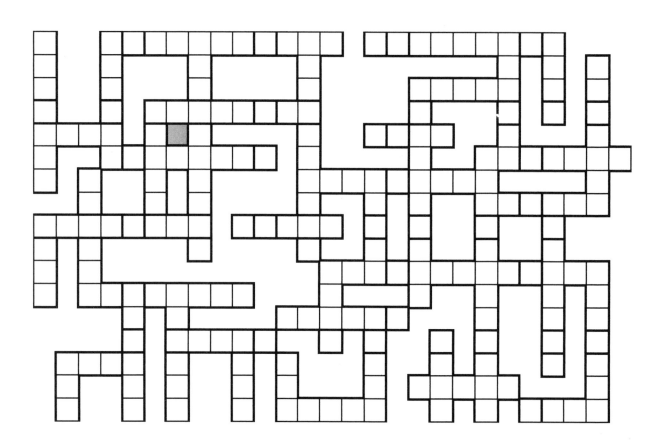

3-letter words
Bop
Jig

4-letter words
Frug
Hora
Hula
Jerk
Jive
Pony
Reel
Shag
Swim

5-letter words
Disco
Polka
Rumba
Swing
Tango
Twist
Waltz

6-letter words
Bolero
Can-can
Minuet
Monkey

Shimmy
Stroll
Troika
Watusi

7-letter words
Foxtrot
Gavotte
Madison
Peabody

8-letter words
Cakewalk
Fandango

Lindy Hop
Misirlou
Time Warp

9-letter words
Bossa Nova
Quickstep

10-letter words
Hucklebuck
Tarantella
Turkey Trot

11-letter word
Schottische

12-letter word
Mashed Potato

13-letter word
Highland Fling

ANSWER, PAGE 222

THE HUMAN ZOO

Sometimes the best way to describe people isn't to describe them as people at all.

ACROSS

1 Intestinal fortitude
5 One of Victoria's Secrets?
8 D-sharp
13 Olympics blade
14 Home for a *srta.* or *mlle.*
15 Combined, as resources
17 Large, gray peanut fancier
19 The Fighting ___ (Midwest team)
20
22 F.I.C.A. funds it
23 Biblical verb ending
24 Gone up
25 Symbolic pole
27 Letters on a shoebox
28 Brown smoke
30 Capital of Ukraine
33
37 Not warring
40 Ski mask cutout
41
43 Strong as ___
44 Do not disturb
45 Mafia bigwig
47 Pretty Boy of the Dillinger gang
50 Bible's first man, alphabetically
52 Country at the tip of Afr.
55 Fleur-de-___
56

59 Ashe Stadium event
61 Striped buzzer
62 Hightailed it
63 Chang's Siamese twin
64 Volcano output
65 Like salad greens
66 "Drop of golden sun" notes
67 Part of Q.E.D.

DOWN

1 Honkers
2 Illuminated from below
3 They're a mouthful?
4 Back-to-school mo., usually
5 Cap with a propeller
6 Ladder parts
7 Empire State Building style
8 Grand-scale movie
9 Word-of-mouth story
10 Guffaw, online
11 Most-wanted invitees
12 On edge
16 Circle meas.
18 *Spenser: For* ___
21 Joins together
26 Parentless one
27 In equal shares
29 Not straight
30 ___-El (Superman's birth name)
31 Personal finish
32 Center prefix
33 Dunker with a string attached
34 Charged particle
35 Day-___ paint
36 Kinsey's subject
38 Steakhouse's premium stock
39 Part of a TV
42 *Boston Public* extra
45 Comings and goings
46 Without repetition
47 Goof
48 Disinfectant brand
49 "___ Mio"
51 French river
52 Construction rod
53 Tom who won at 57 Down in 1983
54 Book ___ (make flight plans)
57 Racetrack a.k.a. "the Brickyard"
58 Actor MacLachlan
60 School grp.

ANSWER, PAGE 221

BLONDE AMBITION

Country music legend Dolly Parton has more than just music on her very sharp mind. We've translated some of her best sayings into simple letter-substitution code. For further instructions and hints on how to solve, see page 7.

1. *G KDW EVVZGPX QO DN NMI TGX WGXP NMDN WDFW

*MVEEFKVVL, DPL *G NMVQXMN, "KVQELP'N GN TI XBIDN GA

WVSILDF *G RVQEL UIBZ NMDN TGX VE' *M LVKP DPL OQN D *L

NMIBI NV SDZI GN *LVEEFKVVL?"

2. *M POOC HGGF SYF *M FGY'X CGGZ USF PGV DA SHO. *M CGGZ

CMZO S JSVXGGY SYALSA, RG LQSX FMPPOVOYJO FGOR MX DSZO?

*M'D SCLSAR HGYYS CGGZ CMZO *FGCCA, CMZO S PVOSZ. UNX *M'D

XQO UORX PVOSZ *M'WO OWOV UOOY.

3. *H AECP SMJQBZ DER PNDY *H PDEY, DER PNDY *H RCE'Y PDEY

HJ YC LC CXY YC IDJYXUQ. *H NDWQ DLUQQR YC ICJQ EXRQ ZCU

*IQEYNCXJQ CE SM CEQ NXERUQRYN KHUYNRDM.

4. TBPFJXVMM YM GIF APMYL *Y NUPBZ IVHF TFFE ZUYEJ VBB VBUEJ

YS *Y LUPBZ IVHF AVZF V BYHYEJ VG YG. YG'M BYQF *Y IVZ GU JFG

XYLI YE UXZFX GU MYEJ BYQF *Y NVM CUUX.

TOM SWIFT
AND HIS AMAZING MENAGERIE

In this installment, Tom takes on a flock of various creatures. Finish each sentence (1-10) with the word (a-j) that makes the most appropriate pun.

a. barked   c. chirped   e. groused   g. nagged   i. snapped
b. blubbered   d. droned   f. kidded   h. roared   j. yakked

____   1. "Get back here with that tennis ball!" Tom …
____   2. "Hey, don't get too close to that turtle!" Tom ...
____   3. "How many times have I told you not to ride that horse?" Tom ...
____   4. "I feel so sorry for that poor beached whale," Tom ...
____   5. "I hate going bird-hunting," Tom ...
____   6. "I much prefer bird-watching," Tom ...
____   7. "I warned you not to tease the lions!" Tom ...
____   8. "I've been just as busy as a bee," Tom …
____   9. "My dad's name is Billy and my mother's name is Nanny," Tom …
____   10. "There are all sorts of beasts of burden, you know. In Peru, they've got their llamas, and in Tibet…," Tom ...

ANSWER, PAGE 222

* * * * *

THE SAME OLD MATH

Small crostic puzzles are solved just like the big ones (directions on page 13) but the first letters of the fill-in words **do not** spell out a hidden message.

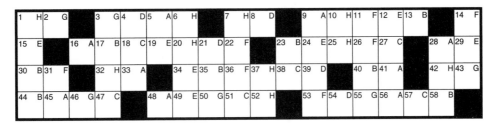

A. Billy Joel song set in Pennsylvania

$\overline{16}\ \overline{56}\ \overline{48}\ \overline{33}\ \overline{41}\ \overline{9}\ \overline{45}\ \overline{28}\ \overline{5}$

B. Edge-of-your-seat kind of movie

$\overline{23}\ \overline{44}\ \overline{58}\ \overline{40}\ \overline{30}\ \overline{17}\ \overline{13}\ \overline{35}$

C. Villain in Uncle Tom's Cabin

$\overline{47}\ \overline{57}\ \overline{18}\ \overline{51}\ \overline{27}\ \overline{38}$

D. Spice found in a fruit pomander

$\overline{4}\ \overline{39}\ \overline{21}\ \overline{54}\ \overline{8}$

E. Smart cookie

$\overline{15}\ \overline{24}\ \overline{49}\ \overline{12}\ \overline{34}\ \overline{29}\ \overline{19}$

F. Tourist-attracting fort in Wyoming

$\overline{31}\ \overline{22}\ \overline{26}\ \overline{36}\ \overline{53}\ \overline{14}\ \overline{11}$

G. Skip down a virtual page

$\overline{2}\ \overline{43}\ \overline{50}\ \overline{46}\ \overline{3}\ \overline{55}$

H. Frequent Roy Rogers second banana (2 wds.)

$\overline{6}\ \overline{1}\ \overline{32}\ \overline{20}\ \overline{37}\ \overline{10}\ \overline{7}\ \overline{52}\ \overline{25}\ \overline{42}$

ANSWER, PAGE 222

FLUGIE & FRIENDS

In the language of politics, a "flugie" is a rule that helps only the rule maker—sort of like the pay raises that Congress gives itself every few years. You'll find more of Uncle John's favorites in the grid.

ACROSS

1 "Dang!"
5 Schoolyard retort
9 The Lion King
14 Mine, to Michelle
15 Boxer Spinks
16 German sub
17 "Your majesty"
18 Moolah
19 Tubular pasta
20 A politician who puts politics ahead of principle
23 Novelist Deighton
24 "___ to Billy Joe"
25 Melodic
29 Rough board for nails
31 Invented rumors intended to smear an opponent
34 Fits ___ (is perfect)
36 Roswell sighting
37 Tiny taste
38 Speechifies pompously
42 Legendary Boston Bruin
45 Married
46 Uppity one
48 Intentionally confusing jargon
52 Construction support
55 Not alfresco
56 ___ de Janeiro
58 16-oz. sizes
59 Meaningless officialese
63 Harem honcho
66 Actor Chad of Life Goes On
67 "Thanks ___!"
68 38th Parallel conflict site
69 Draftable classification
70 Henpecks
71 "This is only ___" (radio phrase)
72 Damsel
73 Spock's journey

DOWN

1 Give a hard time to
2 "Like Toy Soldiers" rapper
3 Small crown
4 Actor Martin of Hill Street Blues
5 Paint category
6 Piddling
7 Big moment for a chorister
8 Small bills
9 Terrific
10 Spain and Portugal, once
11 Day of the wk.
12 Prohibit
13 Downed
21 True-blue
22 Fortuneteller's cards
26 ROTC relative
27 Hit the slopes
28 Paranormal power, for short
30 Brother of 66 Across
32 Pen name of Marie Louise de la Ramée
33 ___ mind (inclined)
35 Second of a group of high-rises, maybe
39 ___ out (relax)
40 Get a kick out of
41 ___ Canals
42 Tokyo tie
43 Did a 5K
44 Country P.O. option
47 Manic-depressive
49 Fuddy-duddies
50 Observe
51 Milwaukee player
53 Larry Fine role
54 "Shame on you!"
57 Optimal
60 Online diary
61 Actress Anderson
62 Big name in men's pants
63 Reggae relative
64 Sexy
65 Prior to

ANSWER, PAGE 222

SCRABBLE BABBLE

Our resident Scrabble™ expert gave us this list of two-letter words that she found in her *Official Scrabble Players Dictionary*. Sure, you can match the words (1-20) with their definitions (a-t), but the real challenge is to remember them the next time you play.

_____ 1. AA	a.	A bone (noun)
_____ 2. AE	b.	Born with the name of (adj.)
_____ 3. AI	c.	A Chinese unit of distance (noun)
_____ 4. AL	d.	The eternal soul in Egyptian mythology (noun)
_____ 5. BA	e.	An East Indian tree (noun)
_____ 6. JO	f.	A Greek letter (noun)
_____ 7. KA	g.	A Hebrew letter (noun)
_____ 8. LI	h.	A hypothetical force of natural power (noun)
_____ 9. NE	i.	A mantra used in contemplation of ultimate reality (noun)
_____ 10. OD	j.	A monetary unit of Vietnam (noun)
_____ 11. OE	k.	The old name for the first tone "do" in the scale sequence do, re, mi, fa, etc. (noun)
_____ 12. OP		
_____ 13. OS	l.	No; not (adv.)
_____ 14. UT	m.	One (adj.)
_____ 15. XU	n.	A part of the psyche (noun)
_____ 16. ID	o.	Rough, cindery lava (noun)
_____ 17. NA	p.	The spiritual self of a human being in Egyptian religion (noun)
_____ 18. OM		
_____ 19. PE	q.	A sweetheart (noun)
_____ 20. XI	r.	A style of abstract art (noun)
	s.	A three-toed sloth (noun)
	t.	A whirlwind off the Faeroe Islands (noun)

ANSWER, PAGE 223

* * * * *

UNCLE OSCAR'S BIG NIGHT #3

More scrambled Oscar-winning stars and the Oscar-winning films they won for.
For complete directions on how to solve, see page 12.

The Stars

1. NENE NAPS (4 4)
2. HIP NUN HEARTBREAK (9 7)
3. RODE TIGERS (3 7)
4. MENDING BRA RIG (6 7)
5. LONG JADE SNACK (6 7)

The Films

a. COACH SO FAULTS (1 5 2 5)
b. GAS LIGHT (8)
c. VIC, IT'S MY ERR (6 5)
d. HILTON TIE-WINNER (3 4 2 6)
e. OH! INFANT TEETHE THIGH (2 3 4 2 3 5)

ANSWER, PAGE 223

THAT'S ABOUT THE SIZE OF IT

Most people never give a second thought to life's most important questions, like how much should a dozen eggs weigh if they want to be called "jumbo"? Here's a look at the standard sizes and measurements attached to a few other everyday objects.

ACROSS

1 Spots on a 49 Down
5 Low-___ pants
10 TV's Griffin
14 *The African Queen* screenwriter
15 Knight's mail?
16 Both ways, as a prefix
17 Attract
18 It should weigh a maximum of 3 pounds, 10 ounces and should be exactly 1 foot, 3 inches tall
20 East-west map line (abbr.)
21 Kind of Buddhist
22 Bridge bid, briefly
23 Sign on some airplane lavs
25 Disappear slowly
28 It should be hung so that its center is 5 feet, 8 inches above the floor
31 Ostrich's kin
32 Big ___ (W.W. I German cannon)
33 Hindu retreat
36 It has to be 28 feet in diameter to work for a 200-pounder
38 Confirms
41 Bottom lines
43 Interstate 1, for short
44 It should be a square no smaller than 12 by 12 inches and no larger than 14 by 14 inches
47 "Let's go ahead with this"
51 Asian land
52 More aloof
53 Flunking letters
55 Soldiers on horseback (abbr.)
56 It has to measure between 27 and 28 inches in circumference and weigh 14 to 16 ounces
59 Present
60 Homophone of 59 Across
61 "Well, ___ a monkey's uncle!"
62 In ___ (bored)
63 *So Big* author Ferber
64 Fished for congers
65 Mistake in print

DOWN

1 Wan
2 Tennessee Williams title lizard
3 Bother
4 Understand
5 Kemo ___
6 Hubbard of Scientology
7 Ore-diggers' org.
8 Like some funds
9 Rat race
10 ___ cum laude
11 Give authority to
12 Stat for a slugger
13 Voice of the Dodgers Scully
19 Maiden-named
21 Football refs
24 Actions to take
25 Irregular geometric shape
26 Surgeons' grp.
27 "Delish!"
29 Other, in Madrid
30 "Eureka!"
33 One who may be anon.
34 Piles of pancakes
35 Greeting on a conventioneer's tag
37 Components of a hearty laugh
38 ___ Lanka
39 Long-distance initials
40 Sammy Davis Jr. story
42 Witchcraft
44 Trill like a bird
45 Get weepy
46 Must
48 Capital of Ghana
49 Craps cube
50 Spine-tingling
53 Hamburg's river
54 Ran for the hills
56 Ursula Andress film
57 British alternative to Webster's (abbr.)
58 The whole shebang
59 Easter parade attention-getter

ANSWER, PAGE 223

TRULY DROOLY

In the 1940s, if you saw a "drooly" guy or a girl who was "date bait," you might have gotten "squirrel fever"—a romantic urge. We've hidden 43 slang terms from the '40s in the squirrel below. After you've circled all the word list items in the grid, the leftover letters will reveal two more examples of '40s slanguage. See the answer section for definitions.

```
                     Y       E
                   T       L
                   H I N G E S
                 E S G O N A T L
                 L N T I A B E T A D
                 F A L L R I D B F E
                 F M Y L O B U U R N
                 I E J I W H I Z Z O
               L H I I U       V Z E
             S M W G K Q
             A E T O A S N P           S
             S Q O O T T M Y       O
             T G U B E U A K C A W
     L K H       F U Y R O A J C E C
   E L S Y G   B D N A S C R R O A
 R T U M B L E E P I P G A B I M V
 O R E V E F L E R R I U Q S A U E E A
 B N S I T B O F R O O S T E H N M R R K
 O S G V B O O B A K E E P D F B E A T N
 M U A O   G E U I J A C K S O N N W I A
 B P G R   D L R I G R E T A E W S D L Y
 E R C Y   O G N I L L O R C N N R Z V
 H E R D   E E S T E P O U T R A S
 A M T O   R S H O R T I E I R H B
   O O M     T A I L E N D C H A R L I E
     N E     S T N E D I S E R P D A E D
```

AQUARIUM	GOBBLEDYGOOK	STEP OUT
BAGPIPE	HARDWARE	SUPREMO
BEAGLE	HERD	SWEATER GIRL
BEAT	HINGES	TAIL-END CHARLIE
BEEFBURGER	IVORY-DOME	TOECOVER
BOOGIEMAN	JACKSON	TTFN
BRIGHTY	JUMP	TUMBLE
BRUSH	PEEK-A-BOO	UNPUTDOWNABLE
BUZZ	ROBOMB	VACKY
COGS	ROLLING	WACK
CRAZY	ROOST	WHIFFLE
DATE BAIT	SHORTIE	WHIZZO
DEAD PRESIDENTS	SLIMLINE	YANK
DEUCE OF HAIRCUTS	SQUILLION	
FALL	SQUIRREL FEVER	

ANSWER, PAGE 224

TAKE A LODE OFF

Directions for solving are on page 13.

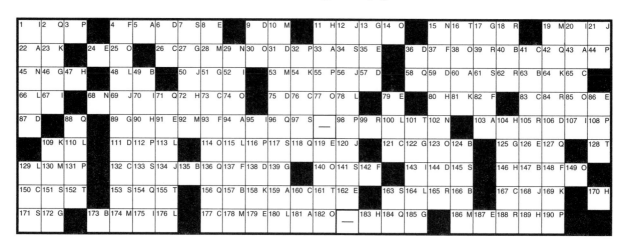

A. Warner Bros.' biggest star in the 1920s (3 wds.)

$\overline{60}$ $\overline{5}$ $\overline{22}$ $\overline{94}$ $\overline{43}$ $\overline{103}$ $\overline{181}$ $\overline{159}$ $\overline{33}$

B. Of great concern

$\overline{63}$ $\overline{124}$ $\overline{135}$ $\overline{147}$ $\overline{40}$ $\overline{49}$ $\overline{157}$ $\overline{173}$ $\overline{166}$

C. Andrew Card, to George W. Bush (3 wds.)

$\overline{26}$ $\overline{76}$ $\overline{41}$ $\overline{73}$ $\overline{150}$ $\overline{160}$ $\overline{83}$ $\overline{132}$ $\overline{177}$ $\overline{65}$ $\overline{167}$ $\overline{121}$

D. Inventor of the *Spruce Goose* airplane (2 wds.)

$\overline{57}$ $\overline{31}$ $\overline{75}$ $\overline{59}$ $\overline{6}$ $\overline{87}$ $\overline{144}$ $\overline{9}$ $\overline{106}$ $\overline{111}$ $\overline{138}$ $\overline{36}$

E. Author of the novel *The Pilot's Wife* (2 wds.)

$\overline{35}$ $\overline{86}$ $\overline{24}$ $\overline{8}$ $\overline{79}$ $\overline{162}$ $\overline{126}$ $\overline{119}$ $\overline{187}$ $\overline{91}$ $\overline{179}$

F. Cancel out

$\overline{93}$ $\overline{37}$ $\overline{142}$ $\overline{148}$ $\overline{137}$ $\overline{4}$ $\overline{82}$

G. "Big D" (2 wds.)

$\overline{139}$ $\overline{51}$ $\overline{46}$ $\overline{13}$ $\overline{122}$ $\overline{17}$ $\overline{125}$ $\overline{172}$ $\overline{185}$ $\overline{27}$ $\overline{89}$

H. Turning-point battle of the Civil War

$\overline{11}$ $\overline{90}$ $\overline{170}$ $\overline{72}$ $\overline{47}$ $\overline{183}$ $\overline{80}$ $\overline{104}$ $\overline{189}$ $\overline{146}$

I. Proof positive that you can't take it with you! (2 wds.)

$\overline{107}$ $\overline{52}$ $\overline{143}$ $\overline{20}$ $\overline{67}$ $\overline{95}$ $\overline{1}$ $\overline{70}$ $\overline{175}$

J. Deuces (hyph.)

$\overline{69}$ $\overline{50}$ $\overline{12}$ $\overline{120}$ $\overline{134}$ $\overline{168}$ $\overline{56}$ $\overline{21}$

K. Capital of Ontario

$\overline{23}$ $\overline{81}$ $\overline{169}$ $\overline{109}$ $\overline{64}$ $\overline{158}$ $\overline{54}$

L. Hint that might be nasty

$\overline{66}$ $\overline{78}$ $\overline{113}$ $\overline{48}$ $\overline{110}$ $\overline{100}$ $\overline{115}$ $\overline{176}$ $\overline{164}$
$\overline{129}$ $\overline{180}$

M. Nick and Jessica's TV reality show

$\overline{53}$ $\overline{174}$ $\overline{178}$ $\overline{28}$ $\overline{186}$ $\overline{19}$ $\overline{92}$ $\overline{130}$ $\overline{10}$

N. Electric distribution systems

$\overline{45}$ $\overline{15}$ $\overline{29}$ $\overline{102}$ $\overline{68}$

O. Hanna-Barbera cartoon duo (3 wds.)

$\overline{123}$ $\overline{85}$ $\overline{114}$ $\overline{30}$ $\overline{140}$ $\overline{25}$ $\overline{149}$ $\overline{38}$ $\overline{77}$
$\overline{74}$ $\overline{14}$ $\overline{182}$

P. Does a U.N. job

$\overline{112}$ $\overline{44}$ $\overline{116}$ $\overline{3}$ $\overline{55}$ $\overline{98}$ $\overline{32}$ $\overline{131}$ $\overline{108}$ $\overline{190}$

Q. Star of TV's *Two and a Half Men* (2 wds.)

$\overline{58}$ $\overline{154}$ $\overline{88}$ $\overline{71}$ $\overline{136}$ $\overline{184}$ $\overline{96}$ $\overline{42}$ $\overline{2}$
$\overline{118}$ $\overline{127}$ $\overline{156}$

R. Nickname of actor William Boyd

$\overline{18}$ $\overline{99}$ $\overline{39}$ $\overline{188}$ $\overline{62}$ $\overline{84}$ $\overline{165}$ $\overline{105}$

S. U.S. electric light and power inventor (2 wds.)

$\overline{145}$ $\overline{141}$ $\overline{34}$ $\overline{171}$ $\overline{133}$ $\overline{153}$ $\overline{117}$ $\overline{61}$ $\overline{163}$
$\overline{7}$ $\overline{151}$ $\overline{97}$

T. Small stream

$\overline{152}$ $\overline{16}$ $\overline{101}$ $\overline{161}$ $\overline{155}$ $\overline{128}$

ANSWER, PAGE 223

JEOPARDY!

The history and lore of America's favorite game show.

How It Came to Be

*VCWB IXU *ROPQIXX *KWQGGQX QXBCXHCU HZC TZEN. TILT *VCWB, "Q VCXHQEXCU ZEN VOAZ *Q PQJCU HZC EPU FOQD TZENT, YOH WCVQXUCU ZCW EG HZC TAIXUIPT. 'NZL XEH KQBC HZCV HZC IXTNCWT HE THIWH NQHZ?' TZC JQUUCU." HZC *RCESIWUL! GEWVIH NIT YEWX.

How It Got Its Name

UY NCKKYL SFY OCIY "*UFCS'R SFY *MVYRSGWD?" TVS C DYSUWZB YEYNVSGJY NWIIYDSYL, "SFY OCIY DYYLR IWZY 'XYWHCZLGYR'," RGSVCSGWDR UFYZY SFY HKCAYZ ZGRBR KWRGDO GS CKK. OWWLTAY, *UFCS'R SFY *MVYRSGWD?', FYKKW *'XYWHCZLA!'

Are You *Jeopardy!* Material?

JBJGD DJOG, EVL IKQCGJC NPNED EILKHOQC TJLTYJ OTTYD NLG OQ OKCPEPLQ. LQYD NPNEJJQ EILKHOQC OGJ UILHJQ NLG EIJ PQPEPOY HUGJJQPQZ JFOR, OQC LQYD NPNEJJQ IKQCGJC AKOYPND EL MJULRJ ULQEJHEOQEH. EIJQ, LQYD NPBJ IKQCGJC OUEKOYYD ROSJ PE LQ EIJ OPG.

ANSWER, PAGE 223

TOUR DE FRANCE

Those faraway places with strange-sounding names that are just begging for a punster to come along.

ACROSS

1 Give the wrong hint
7 Anthony or Antony
11 Old-fashioned winter wear
16 ___ delight
17 Muslim prince
18 Arctic native
19 Jungle vines
20 Cancellation of *le festival de cinema*?
22 Dame Judi
23 Sounds of contentment
24 ___ populi
25 Hotel ending
26 ___ use for (doesn't need)
28 Auto club inits.
29 Nothing but
30 Spoil a *Jeanne d'Arc* tour?
35 Blows it
36 ___-wip
37 RR stop
38 In the manner of
39 Bando or Mineo
40 Run-___
42 Olympian Rudolph
46 "*Quelle surprise* that van Gogh lived here!'"?
50 Sleep noisily
51 52 Across, in Madrid
52 Mr.'s mate
53 MGM motto "___ gratia artis"
54 Tattooing fluid
56 "Well, ___ darned!"
58 A single time
59 Chatty tourist's report on *le voyage*?
62 Cotillion
64 Famous litigant
65 In the ___ of one's family
66 Sidewalk stand drink
67 Boy child
68 Recipe abbr.
69 Not straight

73 Seem suspicious, like a government *de guerre*?
76 Head of the Huns
77 Old photo color
78 Canadian prairie Indian
79 Every seven days
80 Beginning
81 The plaintiff
82 Whirlpools

DOWN

1 Salsa choice
2 *Each Dawn ___* (Cagney flick)
3 English actress Phillips
4 Sea shells
5 Provo resident
6 Snaky shape
7 Boys grow into it
8 Famous cookie guy
9 Rocker Ocasek

10 Upscale tie
11 Saucy gal
12 French article
13 Putting together
14 Señor Castro
15 Alibi
21 Beery and Wyle
23 ___ *Ashes*
27 Singer McLachlan
28 Stop on ___ (halt suddenly)
29 Sign outside a soundstage
30 Does the Tarot
31 Manmade fiber
32 Of Oberon's planet
33 Nonconformist
34 "___ a Very Good Year"
39 Office worker
41 Money exchanges
43 Plain in Spain
44 Thanks, to Thierry

45 Donkeys
47 Sing like a bird
48 Clan
49 Lock of hair
55 Russian ballet company
57 Special interest pusher
58 Central Park planner Frederick Law ___
59 Deletes expletives
60 Seattle team, familiarly
61 Went yachting
62 Deep opera voice
63 Madison Avenue types
67 Louver part
68 You, to a Quaker
70 Pop singer Dee
71 *Vogue* competitor
72 Means' partner
74 Tell a whopper
75 French vineyard
76 Reverence

ANSWER, PAGE 225

ALABAMA KLEENEX REDUX

More of those groovy slang terms, like "Bronx cheer," named for the places
they originated. Match the names (1-10) with their definitions (a-j).

____	1. Arkansas fire extinguisher	a.	an armadillo
____	2. California collar	b.	a chamber pot
____	3. Cincinnati oysters	c.	dice
____	4. Kansas sheep dip	d.	a hangman's noose
____	5. Kentucky breakfast	e.	pickled pigs' feet
____	6. Mississippi marbles	f.	a sandstorm
____	7. Oklahoma rain	g.	sleeping on the ground without cover
____	8. Texas turkey	h.	steak and bourbon
____	9. Tucson bed	i.	sympathy, but little else
____	10. Vermont charity	j.	whiskey

ANSWER, PAGE 224

* * * * *

ROTTEN TO THE CORPS?

Small crostic puzzles are solved just like the big ones (directions on page 13)
but the first letters of the fill-in words **do not** spell out a hidden message.

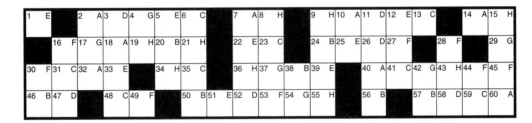

A. Brilliantly beautiful; splendid

‾2‾ ‾18‾ ‾7‾ ‾10‾ ‾14‾ ‾40‾ ‾32‾ ‾60‾

B. Knotted cord or yarn decoration

‾38‾ ‾56‾ ‾50‾ ‾46‾ ‾24‾ ‾57‾ ‾20‾

C. *Rhoda* and *Joey*, e.g.

‾13‾ ‾6‾ ‾48‾ ‾23‾ ‾31‾ ‾35‾ ‾41‾ ‾59‾

D. Tasty tidbit

‾26‾ ‾11‾ ‾3‾ ‾47‾ ‾58‾ ‾52‾

E. Asunción's country

‾33‾ ‾22‾ ‾25‾ ‾51‾ ‾12‾ ‾5‾ ‾1‾ ‾39‾

F. Hardly; not quite

‾49‾ ‾44‾ ‾28‾ ‾30‾ ‾16‾ ‾45‾ ‾53‾ ‾27‾

G. Search about for provisions

‾42‾ ‾4‾ ‾37‾ ‾17‾ ‾29‾ ‾54‾

H. Showy flowers of the amaryllis family

‾21‾ ‾36‾ ‾8‾ ‾9‾ ‾34‾ ‾55‾ ‾43‾ ‾19‾ ‾15‾

ANSWER, PAGE 222

BRITISH SPOKEN HERE

Oh, sure, it's English, but it might as well be a foreign language when Brits start slinging the slang around. Like the 49 words listed below. Once you've found them all in the grid, reading across, down, and diagonally, the leftover letters will reveal a hilarious (and possibly untrue) story about a comment made by England's master of the faux pas, Prince Philip, upon meeting a certain VIP. Also, see the answer section for a translation of the Britspeak terms into "real" English.

```
N  C  H  N  A  M  E  C  I  L  O  P  G  N  I  P  E  E  L  S
T  A  O  H  A  T  A  N  O  R  A  K  W  A  S  A  D  B  T  T
L  R  U  P  E  L  I  C  A  N  C  R  O  S  S  I  N  G  E  A
O  A  S  G  O  D  C  Y  D  M  K  A  T  O  L  B  S  O  R  R
M  V  I  N  H  O  L  A  Y  B  Y  E  O  S  B  U  I  G  R  K
L  A  N  C  O  T  C  T  E  P  M  U  R  C  M  B  Y  H  A  E
I  N  G  K  A  A  S  N  Y  T  T  A  C  S  E  B  O  D  C  R
F  S  E  H  R  P  A  A  K  N  E  R  H  Y  A  L  R  Y  E  S
G  R  S  O  U  A  U  S  N  A  E  L  Y  R  N  E  D  O  L  D
N  U  T  T  E  R  S  W  O  D  K  G  G  O  F  A  N  D  M  E
I  E  A  T  I  A  N  G  N  N  C  Y  G  F  L  N  J  H  O  I
L  H  T  S  H  L  O  I  E  U  A  R  A  P  L  D  U  I  N  D
C  E  E  S  P  Y  M  S  G  D  B  G  O  L  F  S  M  P  Y  O
F  U  L  L  S  T  O  P  N  E  L  P  L  S  P  Q  B  L  E  J
O  H  O  N  K  I  B  S  U  R  I  C  P  M  S  U  L  A  R  C
U  N  F  L  I  C  R  I  O  L  A  R  I  A  K  E  E  P  E  R
K  A  O  T  N  E  O  T  L  H  T  E  E  L  T  A  S  V  K  I
F  I  R  S  T  F  L  O  O  R  A  C  T  L  I  K  A  C  S  S
A  N  M  F  I  N  L  1  L  O  O  H  C  S  C  I  L  B  U  P
E  D  A  R  A  P  Y  T  I  T  N  E  D  I  9  8  E  8  B  S
```

AFTERS
ANORAK
ARGY-BARGY
BROLLY
BUBBLE AND
   SQUEAK
BUSKER
CARAVAN
CHAT UP
CLING FILM
CONKERS
COOKER
CRECHE
CRISPS

CRUMPET
DODDLE
FIRST FLOOR
FLOG
FORM
FULL STOP
GAFFER
GAOL
HOUSING ESTATE
IDENTITY PARADE
JUMBLE SALE
KEEPER
LAY-BY
LOLLIPOP LADY

LOUNGE
MEAN
MINDER
NAUGHTS AND
   CROSSES
NUTTERS
PANDA CAR
PARALYTIC
PELICAN
   CROSSING
PLONK
PUBLIC SCHOOL
REDUNDANT
SCATTY

SKINT
SLEEPING
   POLICEMAN
SLIDE
SMALLS
STARKERS
TAILBACK
TELLY
TERRACE
TORCH
YOBBO

ANSWER, PAGE 225

SIX OF ONE...

When we took these lists of sixes from *Uncle John's Supremely Satisfying Bathroom Reader*, we accidentally dropped one item from each list. Can you complete each list by coming up with the sixth item?

Nobel Prize Categories
Peace
Chemistry
Physics
Physiology & Medicine
Literature

Wives of Henry VIII
Catherine of Aragon
Anne Boleyn
Anne of Cleves
Catherine Howard
Catherine Parr

Rodeo Contests
Saddle bronco riding
Bareback riding
Calf roping
Steer wrestling
Team roping

Parts of the Circulatory System
Heart
Arteries
Arterioles
Venules
Veins

Categories of Dog Breeds
Working
Sporting
Hounds
Nonsporting
Toy

Layers of the Earth
Crust
Upper Mantle
Lower Mantle
Transition region
Inner core

Branches of the U.S. Armed Forces
Army
Navy
Air Force
Marines
Coast Guard

Grades of Meat
Prime
Good
Standard
Commercial
Utility

Hockey Positions
Left wing
Right wing
Left defense
Right defense
Goalie

Sinister Six (Spider-Man's Arch Enemies)
Kraven the Hunter
Mystero
Vulture
Electro
Sandman

Main Vocal Ranges of the Human Voice
Soprano
Mezzo-soprano
Contralto
Tenor
Bass

Six Flags Over Texas
Spain
France
Mexico
The United States of America
The Confederate States of America

ANSWER, PAGE 225

HAIL TO THE CHIEFS

When in the course of human events it became necessary for
Uncle John's Bathroom Reader to Plunge Into the Presidency...

1. Who's buried in Grant's tomb?

   a. Ulysses S. Grant
   b. Ulysses S. Grant and his wife, Julia
   c. No one. Strictly speaking, he's not "buried," but lies in a sarcophagus above ground
      (Mrs. Grant as her own sarcophagus next to him.)

2. When he was a relatively unknown representative, Franklin Pierce was publicly accused of
   lying by John C. Calhoun. Pierce couldn't defend himself because:

   a. he *was* lying
   b. he had told the lie to protect a friend
   c. he had laryngitis

3. Who was the only divorced president?

   a. Thomas Jefferson
   b. Ronald Reagan
   c. Ulysses Grant

4. Besides Him and Her, Lyndon Johnson had a dog named Yuki, given him by his daughter Luci
   who brought him home after she:

   a. found him at a Texas gas station
   b. was given him by the Japanese ambassador
   c. bought him at PetCo

5. He could stand up, put his hands behind his back, and his lips would move while he gave a stirring
   speech. He was the first Animatromic figure created by the Walt Disney team. Who was he?

   a. George Washington
   b. Abraham Lincoln
   c. Franklin Delano Roosevelt

6. At the time of his presidency, the custom was to bow to people when you met them. Which
    president instituted the custom of shaking hands with the people he met?

   a. John Adams
   b. Thomas Jefferson
   c. Andrew Jackson

7. Abraham Lincoln's last words to his wife were, "They won't think anything about it." His wife had
   just asked him what people would think if they:

   a. saw him loosening his tie
   b. knew that he hated going to the theater
   c. saw the two of them holding hands

8. What six presidents were Navy men? (Hint: JFK was the first.)

9. Presidents meet with popes all the time (well, almost). But what president insulted a pope by refusing to meet with him?

   a. Andrew Jackson
   b. Theodore Roosevelt
   c. George H. W. Bush

10. Match each comment about the presidency with the president who said it.

    1. John F. Kennedy
    2. Lyndon Johnson
    3. Richard Nixon

    a. "Being president is like being a jackass in a hailstorm. There's nothing to do but stand there and take it."
    b. "Why would anyone want to be president today?...It's not because the Presidency offers a chance to *be* somebody, but because it offers a chance to *do* something."
    c. "The pay is good and I can walk to work."

What president...

11. ...at age 74, argued and won the *Amistad* case before the Supreme Court?

12. ...was elected president of Princeton University 10 years before he was elected President of the U.S.?

13. ...was president of Columbia University from 1948 to 1950?

14. ...was nicknamed "Buffoon," "Tycoon," and "Illinois Baboon"?

15. ...was sworn into office by U.S. District Judge Sarah Hughes aboard Air Force One?

16. ...never slept in the White House?

17. ...was inaugurated 100 years after George Washington and 100 years before George H. W. Bush?

18. ...once described himself as "a southerner...a Christian...and a lover of Bob Dylan's songs and Dylan Thomas' poetry"?

19. ...spoke of the world food crisis in the first presidential address telecast from the White House?

20. ...served in World War I and World War II?

21. ...declared a bank holiday to prevent bank closings as one of his first acts as president?

22. ...carried 49 states in the 1972 election?

23. ...carried 49 states in the 1984 election?

24. What future president left the state of Tennessee when Tennessee left the Union in 1861?

25. What president, first lady, and their two daughters shared the same three-letter monograms?

26. What president referred to his wife as "the boss" and his daughter Margaret as "the one who bosses the boss"?

27. What first lady, according to a Harris poll, was more popular than her husband?

28. What first lady, the daughter of Republicans, married a Democrat on September 12, 1953?

29. What future president and first lady translated a medieval Latin book on mining and metallurgy?

30. What president and first lady were born and raised in the same small town in Georgia?

ANSWER, PAGE 226

LOOPY LEXICON

Match the word (1-10) with its wacky definition (a-j).

____	1. Abdicate	a.	A Jamaican proctologist
____	2. Absentee	b.	A missing golf peg
____	3. Archive	c.	A person who sprinkles his conversation with Yiddish expressions
____	4. Coffee	d.	Appalled over how much weight you have gained
____	5. Flabbergasted	e.	The person upon whom someone coughs
____	6. Heroes	f.	To give up all hope of ever having a flat stomach
____	7. Oyster	g.	What a guy in a boat does
____	8. Parasites	h.	What trees do in the spring
____	9. Pokemon	i.	What you see from the top of the Eiffel Tower
____	10. Relief	j.	Where Noah kept his bees

ANSWER, PAGE 225

* * * * *

YOU MEAN LIKE THIS ONE?

Small crostic puzzles are solved just like the big ones (directions on page 13)
but the first letters of the fill-in words **do not** spell out a hidden message.

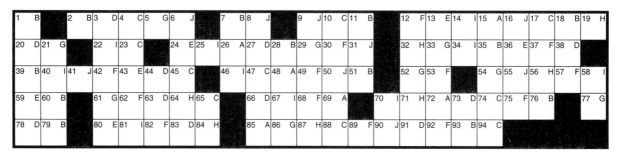

A. Sci-fi character type

$\overline{85}\ \overline{72}\ \overline{69}\ \overline{15}\ \overline{48}\ \overline{26}$

B. Good reason to blush

$\overline{79}\ \overline{39}\ \overline{7}\ \overline{35}\ \overline{28}\ \overline{51}\ \overline{1}\ \overline{76}\ \overline{2}$
$\overline{18}\ \overline{11}\ \overline{93}\ \overline{60}$

C. Highly pleasing or enjoyable

$\overline{65}\ \overline{47}\ \overline{45}\ \overline{74}\ \overline{94}\ \overline{10}\ \overline{17}\ \overline{23}\ \overline{4}\ \overline{88}$

D. Low-key

$\overline{63}\ \overline{20}\ \overline{91}\ \overline{83}\ \overline{78}\ \overline{38}\ \overline{3}\ \overline{44}\ \overline{66}$
$\overline{27}\ \overline{73}$

E. Tyro

$\overline{59}\ \overline{80}\ \overline{24}\ \overline{36}\ \overline{43}\ \overline{13}$

F. Sheer grit

$\overline{12}\ \overline{89}\ \overline{82}\ \overline{75}\ \overline{37}\ \overline{57}\ \overline{92}\ \overline{53}\ \overline{68}$
$\overline{49}\ \overline{42}\ \overline{62}\ \overline{30}$

G. Written declaration sworn before a judge

$\overline{29}\ \overline{33}\ \overline{61}\ \overline{86}\ \overline{5}\ \overline{77}\ \overline{54}\ \overline{52}\ \overline{21}$

H. Leatherworkers

$\overline{71}\ \overline{32}\ \overline{64}\ \overline{84}\ \overline{19}\ \overline{56}\ \overline{87}$

I. Stopoff for a morning eye-opener (2 wds.)

$\overline{46}\ \overline{58}\ \overline{81}\ \overline{34}\ \overline{25}\ \overline{40}\ \overline{70}\ \overline{67}\ \overline{22}\ \overline{14}$

J. Most played radio song of all time

$\overline{6}\ \overline{55}\ \overline{31}\ \overline{9}\ \overline{50}\ \overline{16}\ \overline{41}\ \overline{90}\ \overline{8}$

ANSWER, PAGE 226

THE TALENTED MISS AMERICA

Miss America has demonstrated her talents in any number of ways: She's stomped on broken glass, driven a tractor, shown how to properly pack a suitcase, and told a fishing story with a Norwegian accent. And she's done some—but not all—of the following. Can you tell the real Miss America stories from the phonies?

1943: Miss Ohio planned an ice-skating routine. They built a small rink for her but left it out in the sun and it melted before the pageant began. She had to perform the routine on a bare concrete floor.

1949: Miss Montana rode a horse onto the stage to perform an equestrian routine. The horse stumbled and almost fell into the orchestra pit. Animal acts have been banned ever since.

1957: Miss South Carolina's talent was an impersonation of Marilyn Monroe. (She won.)

1958: Miss Mississippi sang an aria, which turned into a burlesque routine, including a striptease. She only got down to shorts and a slip, but disrobing was banned from any future acts. (She won.)

1959: Another Miss Mississippi became Miss America by performing a dramatic recitation about schizophrenia.

1962: Miss Nebraska accidentally threw a flaming baton into the judges' pit, leading to a ban on pyrotechnics.

1967: Miss Oklahoma won the crown by conducting the Miss America orchestra.

1970: Miss California sang the perennial "I Enjoy Being a Girl" while painting a (not-too-bad) portrait of Bert Parks.

1982: Miss Hawaii played the ukulele and danced the hula in coconut bra and grass skirt. It's a good thing she had that uke—she had to hide behind it when one of her coconuts fell to the ground.

1995: Miss Alabama won after performing a ballet piece. Not unusual, except for the fact that she is deaf—she took her cues from the vibrations coming through the stage from the orchestra.

ANSWER, PAGE 226

* * * * *

G WHIZ

The last name of entertainer Kenny G is:

    a. Gorelick
    b. Gorman
    c. Gottlieb

ANSWER, PAGE 225

CAN WE TALK?

Someday she'll be known as Melissa Rivers' mother, but for now she's still
the Queen of the Red Carpet. A few of Joan Rivers' funniest sayings…

1.
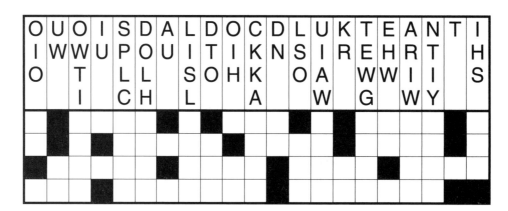

2.
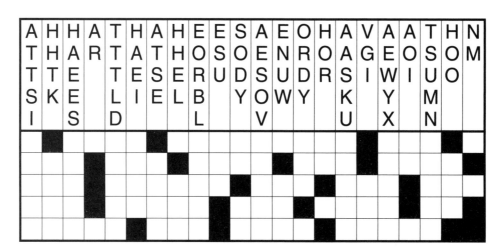

3.
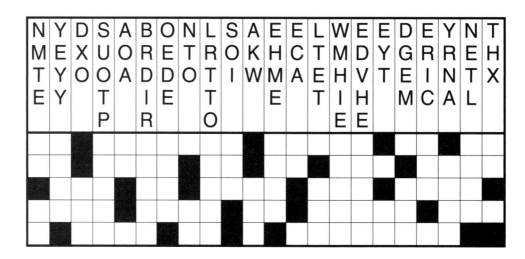

WOULD WE LIE TO YOU AGAIN?

Who, us? This time the questions have to do with word origins, and as before,
you've got three choices for each. Only one is correct, of course.

1. It's easy to see why the word butter is in butterscotch, but what's with the scotch?
    a. The candy was originally a Scottish delicacy.
    b. The original version of the candy (and some modern versions, though none that you can buy at your local grocery store) contained Scotch whisky.
    c. As a verb, scotch means "to cut." The candy is "scotched" into squares as it cools.

2. Why are exercise weights known as dumbbells?
    a. The name has nothing to do with dumbness—the word simply means "two bells," referring to the two bell-shaped weights on the ends of the bar.
    b. The original dumbbell was a cumbersome exercise device that mimicked the contraption that bell ringers used (because bell ringers usually had well-developed chests, shoulders and arms). Since the device had no actual bells, it was called a dumbbell, "dumb" meaning silent.
    c. The first dumbbells were called handweights, but the word "dumbbell" (already a slang term for idiot) was applied to them by social observers who noticed that the people who used them— mostly fighters, wrestlers, and carnival performers—tended to be, well, dumb. Much to the handweight users' chagrin, the new name stuck.

3. How did flea markets get that name?
    a. Yes, it really is because secondhand items have fleas—especially back in the 1800s, when the term was first coined. Flea markets didn't refer to themselves by that name until much later, however.
    b. The name has nothing to do with fleas. In Dutch Colonial days, downtown Manhattan was home to many vallie (valley) markets, abbreviated as vlie markets. The term was later anglicized to "flea markets."
    c. The name comes from Jacob Armand Fleigh, who organized the first open-air market to charge one penny admission. Fleigh swore that his prices were so low, buyers would recover their penny on the first purchase. He died after three short years in business, but his name endured.

4. Why is fruit drink known as punch?
    a. The word derives from panch, a Hindustani word meaning "five." The original recipe for punch had five ingredients: alcohol, water, lemon, sugar, and spice.
    b. "Punch" originally referred to the liquor content, much like "kick" does today. Fruit juice and spices hide the taste of alcohol well, so people tended to drink more punch than they would any other alcoholic beverage—and subsequently get flattened by its "punch."
    c. In 19th century England, mixed fruit drink and scones were referred to as "Punch and Judy," because they went together so well. Anyone hosting a ball was well advised to have plenty of Punch and Judy on hand.

5. How did the word phony come to mean not genuine?
    a. It's a variant of the word funny, as in "suspicious."
    b. When telephones were new, many users commented on how strange people's voices sounded when heard over this new medium. A new word, phoney, was coined to describe the phenomenon (as in "your voice sounds phoney").
    c. It's an alteration of the word "fawney," British slang for a finger ring. A common con game known as a fawney rig involved pretending that a brass ring was a gold one.

ANSWER, PAGE 226

OLD-FASHIONED GIRLS

If you've got a bun in the oven—a little girl bun, that is—feel free to pick a Lily or a Daisy for her from this list of old names that are back in fashion. Then, if you can find all 58 names in the grid, reading across, down, and diagonally, the leftover letters will reveal a piece of modern, but timeless, parental advice.

```
A L L I C S I R P E N A I V L Y S
E E C I R A L C V T E R I M O A N
L M A I R I M E N H E N E L R A O
P Y S Y T I C I L E F N D A E C R
T R I A D E L E L L Y Y A O T M M
E A U D U D E R D L I M I A T A A
I A O D R E C Y O J E C V L A R A
R M L E E C E D I T H I I R E I C
R R C H A N N A H T A L L C D O O
A I L I C E C I L Y Y J O A N N A
H A E N W R M E Y A O P A S A N R
G T M G E O A T T N R E T S E H A
R O E W H L B T O E A A I A O R B
A N N P Y F E E A H N R N N O O E
C I T S S I L N T C G L A D Y S L
E N I D R L O R E N M Y U R O A L
U A N N E M E D I A L E D A H L A
D A E V A B E G I L V E N B I I R
C H A R L O T T E B E O H P T E H
```

ADELAIDE	CONSTANCE	HEDDA	NINA
ADELE	DAISY	HENRIETTA	NORMA
AMELIA	EDITH	HESTER	NOELLE
ANITA	EDNA	IRMA	OCTAVIA
ARABELLA	ELSPETH	JOANNA	OLIVIA
ARLENE	ENID	JOYCE	PEARL
BERTHA	ETHEL	LILY	PHOEBE
BLANCHE	EUDORA	LORETTA	PRISCILLA
CAMILLE	FELICITY	LOUISA	PRUDENCE
CASSANDRA	FLORENCE	MABEL	RAMONA
CECILIA	GLADYS	MARION	ROSALIE
CECILY	GRACE	MILDRED	SARA
CHARLOTTE	GWENDOLYN	MIRIAM	SYLVIA
CLARICE	HANNAH	MYRA	
CLEMENTINE	HARRIET	NAOMI	

ANSWER, PAGE 226

OLD-FASHIONED BOYS

If your bundle of joy turns out to be a boy, how about naming him Dudley or Melvin? Once again, your job is to find all the names in the grid, 59 of them this time. When you're done, the leftover letters will reveal something else that parents should know.

```
H P L O D N A R D E X T E R A I C
N H S A N H C K I R A H T Y L L I
L I C E C J A C S A V E S E I H E
H N J R R U A I I G I O E F S D J
I E E T L S R M D E D F R T T U
A A R N E I I E O E R O E E A O L
R S O B Y A Y D N M R R D M I I I
C O M A E N U E A D H E U R R L U
H L E G E R A R D B C B J E Y E S
E A Y C A N T F T Y O E O L R U A
S G R D E R T R H R N N N Y R M I
T I N V E T D F A O E E A U A E L
E O I B E A C R D N B Z S H H L E
R L L H M Y E L D U D E A C I V U
O I K O H T E S E C Y R U S R I N
G V N M M H Y R U M B O A U A N A
R E A E S I L A S A E B C H M I M
L R R R D R E T N E C N I V R A M
R U F U S U I C U L N T T E M M E
```

ABNER	DEXTER	HARVEY	OLIVER
ABRAHAM	DUDLEY	HERBERT	PHINEAS
ALISTAIR	EBENEZER	HIRAM	RANDOLPH
BASIL	EDGAR	HOMER	REUBEN
BERTRAM	EFREM	ISAAC	RUFUS
BERTRAND	ELIAS	JEREMIAH	SCHUYLER
BYRON	ELIOT	JEROME	SETH
CALEB	EMMANUEL	JONAS	SHELDON
CECIL	EMMETT	JUDE	SILAS
CHESTER	ENOCH	JULIAN	SIMON
CLEMENT	FRANKLIN	JULIUS	THADDEUS
CLIFFORD	FREDERICK	LEMUEL	THEODORE
CLYDE	GERARD	LUCIUS	VINCENT
CYRUS	GILBERT	MARVIN	XAVIER
DAMON	HARRY	MELVIN	

ANSWER, PAGE 227

WHERE AM I?

No, we don't have amnesia. We're just wondering which American cities once proudly bore names like Pig's Eye and Assunpink and—for some crazy reason—changed them to the names they bear today.

ACROSS

1 Heart of the matter
5 Sweet Sixteen grp.
9 Animal in the Chinese zodiac
13 Malt beverage launched by Coors in 1993
17 Attending to a task
18 Couturier Cassini
19 "Oh woe!"
20 Fashion brand with a reptilian logo
21 COLE'S HARBOR
23 PIG'S EYE
25 Lunchtime, for some
26 RUMFORD
28 ___ of mistaken identity
29 Ballot crosses
30 Inquire
32 Qatar's capital
33 Unwelcome guest in most places nowadays
34 FORT DEARBORN
36 What deuce means, in tennis
37 Public utility (abbr.)
41 Brian of rock music
42 MGM lion?
44 Grub
48 Gordon of *Carousel*
50 ___ *Vadis?*
53 Minus
55 Welcome gift in Oahu
56 TERMINUS
58 Run the credit card through the machine
60 Like some high-fiber cereals
62 First- and third-quarter tides
63 ASSUNPINK

65 *Once ___ Mattress* (Carol Burnett musical)
66 Pop up
67 Start of many toasts
68 FORT PONTCHARTRAIN
70 Gunk in cigarettes
71 Bank deal
73 Sewer denizen
75 Peevish complainer
76 Actress Lanchester
78 Dashboard feature
80 Bart Simpson's grandpa
82 Croft of video games
83 Campus square
85 LANCASTER
89 "Truth is ___," to Keats
92 Brand of meatless hamburgers that originated in Florida
93 Bullfight cheer
94 Rodriguez of *Queer Eye for the Straight Guy*
97 Famous marbles at the British Museum
98 NEW AMSTERDAM
100 Speak up (for)
102 NEW CONNECTICUT
104 JUNEAUTOWN
106 Cattle, in olden days
107 Recipe direction
108 "You got a better ___?"
109 Actress Ward
110 Date on a wine bottle
111 Refute
112 Congeals
113 Ivan the Terrible, e.g.

DOWN

1 Pt. of many addresses
2 Silly
3 A Scrabble set has 100 of these
4 Start of many Web addresses
5 ___ de guerre (pseudonym)
6 Punch, as a time card
7 Flying-related
8 Meeting to-do list
9 Hybrid fuel
10 *Pal Joey* author John
11 In the thick of
12 Number for Nadia Comaneci
13 Five-digit address item
14 *The Compleat Angler* author Walton
15 Stuart Little, e.g.
16 Chicago's ___ Planetarium
22 Apple on the teacher's desk?
24 Domesticated
27 Gear tooth
31 1/500 of a ream
33 Formal letter salutation
35 Rooster, to the French
36 Song from the Beatles' "Abbey Road"
37 Give off
38 Sidelong football pass
39 Napoleon's bakery relatives
40 Casino game with a stickman
43 Chow chow's chow
45 Home to a Penn State campus
46 Smaller
47 Anagram for "artisan"
49 Photographer Adams
51 ___-friendly
52 Deed holder
54 Stars and Bars region
57 Easy to get hold of

59 "___ Great Day for the Irish"
61 "The cruellest month," to Eliot
64 "The Biggest Little City in the World"
69 General at Gettysburg
72 Pretty good
74 Washington's Sea-___ Airport
77 Shaking
79 Salon offering
81 Instruction manual

84 ___ *Reader, A Different Read on Life* (magazine)
86 Like an igloo
87 Judd and Campbell
88 River through St. Petersburg
89 ___ Sharp of *Vanity Fair*
90 Doo-wop songwriter Greenwich
91 NASA booster rocket
92 Nigeria neighbor

94 Soda shop music makers, for short
95 Amtrak's fast train
96 The Supremes' "___ a Symphony"
98 Brother in *Six Feet Under*
99 First American woman in space
101 Throw out of office
103 It can take you on a trip
105 Had been

IT'S OIL IN THE WAY YOU SAY IT

Workin' in an oilfield ain't easy, 'specially if you don't know what to call stuff. So if you're thinking about getting a job in the oil field (pun intended), you can practice by solving this quiz. Match the slang terms (1-10) with their definitions (a-j).

____	1. Boll weevil		____	6. Monkeyboard
____	2. Bulldog		____	7. Mousehole
____	3. Christmas Tree		____	8. Pebble pup
____	4. Doghouse		____	9. Rockhound
____	5. Doodlebug		____	10. Roughneck

a. A field geologist.

b. A hole in the rig floor though which drilling pipe is fed.

c. A little shack at the drill site that typically doubles as an office, supply closet, and place to hang provocative calendars of girls in bikinis holding oilfield tools.

d. A person or device (like a divining rod) supposedly able to sniff out oil, gas, or precious minerals.

e. A tall and cluttered setup of valves, fittings, spools, gauges, and so on that's often painted green.

f. An oilfield newbie who is given a hard time—and the worst jobs to do.

g. Any member of a drilling crew.

h. A field geologist's assistant; also a kid who collects rocks.

i. A small oil rig platform a derrick hand stands on when handling pipe.

j. A tool used to fetch broken pipe out of the hole.

ANSWER, PAGE 227

* * * * *

GOING TO EXTREMES

Where did the phrase "the bitter end" originate?

a. Before the days of refrigeration, vats of pub-brewed beer tended to get increasingly bitter as time went on. Some pub owners would automatically throw away unconsumed beer after a set period of time, but others would keep serving it "to the bitter end."

b. In Victorian English parlance, the "bitter end" of a cigar was the end you bit down on. Any man who smoked his cigars "down to the bitter end" was letting his frugality interfere with the pleasures of smoking.

c. It's an old sailing term. The "bitter end" of a mooring line is the end that's attached to the bitts, sturdy wooden or metal posts mounted to the ship's deck.

ANSWER, PAGE 227

LOCATION, LOCATION, LOCATION

Here's a list of places that people have only dreamed about, and recounted to us via fiction, ancient legend—and even television. See if you can fit all 39 of them into the grid, crossword-style. Then visit the answer section for directions on where to find them.

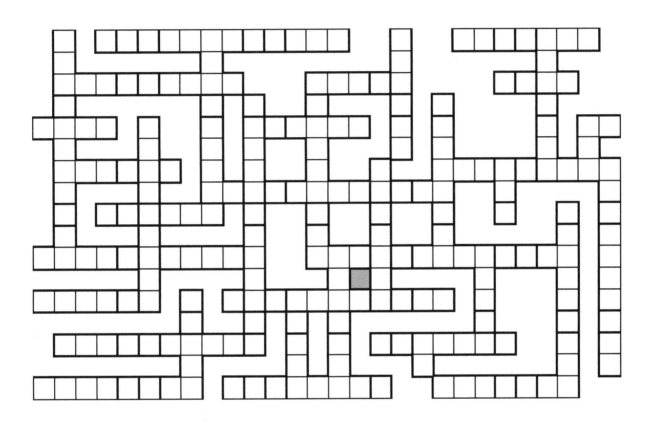

2-letter words
Mu
Oz

3-letter words
Nod
Ork

4-letter words
Tara
Tuna

5-letter words
Adano
Derry
Mongo
Naboo

6-letter words
Avalon
Elysia
Narnia
Utopia
Vulcan

7-letter words
Camelot
Elbonia
Erewhon
Genovia
Honalee
Oceania

8-letter words
Bacteria
El Dorado
Greyhawk

9-letter words
Brigadoon
Funkytown
Manderley
Neverland
Shangri-la
Twin Peaks

10-letter words
Centerburg
Spoon River

11-letter words
Lake Wobegon
Middlemarch
Santa Teresa

12-letter words
Grand Fenwick
Knots Landing
Wisteria Lane

13-letter word
Yoknapatawpha

ANSWER, PAGE 228

THAT'S WHY THEY CALL IT TRIVIA

Because it doesn't get any more trivial than this.

1. On applications requesting ethnic identity, Tiger Woods has described himself as:

    a. Creole
    b. African-American
    c. Asian

2. *Xena: Warrior Princess* star Lucy Lawless:

    a. got the part of Xena by a fluke, when the original actress became ill.
    b. once worked as a grape-picker in Germany.
    c. had another job working in a gold mine in Australia.

3. Actor Kevin Spacey (*American Beauty*):

    a. once played an Elvis impersonator on *The Golden Girls*.
    b. was once considered not talented enough to appear on *The Gong Show*.
    c. was once caught climbing over the wall to Graceland.

4. True or False: *The Golden Child*, the 1986 Eddie Murphy adventure-comedy, was originally intended as a serious adventure drama with Mel Gibson in the starring role.

5. Singer John Mellencamp and wife Elaine Irwin have sons named:

    a. Audio Science and Elijah Bob Patricius Guggi Q.
    b. Geoffrey Crayon and Launcelot Wagstaffe
    c. Speck Wildhorse and Hud

6. Comedian-actress Wanda Sykes:

    a. wrote a book on stand-up comedy titled *For Goodness Sykes!*
    b. speaks fluent Swahili.
    c. worked for seven years at the National Security Agency, buying spy equipment.

7. When she checks into a hotel, pop diva Britney Spears sometimes uses the alias:

    a. Snit Beardsley
    b. Alotta Warmheart
    c. Ivana Behalone ("I vanna be alone," get it?)

8. Which two of these statements about *American Idol*'s Simon Cowell are true:

    a. He was a high school dropout.
    b. He has volunteered as a walker of stray dogs at a London shelter.
    c. He was born Simon Cowbell, but later dropped the "b."

9. Pop singer Christina Aguilera:

    a. loves satin sheets because her first name is an anagram of RICH SATIN.
    b. still sleeps with lights on because she's afraid of the dark.
    c. can recite the alphabet backwards in Estonian.

10. "Left to my own, I'd rather look like trash. I love tacky clothes." Who said it?

    a. Ashley Judd
    b. Dolly Parton
    c. Gwyneth Paltrow

11. David Boreanaz of *Angel* and *Buffy the Vampire Slayer*:

    a. is a third cousin of Orlando Bloom.
    b. was chased out of the Creative Artists Agency for dropping by unannounced with
       copies of his résumé.
    c. didn't learn to read until age 12.

12. Hoops legend Shaquille O'Neal's first name translates to:

    a. "Little One"
    b. "He Who Overcomes"
    c. "Large Warrior"

13. Late-night host Conan O'Brien is related to:

    a. actor-comedian Mike Myers (cousin)
    b. actor Tobey Maguire (half-brother)
    c. actor Denis Leary (cousin)

14. Actor Rob Lowe went to high school with:

    a. Sean Penn and Charlie Sheen
    b. Judd Nelson and Demi Moore
    c. Molly Ringwald and Andrew McCarthy

15. Which of these statements about singer-songwriter Ashanti is true:

    a. An honor student and high school track star, she turned down Princeton University to
       pursue her singing career.
    b. Calls her mom "Momager" because her mom is her manager.
    c. In 2002, became the first artist since the Beatles to have three Top 10 hits simultaneously.

16. Actress Cate Blanchett has the bad habit of:

    a. sucking her thumb before auditions.
    b. biting her nails.
    c. chewing pencils so much that her mother once coated them with Tabasco sauce.

ANSWER, PAGE 227

SCHOOL'S OUT FOREVER

Some school dropouts who went on to become self-made
millionaires and billionaires. Don't try this at home, kids.

ACROSS

1 Old Steven Bochco show
6 *The Lion King* lion
10 Thom ___ shoes
14 Not the best roommates
19 Oft-upsetting bacteria
20 Early role for Shirley
21 John Kerry's old school
22 *Glengarry Glen Ross* Pulitzer winner
23 Heart, say
24 Govt. division
25 Animator who dropped out at 16 to drive a W.W. I Red Cross truck
27 Camera pioneer who dropped out at 14 to support his mother and two sisters
30 Kay Thompson's Plaza Hotel hoyden
31 Faith of 1.2 billion
32 Jazz trumpeter Eldridge
33 Wearing less
35 Merged labor union, briefly
38 Grammy division
39 Singer/businessman who dropped out at 16 to join the Merchant Marines
43 ___ *Geordie* (1956 Bill Travers film)
44 Excellent
47 Hot chips dip
48 ___ mater
49 A Baldwin brother
51 Small battery size
52 EarthLink competitor
53 Trite
55 Hebrew T
56 Dropout at 17 whose headmaster predicted he'd either go to prison or become a millionaire
61 TV exec Arledge

63 Breathed out
64 Two-seater auto
65 Church songbook
66 Hardly the original one
69 Not a pretty sight
71 Music played at a rave
74 No-___ (gnat)
76 Prepare to wallop
80 Others, to José
81 Captain of industry who dropped out at 13 to work as a bobbin boy in a cotton mill
84 Beam
85 Reaction at the circus
88 Lo-o-o-ng time
89 Take part in a ten-K
90 Blab to the fuzz
91 Capital of Samoa
93 With great force, old-style
95 Kung fu cousin
98 That's a moray
99 Dropout at 16 who became a machinist's apprentice
101 Humdinger
102 Worried states
104 Dewy
105 Button on a VCR
106 Oscar winner for *Blue Sky*
108 Flyer of myth who suffered meltdown
111 Resort king who dropped out in the eighth grade to become a boxer
116 Fast-food mogul who dropped out at 15 to work as a busboy and cook
119 Garlic, to a vampire
120 10:1, say
121 From Cork
122 Subside
123 *Chocolat* actress
124 Slither
125 Knightly exploits

126 Squared up now
127 Lucy Lawless' TV role
128 Flop of the '50s

DOWN

1 *Topper* actor Carroll
2 Ranch unit
3 NBC's peacock, e.g.
4 Visigoth who sacked Rome in 410
5 Plays without a script
6 Hit half of a 45
7 Eric Clapton's trio
8 Roadie's burden
9 Rundown dwelling
10 Big Sinatra hit
11 *The Godfather* actor
12 Tide rival
13 Lets touch this
14 Le Carré's agent
15 Dodgers manager Tommy
16 Onetime online science mag
17 Ulee's "gold" producers
18 Eyelid affliction
26 Skin-related
28 *The Time Machine* people
29 Swiffer, e.g.
33 Puppeteer Baird
34 Schoolyard retort
35 Cognizant
36 Comics cat
37 Swamp thing that won't let go
38 Laugh heartily
39 Old crate
40 John of England
41 Name on a fridge
42 Kind of orange
45 Rice field
46 Key next to the Q
47 "See if I care!"
50 Mambo kin
52 Year in the Yucatán

54 Test

57 King in *The Tempest*

58 Bank take-back

59 Did something about

60 Maiden name intro

62 Something for brunch, perhaps

65 Icy coating

67 Gen. Lee's org.

68 Tale about a Troy survivor

70 Journalist Alexander

71 Synagogue study

72 A day's march

73 "For ___ out loud!"

75 Garden planter

77 S-shaped moldings

78 Serving of sole

79 Cuts down

82 Low-fat sandwich

83 Lowlife

86 Clumsy

87 Options for med. care

92 Plane seat divider

94 Some hangings

95 Fight with your foot

96 Sleeveless top

97 Eat like a glutton

100 Schoolboys

101 For each

103 Jimmy's predecessor in the Oval Office

105 Gone up

106 First Soviet premier

107 Set for *Gladiator*

108 "It's cool"

109 Part of TLC

110 Bird, to Brutus

111 Batman creator Bob

112 Cabbage kin

113 Sinus attachment?

114 Secretary, for one

115 Playwright Coward

117 Be behind

118 Dallas hoopster, for short

ANSWER, PAGE 228

SUBURBAN LEGENDS

Last time, we debunked the misconception that human beings only use 10 percent of their brains. This time we're back for more. Can you separate the following urban and suburban legends into "true" or "false"?

_____ 1. There are no straight lines in nature.

_____ 2. The Eskimo language has hundreds of words for "snow."

_____ 3. Monkeys and apes groom each other by picking off fleas and ticks. And then they eat them.

_____ 4. More suicides occur during the Christmas season than at any other time of year.

_____ 5. Bats are rodents.

_____ 6. If you get arrested, you're entitled to one phone call.

_____ 7. TV Channel One is reserved for emergency broadcasts in the case of nationwide disaster.

_____ 8. Doctors have found that there is at least one health benefit of smoking.

_____ 9. Sitting too close to the TV will damage your eyes.

_____ 10. Eating a bagel with poppy seeds will cause you to fail a drug test.

ANSWER, PAGE 229

* * * * *

MAKING HEADLINES

More of those silly headlines, only this time your task is to find the missing word and tack it on to the correct, but goofy, headline.

| CRACK | HEARING | HOSIERY | MOON | NUTRITION |
| DEAD | HOOKERS | HURT | NOSES | WEAPONS |

1. BODY SEARCH REVEALS $4,000 IN _____

2. DR. TACKETT GIVES TALK ON _____

3. FEDERAL AGENTS RAID GUN SHOP, FIND _____

4. GREEKS FINE _____

5. MAN GOES BERSERK IN CAR SALESROOM, MANY VOLVOS _____

6. MEN PICKY ABOUT _____

7. NEW HOUSING FOR ELDERLY NOT YET _____

8. ROBBER HOLDS UP ALBERT'S _____

9. SHOUTING MATCH ENDS TEACHER'S _____

10. YELLOW SNOW STUDIED TO TEST _____

ANSWER, PAGE 228

TILT!

We've hidden 42 pinball-related words and phrases in the flipper-and-ball grid below. When you've found them all, the leftover letters will reveal what Jack Handey of *SNL*'s "Deep Thoughts" said in response to his own question: "Why do people in ship mutinies always ask for 'better treatment'?"

```
                        P D G I
                      O U T L A N E D
                    E A S K E U F I R O
                    R X S P I N N E R S
                  A P I T N F B P G A P P
                  L S L M R Y L A C E I S
                  S H O O T A G A I N R H
                  I A N E Y L B B B E C A
                  K S L A P S A V E W
                  E A K C O L L L A B
                  B A L L Y U R L
          S E W I T H         W A L D
        S O L E N O I D L I
      P T Q U A R T E R Z H A T
      A F R D R O P T A R G E T T
      R O L L O V E R I O C K L I N G B
      T A D I N G D I N G D I N G D I N G C K
      R E I L P I T L U M T A N T O H S G N I L S
        J A C K P O T D F O S U N O B R H T S P M A R E
        H Y O D E A F D U M B A N D B L I N D K I D E G U
          D P R R B L I N K I N G L I G H T S O M K D B B
            S C I H P A R G A B E L H T Y B A E C U A B
              L E H C T A M T H O S O G G E M I N T
                N R U T R U O Y C K E P A L K O
                  T E O F L F O E D A C R A
                    R E E R R N E G A
                      M F E E S
```

ARCADE	DRAIN	MATCH	SHAKE
AWARD	DROP TARGET	MULTIPLIER	SHOOT AGAIN
BALL LOCK	EXTRA BALL	NUDGE	SLAP SAVE
BALLY	FLIPPERS	OUTLANE	SLINGSHOT
BLINKING LIGHTS	FREE GAME	PINBALL WIZARD	SOLENOID
BONUS	GATE	PLAYFIELD	SPINNERS
BUMPER	GOBBLE HOLE	PLUNGER	SPRING
DEAF, DUMB, AND	GRAPHICS	QUARTER	TILT
BLIND KID	HIGH SCORE	RAMPS	TOKEN
"DING-DING-DING-	JACKPOT	REPLAY	TRAP
DING"	KICKER	ROLLOVER	"YOUR TURN!"

ANSWER, PAGE 229

WHICH HUNT

Life is full of choices—and some are easier to make than others. Pick the right answer to each question.

1. Which is larger?
The planet Jupiter
All the other planets of the solar system put together

2. Which are more valuable, carat for carat?
Diamonds
Rubies

3. Which group is larger?
Americans who have visited a dentist at least once in their lives
Americans who haven't

4. Which sock do more people put on first?
The left one
The right one

5. In which direction do forest fires move faster?
Uphill
Downhill

6. Which is the more likely outcome of being struck by lightning?
Survival
Death

7. Which group is larger?
People with type O blood
People with any of the other three blood types

8. Which are there more of in the Witness Protection Program?
Witnesses in Mafia cases
Witnesses in drug cases

9. Which is larger?
The United States
The Sahara Desert

10. Which is the more likely cause of poisoning in children?
Household chemicals
Toxic houseplants

11. Which does the U.S. treasury print more of?
One-dollar bills
All the other denominations combined

12. Which is the stronger force?
Magnetism
Gravity

13. Which video game was a bigger seller?
Super Mario Bros.
Tetris

14. Which group is larger?
Tattooed NBA players
Tattoo-less NBA players

15. Which does the average traffic light display more often?
Red
Green or yellow

16. Which beat faster?
Girls' hearts
Boys' hearts

17. Which provides better gas mileage?
Warm gasoline
Cold gasoline

18. Which pet lives longer, on average?
A guinea pig
A hamster

19. Which does Hollywood make more money from?
Ticket sales
Video rentals

20. Which spin faster?
Music CDs
Computer CD-ROMs

21. Which has a higher IQ?
The average stutterer
The average non-stutterer

22. Which group is more likely to breastfeed?
College-educated women
Non-college-educated women

23. Which do more employees do?
Attend the office Christmas party
Skip the office Christmas party

24. Which person is more likely to be obese?
The average married man
The average single man

25. Which does your body produce more of in a day?
Saliva
Sweat

26. On which type of day are you more likely to be stung by a bee?
A calm day
A windy day

27. Which does the average person spend more of their life doing?
Talking on the phone
Sitting on the toilet

28. Which requires more milk to make?
A pound of cheese
A pound of butter

29. Which group dreams more?
Smokers
Nonsmokers

30. Which do more stage and screen stars use?
Their real names
Stage names

31. Which are there more of on a dollar bill (not counting serial numbers)?
"1"s
"One"s

32. Which nation has more time zones?
The U.S.
China

33. Which group's members are more likely to have cats as pets?
Democrats
Republicans

34. Which is the more popularly cited reason for not voting in elections, according to the U.S. Census?
"I didn't like either candidate"
"I was too busy"

35. Which would take longer?
Taking the escalator to the top floor of Toronto's CN Tower
Falling from the peak of Mount Everest to the base

36. Which can hold more pounds per square inch of pressure?
A car tire
A can of soda

37. Which group comprises more Americans, according to a poll?
People who make their bed every day
People who never make their bed

38. Which costs the airline more?
One first-class meal
Ten coach-class meals

39. Which is taller?
The Empire State Building
The Eiffel Tower

40. Which weighs more?
A stone at the equator
The same stone at the North Pole

ANSWER, PAGE 230

HOPE FOR THE BEST

He was a red-stater before they coined the term, but that didn't stop Bob Hope from
lambasting Republican VIP's whenever he had the chance. A few of his best....

1.

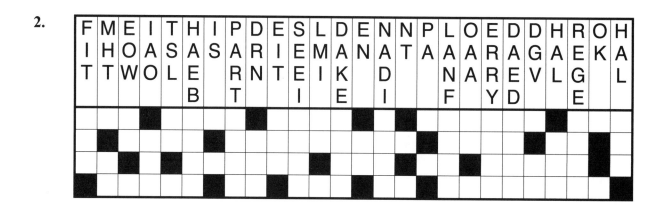

A	I	S	E		T	P	E	C	S	S	S	S	S	N	D	E	E	A	A	O	L	O	W	O	C	W
N	K	S			R	R	R	E	R	O	D	W	A	T	E	T	Q	U	R	E	T	M	A	H	I
V	Y	C			O	O		V	O	I		E	T	T	H		U	R	P	Y	E	T	T		

2.

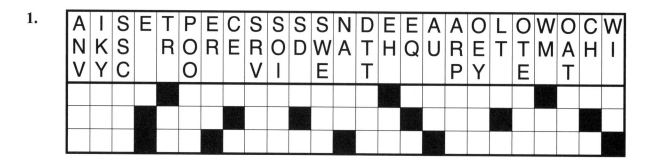

F	M	E	I	T	H	I	P	D	E	S	L	D	E	N	P	L	O	E	D	D	H	R	O	H
I	H	O	A	H	S	S	A	R	I	I	E	N	N	T	A	A	R	A	A	A	A	E	K	A
T	T	W	O	O	E		R	N	T	E	M	A	A		N	A	R	G	E	L	G			L
			L	L	B		T		I	I	K	D	D		F		Y	D	D		E			

3.

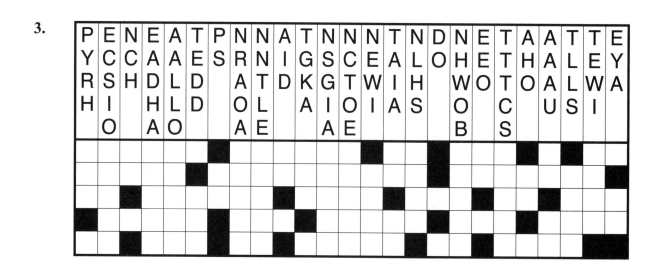

P	E	N	E	A	T	P	N	N	A	T	N	N	N	T	N	D	N	E	T	A	A	T	E
Y	C	C	A	A	E	S	R	N	I	G	S	C	E	A	L	O	H	E	A	A	T	E	Y
R	S	C	D	L	D		A	T	D	K	G	T	W	I	H		W	O	H	A	L	W	A
H	I	H	H	L	D		O	L		A	I	O	I	A	S		O		O	U	S	I	
	O		A	O			A	E			A	E		S			B		C				

LISTOMANIA

Put your smarty pants on. We've put together 16 lists from literature, history, and various other highbrow subjects—some easy to identify, some not so easy. See if you can figure out the category for each of them.

1.
Athos
Porthos
Aramis

2.
Goneril
Regan
Cordelia

3.
Melchior
Caspar
Balthazar

4.
Id
Ego
Superego

5.
Clotho
Lachesis
Atropos

6.
Brahma
Vishnu
Shiva

7.
Strings
Woodwinds
Brass
Percussion

8.
Woodrow Wilson
David Lloyd George
George Clemenceau
Vittorio Emanuele Orlando

9.
Charlotte
Emily
Anne
Branwell

10.
Germany
Italy
Japan
Hungary
Romania
Bulgaria

11.
Light
Heaven
Earth, seas, and plant life
Sun, moon, and stars
Sea life and birds
Land animals and mankind
Rest

12.
Palatine
Capitoline
Quirinal
Viminal
Esquiline
Caelian
Aventine

13.
Pride
Envy
Wrath
Sloth
Avarice
Gluttony
Lust

14.
The Nile turns to blood
Frogs
Lice
Flies
Death of livestock by pestilence
Boils
Hail
Locusts
Darkness
Death of firstborns

15.
Reuben
Simeon
Levi
Judah
Dan
Naphtali
Gad
Asher
Issachar
Zebulun
Joseph
Benjamin

16.
Lancelot
Galahad
Bors
Perceval
Gawain
Tristan
Lamorack
Torre
Kay
Gareth
Bedivere
Mordred

ANSWER, PAGE 231

FAMILIAR PHRASES

Sure they're familiar—you hear them all the time. But where the heck did they come from?

ACROSS

1 Old Spanish fleet
7 Mafia
10 Garden walkway
14 *Ninotchka* actress
19 One who's gung-ho and then some
20 Fire
21 Eight, in Oaxaca
22 Eskimo kin
23 Request
24 Phrase from a line notched in the ground that a boxer had to cross before a new round could begin
27 Author of *To Kill a Mockingbird*
28 Schism
30 Denny Crane of TV, e.g.
31 ___ v. Wade
32 Luncheon finish?
34 Lifeline locale
36 Calendar abbr.
37 Impart, as values
39 Potok's *My Name Is ___ Lev*
41 Go at a gift eagerly
44 Ballet barre
45 Composer Stravinsky
47 Tel. book listings
48 Resort city on the Pacific
52 RR stop
54 Phrase from a boundary marker on the other side of which lived people considered uncivilized
59 Whiny mate
60 Fluid swellings
61 Tax-___ (duty-free)
62 Hammarskjöld of the U.N.
65 Dark volcanic glass
67 Feature of Letterman's smile
68 Final authority
70 '50s Braves pitcher Bob
71 Phrase from the Middle Ages, when a certain food was added to a tankard of ale to improve the taste

77 Fit together
78 Down-in-the-dumps feeling
80 Put away
81 Mineral used as an abrasive
83 Baked ham side
84 Depth charge
88 Exercise too hard
90 Musical brother of George
91 Phrase from early U.S. settlers who chewed tree sap and found that it stuck to their hair and clothes
93 Actor Beatty
94 Prompt
98 Org. concerned with emissions
99 New York City river
101 Ibsen heroine
102 1990 U.S. Open champ Gabriela
107 "Hurray!"
110 Marble choice
114 Watchdog's warning
115 PBS science show
117 Prefix with physical
118 Grren card agcy.
119 Replacing
122 IBM competitor
124 Stir-frying equipment
125 Phrase from the 12th century that referred to dodging a municipal tax
128 As well
130 Actress Berry
131 Hercules' love
132 Egg cells
133 Ring of color
134 Kilmer work
135 NFL receivers
136 Set
137 Pete Rose, once

DOWN

1 Bright garden shrub
2 Adjusts the alarm clock
3 Phrase from the cotton industry about fixing loose screws on broken machines

4 Old politico Landon
5 Way out
6 "...___ to the moon on gossamer wings"
7 Yankees legend
8 Big name in kitchen implements
9 Tag for the second brightest star in a constellation
10 Easy-open can
11 Broadway opening?
12 Author Heyerdahl
13 Egyptian president Mubarak
14 Actors Burghoff and Busey
15 In the manner of
16 Hung-jury upshot
17 Pastoral
18 He "lov'd not wisely but too well"
25 Nth degree
26 Fivescore yrs.
29 The marbling in meat
33 Head exam.
35 Gift from heaven
38 Robert Morse's one-man show
40 Clad for the spa
42 Fishing shack lineup
43 It may be covered by a boa
46 Made over
49 Engine disk
50 High spot of a European vacation?
51 They vacation at kennels
52 Patronizing
53 ___ rasa (clean slate)
55 Used car info
56 Old Atlanta arena
57 Winter budget item
58 Brave opponent, once?
62 Phrase based on the discovery that yarn retained its color better when treated before it was woven, rather than after
63 Give a guarantee
64 Saw red
66 Martinique, *par exemple*
67 Pistol, in old slang

69 The Beach Boys' "Barbara ___"
72 Kind of tide
73 *Critique of Pure Reason* philosopher
74 Phobia start?
75 Fly like an eagle
76 Kid's wheels
79 Herb for stuffing
82 Retract a statement
85 South, south of the border
86 Med. plan choice
87 Eliminates
88 One of a familiar doz.

89 Shania who sang "You're Still the One"
92 Discover
94 How some are recognized
95 Far removed from
96 Support for a railroad bridge
97 Possess, to Scots
100 Waterston of *Law & Order*
103 From way back when
104 Roughnecks
105 "Forget it!"
106 TV oldie ___ *Got a Secret*
108 Best Actor nominee for *My Favorite Year*

109 Purchase for a school project
111 Still ___ (paintings of fruit bowls, e.g.)
112 Shortstop's pos.
113 Girlfriend in the song "Cabaret"
116 Bachelor's last stand?
120 Computer screen symbol
121 Enchanted prince, perhaps
123 Folk wisdom
126 Corrida cheer
127 First lady
129 Stratum

ANSWER, PAGE 231

TROUBLE AND STRIFE

The Cockney rhyming slang for "wife" is "trouble and strife." So if we were to give you a few more words, could you fill in the blank to finish off the slang term?

Ass:
  Khyber _____

Believe:
  Adam and _____

Boots:
  Daisy _____

Car:
  Jam _____

Check:
  Gregory _____

Crap:
  Pony and _____

Dance:
  Kick and _____

Daughter:
  Bricks and _____

Dead:
  Brown _____

Deaf:
  Mutt and _____

Face:
  Boat _____

Feet:
  Plates of _____

Flying Squad:
  Sweeney _____

Hat:
  Tit for _____

Head:
  Loaf of _____

Jewelry:
  Tom-_____

Judge:
  Barnaby _____

Kid:
  Dustbin _____

Lies:
  Porky _____

Lodger:
  Artful _____

Mate:
  China _____

Moan:
  Darby and _____

Money:
  Bread and _____

Mouth:
  North and _____

Pissed:
  Brahms and _____

Pocket:
  Sky _____

Pub:
  Rub-a-_____

Rent:
  Duke of _____

Road:
  Frog and _____

Shirt:
  Dicky _____

Sister:
  Skin and _____

Soap:
  Bob _____

Stairs:
  Apples and _____

Stink:
  Pen and _____

Suit:
  Whistle and _____

Tea:
  Rosie _____

Ten:
  Cock and _____

Turd:
  Richard the _____

Windy:
  Mork and _____

Word:
  Dicky _____

ANSWER, PAGE 231

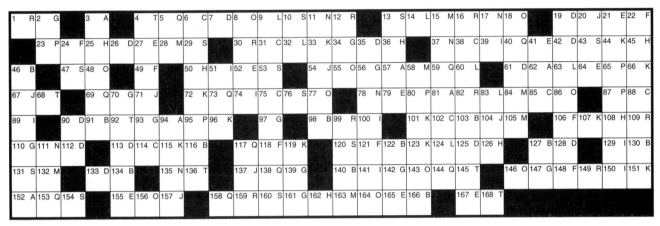

A MYSTERY SOLVED

In this puzzle, the acrostic—the first letters of the words in the word list—finishes
the quote. Complete directions for solving are on page 13.

A. Party treat you get to beat

___ ___ ___ ___ ___ ___
81 152 94 3 57 62

B. According to him, you got all the rules! (2 wds.)

___ ___ ___ ___ ___ ___ ___ ___ ___
130 166 116 103 134 46 127 122 140

___ ___
98 91

C. Roadster with an open top

___ ___ ___ ___ ___ ___ ___ ___
114 6 88 31 102 85 38 75

D. Opera star author of *The Inner Voice* (2 wds.)

___ ___ ___ ___ ___ ___ ___ ___ ___
42 125 26 35 128 113 90 19 61

___ ___ ___
133 7 112

E. John Hertz invention of 1915 (2 wds.)

___ ___ ___ ___ ___ ___ ___ ___ ___
52 165 21 27 79 155 41 64 167

F. Apostle originally called Levi

___ ___ ___ ___ ___ ___ ___
148 49 24 121 118 22 106

G. Fourth-longest running Broadway musical (3 wds.)

___ ___ ___ ___ ___ ___ ___ ___ ___
97 56 70 147 93 142 2 161 110

___ ___
34 139

H. Tatar word meaning "Sleeping Land"

___ ___ ___ ___ ___ ___ ___
126 162 50 45 36 108 25

I. Evinrude product

___ ___ ___ ___ ___ ___ ___ ___
141 74 100 39 51 150 129 89

J. Cruise the World Wide Web

___ ___ ___ ___ ___ ___ ___
67 71 137 157 104 20 54

K. Oscar winner for *The Pianist* (2 wds.)

___ ___ ___ ___ ___ ___ ___ ___ ___
101 96 107 66 119 151 44 123 115

___ ___
33 72

L. Health care profession

___ ___ ___ ___ ___ ___ ___
60 14 32 9 124 83 63

M. Short, simple songs

___ ___ ___ ___ ___ ___ ___
132 58 105 15 84 28 163

N. Trig right triangle ratio

___ ___ ___ ___ ___ ___
78 17 37 135 111 11

O. Annual red carpet event (2 wds.)

___ ___ ___ ___ ___ ___ ___ ___ ___ ___
48 77 146 156 18 86 55 8 164 143

P. Puzzle page offerings

___ ___ ___ ___ ___
80 87 65 95 23

Q. Fashion model's venue, often (2 wds.)

___ ___ ___ ___ ___ ___ ___ ___ ___ ___
158 144 59 117 153 40 138 73 5 69

R. "Prey" of a certain hunter

___ ___ ___ ___ ___ ___ ___ ___ ___
1 159 109 99 30 12 82 149 16

S. 1977 comedy flick about nuns (2 wds.)

___ ___ ___ ___ ___ ___ ___ ___ ___
154 13 53 10 29 76 131 160 43

___ ___
47 120

T. Exuberant; ebullient

___ ___ ___ ___ ___ ___
4 68 92 145 136 168

CHEESE, LOUISE!

And now, a bizarre moment in postal history: two states' honor at stake, all over a hunk of smelly Limburger cheese. Can you pick out the bizarre truth from the bizarre fiction?

In 1935, a doctor from Independence, Iowa, prescribed a hunk of smelly Limburger cheese for his ailing wife, who suffered from **(malnutrition, clogged sinuses, insomnia)**. So he put in an order to **(Monroe, Wisconsin; Lansing, Michigan; St. Louis, Missouri)**, the Limburger capital of America.

The local postmaster there, John Burkhard, approved the package and sent it on its way. But Warren Miller, the postmaster of Independence, Iowa, rejected the package because of its smell, returning it with a note that the smell could "**(stagger a goat, choke a horse, fell an ox)** at twenty paces." Burkhard, insulted, rewrapped it and re-sent it; Miller re-rejected it. This meant war!

Burkhard took his complaint all the way to **(the Postmaster General, the U.S. Vice President, the Supreme Court)**, who declared that, while it smelled pretty bad, the cheese was not hazardous and had to be delivered. But Burkhard, still offended by Miller's attitude, offered him a personal challenge: If Miller could sit at a table and not **(fall over, retch, tear up)** from the stench of the cheese, then he would never again complain about Burkhard's state's cheese. Challenge accepted!

The news media got ahold of the story, so the whole world was watching as Burkhard jokingly offered Miller **(a clothespin and a gas mask, a blindfold, a fork and knife)** as he sat down, but Miller shook his head. He was forced to admit that **(he had Limburger at home in his refrigerator, he had no sense of smell, his eyes could not form tears)**. The challenge was over.

But the war wasn't. Miller remembered Burkhart saying that Limburger was the best accompaniment for beer, and took issue with that, claiming that **(freshly baked wheat bread, smoked whitefish, Cheez-Its)** should properly claim that honor. So he challenged Burkhart to a return contest, this time for the honor of **("Best Snack in the World," "Most Incredible Edible," "Midwest Food-Off Champion")**.

At the rematch, both sides tried to win by **(tampering with the opponent's dish, packing the area with cheering supporters, bribing the judges with beer)**. The competition consisted of many rounds of both entries, accompanied each time by more beer. Eventually the least inebriated judge came up and declared **(a tie, a mistrial, a hung jury)**.

The next time a Cheese Day Parade was held, Limburger was the star, and Warren Miller even came up to see it, sitting right next to his new friend John Burkhard.

ANSWER, PAGE 230

TOTALLY TEXAS

The Lone Star State has more dad-blamed "official" stuff than anywhere else on the planet. The grid contains a passel of things Texan—30 in all. Once you've circled all the capitalized words and phrases, the leftover letters in the grid will spell out four more items that are, respectively, the official Texas State Flying Mammal, Plant, Stone, and Shell. Good huntin', pardner!

```
                    G M E X O
                    U I D M F
                    A E A J R
                    D L L R I
                    A P L E E
                    L A A W N C
                    U S S I D E O A T S G R A M A A
                    P O N N S U L E O C O R U E L P T
                    E F N G H E I W O B M I J C R X O
                    B R E E I E T A I A Z L E N D X R B
          T O R T I L L A C H I P S A N D S A L S A A O N T P
            I R I R A T S E N O L A C I K L P Y P D D F A E A
          R L C N I T S U A A C B L U E B O N N E T E D T U
            S I U P A N H A N D L E A P H T E O R T I O R I
              G H E F I       O E D R J S E P A A L M E M W
              W A C O O       O D A L U U E I U G A S H
                  T A N       I N C B L M N Q G J
                    N       W C O W B O Y S
                            H T E S D H
                            E T G A O
                            S O R X R
                            N O E T
                            E E T S
                              G L A K
```

State Dinosaur
PLEUROCOELUS

State Dish
CHILI

State Fabric
COTTON

State Fish
GUADALUPE BASS

State Dance
SQUARE DANCE

State Flower
BLUEBONNET

State Gem
TEXAS BLUE TOPAZ

State Grass
SIDEOATS GRAMA

State Mammal (Small)
ARMADILLO

State Motto
"FRIENDSHIP"

State Musical Instrument
GUITAR

State Nickname
LONE STAR (State)

State Pepper
JALAPEÑO

State Snack
TORTILLA CHIPS
          AND SALSA

State Tree
PECAN

Famous People From Texas
JIM BOWIE
GEORGE W. BUSH
J. R. EWING
JAMIE FOXX

Texas Cities
AUSTIN
DALLAS
EL PASO
WACO

Things Texas Is Known For
ALAMO
ASTRODOME
COWBOYS
PANHANDLE
RANCHES
RODEO
TORNADOES

ANSWER, PAGE 232

WHO SAID THAT?

Notable quotes from some notable folks....

ACROSS

1 MasterCard rival
5 Locale of Pigalle
10 Sidewalk eatery
14 Make sense
19 Russia/China border river
20 Busch Gardens myopic heavyweight
21 "I'll take Crossword Clues for $200, ___"
22 Everyday writing
23 Gift-wrapping aid
24 "Biography lends to death a new terror"
26 *Nashville* actress Blakley
27 Shooting script
29 Get beat, so to speak
30 Protection on the slopes
32 Rampaging pterodactyl in a 1956 film
33 Dr. Barry Sears' ___ Diet
35 Christmas Eve music
36 Subtly imply
38 Gds. for sale
41 Sierra Club cofounder John
43 Driller who works in an off.
46 Time gone by
47 "If everything's under control, you're going too slow"
51 Uncle, in Uruguay
52 Zero score, in tennis
54 M.I.T. grad
55 What a medium senses
56 Official in the ring
57 "A doctor can bury his mistakes but an architect can only advise his clients to plant vines"
62 Sudden breeze
63 He reached #1 with "When I Need You"
64 Teen spots?
65 Spam producer

67 Kind of professor
70 Big Apple parade sponsor
72 Impressive array
73 Evening affair
74 Six-mile run, for short
75 1930s heavyweight Carnera
76 Pompous response to a knock
77 "This living in a democracy is a problem, isn't it?"
84 New Haven collegian
85 Burt's co-star in *The Rose Tattoo*
86 Raw linen color
87 Easy to sail, to a sailor
88 Bk. after Ezra
89 "First they ignore you, then they laugh at you, then they fight you, then you win"
94 ___ populi (popular opinion)
95 Salon job
96 Bring home
97 Just fair, not great
98 Part of AWOL
100 John Edwards' st.
102 Yugoslav unifier
105 Displays of enthusiasm
106 Revised, in a way
109 Elisabeth of *Leaving Las Vegas*
111 How big purchases may be paid for
114 Headless sculptures
115 "If you can count your money, you don't have a billion dollars"
118 Ending for sock or switch
119 Upper class
120 Where shahs ruled
121 Path beginner?
122 Clobber, slangily
123 Philly hoopster, briefly
124 Win by a ___
125 Treat with contempt
126 Fencing sword

DOWN

1 Winery containers
2 Apple computer
3 Exploding star
4 Retort to "Am too!"
5 Proportionately
6 Bret Harte's Chinese cardplayer
7 *Little Caesar* role
8 ___ fix (stuck)
9 Alphabetize
10 *Aïda* premiered there
11 *Zelig* moviemaker
12 Spoon-___
13 They've split
14 Presupposed, as a judgment
15 Aero or hippo ender
16 "Deals are my art form"
17 Takes advantage of
18 Sneaky look
25 Shrivel up
28 One of the Arkins
31 Heal, as bones
34 Come to the surface
36 Show time at the Bowl
37 Maestro Stravinsky
38 Underage one
39 Stray calf
40 Quartz variety
42 Bryce Canyon locale
44 *XXX* star
45 P, to a pianist
48 Rent out anew
49 *Pride and Prejudice* character
50 Pompeii attraction
53 Guarantee
58 Carol of *Taxi*
59 High school for Henri
60 Looney-toon
61 Bangkok natives
62 Hip, to a hippie

66 "This one's ___"
67 Scale
68 Tom made famous by the Kingston Trio
69 "Once you're dead you're made for life"
70 Destined (for)
71 Area of Vietnam
72 Kvelling
74 Flat dweller
75 Dirt on the screen?
78 Cowardly Lion player
79 ___ Park, Queens
80 Some HDTV's
81 What yentas may do
82 Scientologist Hubbard
83 What you're reading
89 Richer in content
90 Swiss river
91 "Don't tell ___!"
92 Tranquil, as a poet's days
93 Structural beam
99 Elicit a gesundheit
101 Rung of a social system
103 Science writer Asimov
104 "Who'da ___ it?!"
105 Stage direction
106 Salt Lake City college team
107 ___ sci (college major)
108 Muslim magic spirit
110 Swelled heads
111 *Beetle Bailey* pooch
112 Actress Skye
113 Cig drag
116 Opposite of post-
117 PC key

ANSWER, PAGE 232

YOU KNOW THE OLD SAYING

It turns out that foxes are pretty sly, after all. Let's debunk
a few more of those overworked myths about animals.

Crazy as a loon:

OQQMA YVH Y AZUJQO QD BWH *MQVBW *YUHVNGYM

PNOXHVMHAA — YMX KHVDHGBOZ AYMH. BWH NXHY QD

BWHNV JHNML "GVYIZ" GQUHA DVQU BWH OQQM'A BVHUQOQ

GYOO, PWNGW AQEMXA ONTH Y ABVYMLH OYELW, JEB GYM JH

EAHX BQ LVHHB QBWHV OQQMA QV ANLMYO PQVVZ QV

YOYVU.

Strong as a horse:

YGTJAJ YVUA DTVPEIA IAPJ VKS DAAQ DGT QYAET MAEPYQ

VKS JEWA. QYEJ HVK LVXA QYAL CTGKA QG EKONTR VKS

IVLAKAJJ. ED RGN'UA AUAT JAAK VK GF VQ MGTX, RGN'II

XKGM QYVQ "JQTGKP VJ VK GF" EJ LNHY LGTA

VCCTGCTEVQA.

The noble male lion:

LXZ *GQHN AW *EZYFLF QF YPLJYRRV FAKZLXQHN AW Y EJK.

XQF KQNXLV DAYD QF JFZM LA FPYDZ NYKZ QH LXZ

MQDZPLQAH AW XQF KYLZ, BXA QF LXZ DZYR XJHLZD. BXQRZ

LXZ KYRZF FQL YDAJHM RAAGQHN EDYSZ YHM HAERZ, QL'F

YPLJYRRV LXZ WZKYRZ RQAHF QH LXZ TDQMZ BXA MA YRR

LXZ XJHLQHN.

EUREKA!

They found it! While rummaging around in their labs and workrooms, these 40 innovators came up with something new and different enough to guarantee that their names would go down in history. See if you can experiment a little, too, and fit them all in the grid, crossword-style. Then visit the answer section to find out what they're famous for.

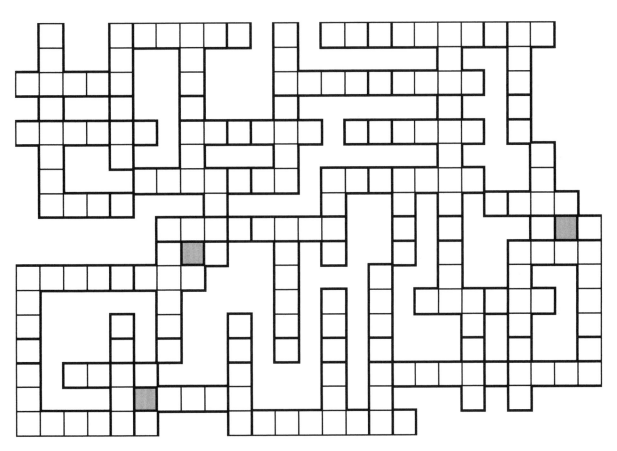

4-letter words
Bell
Benz
Colt
Cray
Ford
Howe
Otis
Watt

5-letter words
Gates
Morse
Nobel
Rubik
Tesla
Volta

6-letter words
Carver
Edison
Eiffel
Ferris
Fuller
Fulton
Jarvik
Lamarr
Teller
Tupper

7-letter words
Babbage
Braille
Burbank
Marconi

Pasteur
Strauss
Whitney
Zamboni

8-letter words
Bushnell
Franklin
Leonardo
Sikorsky

9-letter word
Macintosh

10-letter words
Archimedes
Farnsworth

12-letter word
Westinghouse

ANSWER, PAGE 233

TO YOUR HEALTH!

Directions for solving are on page 13.

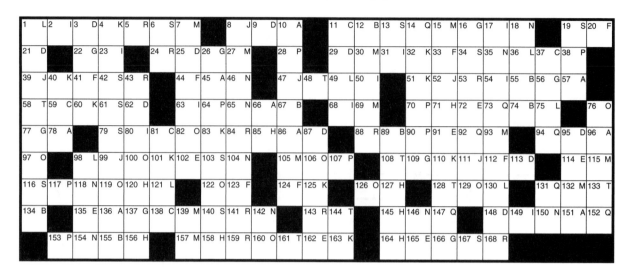

A. Foolishly rash

$\overline{151}\ \overline{66}\ \overline{96}\ \overline{10}\ \overline{57}\ \overline{136}\ \overline{86}\ \overline{45}\ \overline{78}$

B. California town in the Mohave Desert

$\overline{12}\ \overline{134}\ \overline{89}\ \overline{55}\ \overline{155}\ \overline{74}\ \overline{67}$

C. Country estate

$\overline{81}\ \overline{11}\ \overline{37}\ \overline{138}\ \overline{59}$

D. "The Magic Fingers of Radio" in the 1930s (2 wds.)

$\overline{113}\ \overline{29}\ \overline{148}\ \overline{62}\ \overline{21}\ \overline{95}\ \overline{3}\ \overline{9}\ \overline{25}\ \overline{87}$

E. High point of San Francisco (2 wds.)

$\overline{162}\ \overline{165}\ \overline{135}\ \overline{114}\ \overline{102}\ \overline{72}\ \overline{91}$

F. Cash crop of the South

$\overline{41}\ \overline{33}\ \overline{124}\ \overline{20}\ \overline{44}\ \overline{112}\ \overline{123}$

G. Maker of the QX and FX autos

$\overline{166}\ \overline{26}\ \overline{109}\ \overline{22}\ \overline{56}\ \overline{77}\ \overline{16}\ \overline{137}$

H. Powdered chocolate milk maker

$\overline{158}\ \overline{164}\ \overline{71}\ \overline{156}\ \overline{145}\ \overline{85}\ \overline{127}\ \overline{120}$

I. Sure signs that you're on the Great White Way (2 wds.)

$\overline{80}\ \overline{2}\ \overline{17}\ \overline{23}\ \overline{54}\ \overline{149}\ \overline{63}\ \overline{68}\ \overline{50}\ \overline{31}$

J. Beat at bridge or chess, perhaps

$\overline{52}\ \overline{99}\ \overline{8}\ \overline{39}\ \overline{111}\ \overline{47}$

K. Home of the 2004 World Series champions (2 wds.)

$\overline{110}\ \overline{125}\ \overline{83}\ \overline{51}\ \overline{40}\ \overline{163}\ \overline{32}\ \overline{4}\ \overline{60}\ \overline{101}$

L. Worked at occasionally

$\overline{75}\ \overline{49}\ \overline{36}\ \overline{1}\ \overline{98}\ \overline{130}\ \overline{121}$

M. Crept forward (2 wds.)

$\overline{30}\ \overline{15}\ \overline{157}\ \overline{105}\ \overline{7}\ \overline{139}\ \overline{115}\ \overline{93}\ \overline{69}\ \overline{132}\ \overline{27}$

N. Process used in copy machines

$\overline{150}\ \overline{118}\ \overline{18}\ \overline{154}\ \overline{142}\ \overline{65}\ \overline{35}\ \overline{46}\ \overline{146}\ \overline{104}$

O. On a roll, in gambling (3 wds.)

$\overline{106}\ \overline{119}\ \overline{122}\ \overline{76}\ \overline{82}\ \overline{100}\ \overline{129}\ \overline{126}\ \overline{160}\ \overline{97}$

P. Janet Jackson #1 "antic" of 1990

$\overline{64}\ \overline{107}\ \overline{70}\ \overline{28}\ \overline{117}\ \overline{90}\ \overline{153}\ \overline{38}$

Q. Oscar winner Holm of *Gentleman's Agreement*

$\overline{94}\ \overline{14}\ \overline{73}\ \overline{152}\ \overline{131}\ \overline{92}\ \overline{147}$

R. Star of *Kill Bill* (2 wds.)

$\overline{53}\ \overline{24}\ \overline{143}\ \overline{84}\ \overline{88}\ \overline{5}\ \overline{43}\ \overline{159}\ \overline{168}\ \overline{141}$

S. Creator of TV's Ernest G. Bilko (2 wds.)

$\overline{116}\ \overline{19}\ \overline{79}\ \overline{167}\ \overline{34}\ \overline{140}\ \overline{103}\ \overline{13}\ \overline{42}$
$\overline{61}\ \overline{6}$

T. Tolerate

$\overline{144}\ \overline{128}\ \overline{108}\ \overline{133}\ \overline{161}\ \overline{58}\ \overline{48}$

ANSWER, PAGE 232

HEY, DADDY-O!

Dig it, hipster. We've hidden 44 slangy words and phrases from the 1950s in the cube-shaped grid (a "cube" being someone who's squarer than square). After you've circled all the listed lingo in the grid, the leftover letters will reveal a few more examples of '50s slang. See the answer section for definitions.

```
        E E P O T G A R A B B I T I
      L L B S I L V E R J E F F S C
    B K N U C K L E S A N D W I C H
  A C R K C O W E S A L G A H O N R
 S I S S A H C Y S S A L C H E M E O
D T A N S S S A M A J I K S S S N S M
U G P E E P I E C R E E P I E E E I G E
S I   A L   T   O B     M I H P B A P
B L E A Z G I R U L L N G   S T T I N B L
U L N W I G O U T O P A S S I O N P I T A
M A E B T I E C W N K M E   P O I N S E T
E B C L U M P Y R I A N R R A C E I A K E
N E S N E A O N N Z I O U   N S D A A C D
T Y E H I U P O E A S W T P I U A R A U E
A E H D R E N T B T R H S   C A M D N B
L N T J I N T O X I M E T E R I L T E
C A E A R A T I Y O M R E   A I N A
A T K S T T W R O N N E D E B R T
S S A F L S B A T B A L F   U N
E A M E G R A H C E G R A L I
L C U T T H E C H E E S E K
```

AD-LIB
BEATNIK
BIG TICKLE
BLOW YOUR JETS
BOTTLE
BUCKET BAGS
CAST AN EYEBALL
CHARIOT
CHROME-PLATED
CLASSY CHASSIS
COCA-COLONIZATION
COOTIES
CUBE
CUT THE CHEESE
DRAINPIPES

FLABTABS
HI SI
IGGLE
INTOXIMETER
KNUCKLE SANDWICH
LARGE CHARGE
LUMPY
MADE IN THE SHADE
MAKE THE SCENE
MENTAL CASE
NERD
NOWHERE
PANIC
PASSION PIT
PEEPIE-CREEPIE

PUNK OUT
RABBIT
RAGTOP
SILVER JEFF
SIN BIN
SKIJAMAS
SLIP
SMAZE
SUDSABLE
TATT
TONY CURTIS
UNREAL
WIG OUT
WOCK

ANSWER, PAGE 234

IT'S A LIVING

Before he wrote *Lolita*, Vladimir Nabokov made his living in part by constructing crossword puzzles. Some of his fellow literary lights made their money the hard way, too, before they made it to the big time.

ACROSS

1 ___ *diem* (seize the day)
6 Gregory Peck played him
10 Moose ___, Saskatchewan
13 Popular Mexican beer brand
19 Shun
20 *Hacienda* room
21 In the manner of, on menus
22 Big name in mysteries
23 Samuel Taylor Coleridge, before
26 Houses without furnaces
27 Frasier's ex
28 Loser to VHS format
29 Kind of infection
31 Jimmy
32 "Or ___!"
33 Neighbor of Scot.
35 Sex finish
37 Unassertive
39 Dorothy Parker, before
47 O.R. workers
50 Oakland A's general manager Billy
51 Cosmetician Lauder
52 Sturdy material
53 *Alice in Wonderland* message
55 "Tubular!"
57 Infield protector
59 A 135 Across produces a good one
60 Ranch division
61 Half of Hispaniola
64 Points (to)
66 Admiral's org.
67 Robert Frost, before
70 Slanted type (abbr.)
72 Chesterfields and balmacaans
73 Feedbag morsel
74 Waking from a faint
78 Make like a dog in the heat
79 John Keats, before

81 Brouhaha
83 Make ten straight shots, maybe
86 *The Highwayman* poet
87 Pulitzer winner for *Picnic*
88 Where the Dutch boy stuck his finger
90 Be fishy
91 Leo and Claire's *Romeo & Juliet* director Luhrmann
92 Secret chili ingredient, maybe
93 Ocean floor, with "the"
95 Spinning
97 Wally Cleaver's troublemaking pal
101 Course for U.S. immigrants
102 Maya Angelou, before
106 Hosiery shade
107 Midwest Indian
108 German "you"
109 Govt. meat grader
113 Jefferson Davis was its pres.
116 Home on the range
119 "Take ___!"
121 Chatterer
123 *Law & Order* alum Angie
125 Sappho, before
128 Start of a rumormonger's report
129 ___ Beta Kappa
130 Quay
131 National body shop name
132 Upscale-looking
133 Say yes without saying yes
134 Volcano in Sicily
135 Barber's implement

DOWN

1 Stereo connector
2 Pop star Lavigne
3 Agitates
4 Felt for
5 Work on *Time*

6 Bat material
7 Ex-star
8 Crabtree & Evelyn uses a lot of it
9 Tallinn's sea
10 ___ alai
11 Sam Adams products
12 Unsightly bump
13 City on the Formosa Strait
14 Brainy guy
15 Golden Bears' school, for short
16 On
17 Thunderbolt hurler
18 Idiotproof
24 Liking
25 Like lane lines
30 Current measure
34 Elvis' record label
36 Yr. divisions
38 Cap location
40 Old White House nickname
41 Mattress maker
42 Playful mammal
43 Item on Canada's flag
44 Papal grant
45 John Hancocks, for short
46 Eliot Ness and colleagues
47 Do a double-take
48 Salsa dipper
49 Game where you can lose your shirt
54 Where a hadji has been
56 Get rid of a smell, maybe
58 "Sailing the Seas of Cheese" band
61 Fastball
62 One of the creepy crawlers
63 Conditions
64 Commercial wrinkle remover
65 Move to tears
68 Donkey ___ (arcade game)
69 Sixth-day creation

71 Surgery with balloons, for short
74 "Wolf!," for one
75 Sugar suffix
76 Quiznos alternative
77 1993 NBA Rookie of the Year
79 Wild card
80 Moved like molasses
81 Mixes in
82 Most everyone's on one or another
84 Disney World vehicle
85 Mrs. Zeus

89 Blunted sword
91 Loaded
92 Co. head
94 Defense zones, to the military
96 *Foucault's Pendulum* author
98 Torquay trash collectors
99 Half of MCCII
100 Gossip column tidbits
103 Mod
104 What a lost cause has
105 Little tyke
110 Portion of asparagus
111 Mirror-ball music genre

112 Man of morals?
113 Like Kate Spade bags
114 Satirist Mort
115 Zone
117 Where to see *Stump the Schwab*
118 Bounce off the walls
120 Got down
122 $$$ sources
124 More, in Madrid
126 Secreted
127 Paul's cousin in *Mad About You*

ANSWER, PAGE 233

WRIGHT AGAIN

More Steven Wright pearls of…whatever that stuff is.

1.

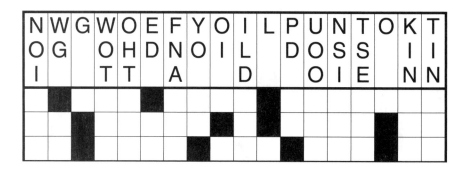

2.

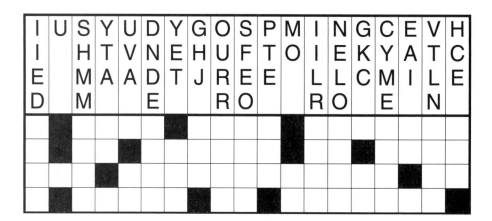

3.

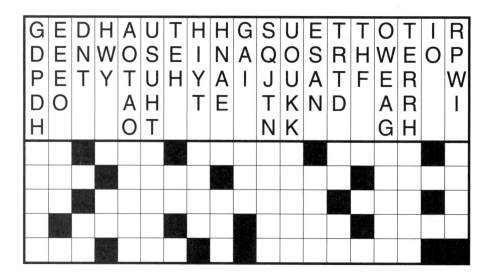

ANSWER, PAGE 232

SONS OF TOM SWIFTIES

Then there are the variations that don't use the usual "-ly" words—the Tom Swifties that defy all limits of levity. That's why we love 'em. Finish each sentence (1-10) with the word (a-j) that makes the most appropriate pun.

a. admitted   c. entranced   e. nonplussed   g. pondered   i. stated
b. being frank   d. in dismay   f. off the top   h. rehearsed   j. with relish
                                              of his head

_____ 1. "Dat's de end of April," Tom said…
_____ 2. "I have a split personality," Tom said,…
_____ 3. "I just came in through the door," Tom said,…
_____ 4. "I'm crazy about hot dogs," Tom said…
_____ 5. "I've been to Alabama, Wyoming, and everywhere in between," Tom…
_____ 6. "It's time for the second funeral," Tom…
_____ 7. "Oops! There goes my hat!" Tom said…
_____ 8. "That just doesn't add up," Tom said,…
_____ 9. "There's room for one more," Tom…
_____ 10. "Where should I plant these water lilies?" Tom…

ANSWER, PAGE 233

* * * * *

MORE LISTOGRAMS

See page 52 for directions and hints on solving.

7 Vegetables That Are Really Fruits	The 7 Deadliest Dogs
IBIBFLRN	GQW JKPP
HUNT	*SODIRU YXOGXODT
RWWAGTVM	FXHC
MHFTMH	IRPRIKWO
ABFAUDV	XKYMZ
ZCBTZX	CHPB XZJDQT
TQHITOH	RMQWR

ANSWER, PAGE 234

LIFESTYLES OF THE
NOT YET RICH AND FAMOUS

Sure, they're R&F now, but there was a time when these celebs flipped burgers, walked dogs, and had other regular jobs, just like the rest of us. Did we say regular? Get a load of some of these early occupations.

1. Before he hit it big as a fashion designer, Giorgio Armani once worked as:

    a. A medic's assistant in the Italian military
    b. A cucumber sizer in a pickle factory

2. Actress Kathy Bates (*Misery, Dolores Claiborne*) used to be:

    a. An accountant for H&R Block
    b. A singing waitress in the Catskills

3. Jason Biggs made his breakthrough, as it were, as an actor in *American Pie*, where he had a famous scene "practicing" with baked goods. Before that he was:

    a. A sandwich-maker in a Subway shop
    b. A carnival artist

4. Actress Annette Bening (*American Beauty*) once worked as:

    a. A Domino's Pizza delivery girl
    b. A cook on a charter boat

5. Singer-songwriter Jon Bon Jovi's original job was as:

    a. A floor sweeper at the Record Plant, a recording studio
    b. A pasta dough maker in a commercial spaghetti factory

6. Country star Garth Brooks joined the San Diego Padres for spring training in 1999, but didn't make the team. Aside from that, he once worked as:

    a. A nightclub bouncer
    b. A bonsai instructor

7. Director Mel Brooks goes way back—he fought in the Battle of the Bulge in World War II and was co-creator of the TV classic *Get Smart*. Once upon a time he also worked as:

    a. A drummer
    b. A shoe salesman

8. As a teenager, Pierce "007" Brosnan:

    a. Ran away with the circus as a fire-eater
    b. Sold Bibles door-to-door

9. Before becoming famous as *Alfie* and then winning two Oscars for other films, Michael Caine worked as a:

    a. Tutu maker
    b. Cement mixer

10. Drew Carey got into comedy as a gag writer who decided to try out his own material onstage. Before that, he was employed as:

    a. A shark feeder at an aquarium
    b. A waiter at a Denny's in Las Vegas

11. Actor George Clooney is riding high now, but once upon a time he:

    a. Picked grapes in Napa Valley
    b. Drew caricatures in a mall

12. Director Oliver Stone (*JFK, Natural Born Killers*) may have developed his in-your-face style while working as:

    a. A taxi driver in New York City
    b. A radio shock jock in Brooklyn

13. Multiple Grammy winner Sting once turned down the villain's role in the James Bond film *A View to a Kill.* Could that be because he considered his onetime real-life job villainous enough? He used to be:

    a. A dentist
    b. A clerk for Inland Revenue, Britain's version of America's IRS

14. Jerry Seinfeld forced himself to succeed at comedy to get away from such jobs as:

    a. Peddling costume jewelry on the street of Manhattan
    b. Selling light bulbs over the phone

15. Before the lady sang the blues, Diana Ross worked as:

    a. A cafeteria bus-girl
    b. A receptionist at an automotive plant

16. Comedian-actor Ray Romano was once employed as:

    a. A futon delivery man
    b. A stem chopper in a mushroom cannery

17. Before she wrote and starred in *My Big Fat Greek Wedding*, Nia Vardalos worked as:

    a. An air-brusher in a photography studio
    b. A box office cashier

18. She's America's sweetheart on *Lost,* but you might have been surprised to see Evangeline Lilly:

    a. As spokesperson for a "chat-line" where you could "meet local singles"
    b. In a shampoo comercial

19. *Tonight Show* Jay Leno host once made ends meet by working as:

    a. A truant officer
    b. A Rolls-Royce mechanic

20. Mariah Carey, who's had more #1 songs than anyone but Elvis and the Beatles, wasn't always on Easy Street. She once worked as:

    a. A janitor in a beauty salon
    b. A fly feeder in a nursery that raised carnivorous plants

21. When his father lost his job, Jim Carrey quit high school to work as:

    a. A janitor
    b. A Zamboni driver in an ice hockey rink

22. Speaking of Jim Carrey, his once-flame Renée Zellweger's original job was as:

    a. A ukulele tester
    b. A bartender's assistant

23. As a teenager, Marg Helgenberger of *CSI* worked:

    a. In her father's meat-packing plant
    b. As a carhop at a fancy Hollywood drive-in

24. Dustin Hoffman slept on Gene Hackman's kitchen floor while looking for acting work. In the meantime, he worked at such jobs as:

    a. Selling toys at Macy's
    b. Cleaning a dance studio

25. Once upon a time, Jeremy Irons earned his daily crumpets by:

    a. Singing and playing guitar outside movie theaters
    b. Working in the bird department of a large pet shop

26. Before Anthony LaPaglia of *Without a Trace* got into acting, he was:

    a. A policeman
    b. A teacher

ANSWER, PAGE 235

PLEASED TO MEAT YOU

Ever since Uncle John saw a sign on an electrician's truck that said "Let us fix your shorts," he's been collecting wacky business mottoes—a bunch of which you'll find in the puzzle below.

ACROSS

1 Ne'er-do-wells
5 Jason's ship
9 Lisping Warner Bros. character
14 Beast of burden's tow
18 At the peak of
19 It might be over your head
20 Amin's predecessor
21 Good, in Guatemala
22 Window cleaner's motto
26 Render openable, as a door
27 Like crab apples
28 Big name in truck rental
29 Pastry shop's motto
35 2003 Will Ferrell film
37 Super Bowl broadcast debuts
38 Santa's sleighful
39 Tale of Troy
40 Surrounded by
41 Rug rats
43 Actresses Tyler and Ullmann
44 More cautious
46 Bakery's motto
52 ___ State (Oklahoma's nickname)
53 Sacramento-to-Berkeley dir.
54 Parenthetical comment
55 Free sample, e.g.
56 Flat-topped formations
58 Hay fever inducer
63 1975 Wimbledon champ
64 Concrete company's motto
68 Humorist Bombeck
69 Last-minute subway boarder, maybe
71 In the lead
72 Snowshoe strand

73 Brewery kilns
76 Former Texas governor Richards
77 ___ Strait (U.S.-Russia separator)
78 Massage studio's motto
84 Certain U.S. bonds
85 Raiment
86 Scandinavian capital
87 Poker champ Phil
88 *Tempus* ___ (sundial motto)
89 It's one foot long?
91 Expand unnecessarily
94 Overly glib
95 Dry cleaner's motto
100 Fold down a corner
102 Divide into piles
103 Merchandise from Saturn
104 Car wash's motto
110 Sent a letter
111 Sing à la Jimmie Rodgers
112 Fictional sleuth Wolfe
113 Common flag symbol
114 Psychiatrist's refrain
115 Pig-keeper's shout
116 Cubs legend Maddux
117 "This is only a ___"

DOWN

1 Lake at Cornell
2 Undid the damage
3 Reservations
4 Use an atomizer
5 "I thought so!"
6 Tricky Dick's press secretary Nessen
7 Elapses
8 Loathsome
9 Entrance threshold

10 Aladdin's pal
11 Gift tag word
12 System for sending info from a PC
13 Cried out in pain
14 Face, slangily
15 Blood disease
16 Receiving government aid
17 Tribulation
21 Poisonous plant name suffix
23 Ultracompetent one
24 Hindrance when catching pop flies
25 Shakespearean "always"
30 Out-and-out
31 Promising
32 Tennis star Nastase
33 Skin care brand
34 Padlock holders
36 Pres. of the '30s-40s
40 "A Long Time ___" (Jim Croce song)
41 1987 Dreyfuss/DeVito comedy
42 Butter alternative
44 Moth-repelling wood
45 "Break ___!"
46 1970 album "The ___ of Jefferson Airplane"
47 Commotion
48 Outstanding, in a way
49 CCCP, translated
50 Go back and forth
51 1989 bio-flick of John Belushi
52 Big tubs
56 Reagan cabinet member Edwin
57 ___ Na Na
59 Screwball

60 Hall-of-Famer Banks
61 Make changes to
62 Hi and Lois' pet
64 Has on
65 Scarred captain of literature
66 Philosopher Descartes
67 Clammy
70 Genoan magistrate of old
72 Blob of wax, perhaps
74 Touch base?
75 Like amateur theatricals
77 Hemmed in
78 ___ *From Mars* (1953 horror classic)

79 How boxers slug it out
80 Farm enclosure
81 Cream, e.g.
82 Without thinking
83 Time of many chimes
84 Good recommendation
88 Outings
89 Activated, as a trap
90 "Mad" Carroll character
91 Pleasingly small
92 Clues to what's cooking
93 Roughly $1/3$ of the Earth's land surface

95 Astronaut Slayton
96 ___ Dawn Chong
97 Hundred Acre Wood resident
98 Hang low
99 English soccer legend Geoff
101 Mansion's outer defense
104 Pershing fought in it (abbr.)
105 Ghost word?
106 Altar answer
107 Driving area
108 Miners' quarry
109 Visibility impairer

ANSWER, PAGE 235

DANCE, DANCE, DANCE

Feel like going dancing...for a few weeks? No? Well, then maybe you'd just like to read about the people who did. Try to pick out the truth from the available choices as you enjoy the history of dance marathons.

After World War I, the country was in the mood for entertainment. Crosswords and mah-jongg became huge fads, and record-breaking contests were common: kissing contests, eating marathons, you name it. A man named Shipwreck Kelly became nationally known after **(preaching, walking backwards, sitting atop a flagpole)** for more than seven days. Another gent, Bill Williams, won a $500 bet by pushing a peanut **(across Delaware, up Pike's Peak, through Death Valley)** with his nose. The biggest fad of them all though, were the dance marathons.

The first American dance marathon took place in 1923 in the Audubon Ballroom in **(New York City, Atlanta, Las Vegas)**, where Alma Cummings went through **(two, four, six)** male partners over a span of 27 hours. A French college student beat her record within a week. Then Cummings beat that, and then a Cleveland salesgirl beat that, and then ... well, a craze was born.

A Houston dance hall owner started charging admission to watch, and soon lots of other dance halls were doing the same. And the prizes got bigger: One dancer named Bernie Brand went home with $5000 in prizes after dancing for just over **(four days, nine days, two weeks)**.

Owners of **(movie theaters, bingo parlors, bowling alleys)** saw the contests as competition, so they joined forces with church groups and local officials to try to ban them. Sinfulness aside, the marathons certainly could be dangerous; one healthy 27-year-old man died from **(dehydration, starvation, heart failure)** after a multi-day competition.

How did people eat, sleep, powder their noses, and so on? Organizers started adding rest periods—perhaps 15 minutes per hour for a while, to be decreased as the competition went on. Food was typically **(held out by spectators, on buffet tables on the dance floor, hung from the ceiling)**, and contestants would actually eat while dancing.

The record, according to *The Guinness Book of World Records*, was a couple who danced for **(four months, seven months, more than a year)** in the early 1930s. But the ultralong contests eventually were seen as a struggle for survival, much like what the country was already going through, and during the Depression, the fad began to attract contestants who simply wanted the free food and medical attention. A 1935 book called **(*They Shoot Horses, Don't They?*; *A Tree Grows in Brooklyn*; *Butterflies Are Free*)** was about just that: couples who danced because it was better than being on the streets.

With the glamour gone, cities and states began to ban the competitions, with the last ones taking place in **(the mid-1940s, the late 1950s, the early 1970s)**. It was finally time for the dance marathons to sit one out.

ANSWER, PAGE 235

WEATHER SYSTEM

This puzzle is all over the weather map. We've hidden 48 words and phrases commonly heard in weather forecasts in the grid, the shape of which is the meteorological symbol for a hurricane. It's up to you to enter the eye of the storm and find them all. After you've weathered that, the leftover letters will spell out a quote that begins, "The trouble with weather forecasting is that …"

```
                      E L Z Z I R D
                  Z I
                A
              H
            M   U N I P P Y D T
          I R C F R O S T S N R I R
          G O E H G R I S U I S L E C
        B L T T C L N I T T W L O W O O
      Y D A S T R O P I C A L S T O R M F
      D T S R A E W R N T A T F E H O G W
    D U N R E O U P S D U S N I M S T N E C
    E O O L D I M R G Q H D U E P N L I A H
  W L C N N O T E S R E I I G E I T Z T I
  P C A D U S T S T O R M G N R A C E H L
  O Y O D H W D S I E R U O H A R N E E L
  I L G Z T O S U N M R H G T T O O R R Y
  N T Y G O L O R O E T E M F U O O F M P
  T R O L U N F E T V E T N O R F M R A W
    A F S N M E C F Y E O O R E S L R N
    P H U Y Z E E R B N R S E T U L O R
      L I G H T N I N G N C C E N U L
        E V A W T A E H A U A Y S F
          G O F E S N E D O S S E N
            I R H G U O R T   T
                          E
                        E
                    T L
          C U M U L U S
```

BAROMETER
BREEZY
CELSIUS
CHILLY
CLEAR
COLD
CUMULUS
DENSE FOG
DEW POINT
DRIZZLE
DUST STORM
FLOODS
FORECAST

FREEZING
FROST
FULL MOON
GUSTING
HAIL
HAZE
HEAT WAVE
HUMID
HURRICANE
LIGHTNING
LOW PRESSURE
CENTER
METEOROLOGY

MIST
MUGGY
NIPPY
OVERCAST
OZONE
PARTLY CLOUDY
PRECIPITATION
RAIN SHOWER
RECORD HIGH
SLEET
SLUSH
SNOW
SQUALL

SUNNY
SUNSET
TEMPERATURE
THUNDERSTORM
TORNADO
TROPICAL STORM
TROUGH
WARM FRONT
WEATHERMAN
WIND

ANSWER, PAGE 235

LOST IN TRANSLATION

In this puzzle, the acrostic—the first letters of the words in the word list—answers
a question posed in the quote. Complete directions for solving are on page 13.

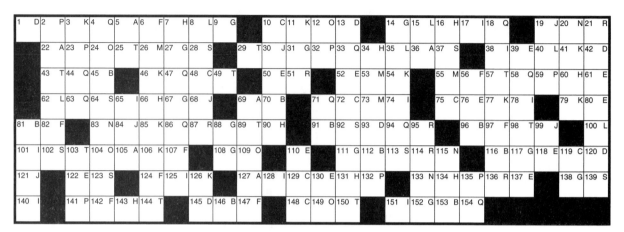

A. Bronze base

$\overline{22}$ $\overline{69}$ $\overline{105}$ $\overline{127}$ $\overline{5}$ $\overline{36}$

B. "The posse is coming!" sounds

$\overline{112}$ $\overline{81}$ $\overline{153}$ $\overline{70}$ $\overline{96}$ $\overline{45}$ $\overline{146}$ $\overline{116}$ $\overline{91}$

C. Penetrating discernment

$\overline{129}$ $\overline{48}$ $\overline{10}$ $\overline{119}$ $\overline{75}$ $\overline{72}$ $\overline{148}$

D. Enya or Yanni's genre (2 wds.)

$\overline{120}$ $\overline{13}$ $\overline{145}$ $\overline{93}$ $\overline{42}$ $\overline{1}$

E. DeNiro-Crystal comedy caper sequel (2 wds.)

$\overline{50}$ $\overline{61}$ $\overline{76}$ $\overline{39}$ $\overline{118}$ $\overline{130}$ $\overline{137}$ $\overline{52}$ $\overline{80}$

$\overline{110}$ $\overline{122}$

F. Texas Hold 'Em finale

$\overline{147}$ $\overline{142}$ $\overline{97}$ $\overline{82}$ $\overline{107}$ $\overline{56}$ $\overline{124}$ $\overline{6}$

G. Catchphrase of Alfred E. Neuman (3 wds.)

$\overline{111}$ $\overline{152}$ $\overline{138}$ $\overline{108}$ $\overline{31}$ $\overline{27}$ $\overline{14}$ $\overline{67}$ $\overline{88}$

$\overline{117}$ $\overline{9}$

H. 4/4 at the craps table (2 wds.)

$\overline{34}$ $\overline{143}$ $\overline{16}$ $\overline{90}$ $\overline{131}$ $\overline{66}$ $\overline{60}$ $\overline{134}$ $\overline{7}$

I. Park Avenue types (2 wds.)

$\overline{17}$ $\overline{38}$ $\overline{65}$ $\overline{101}$ $\overline{151}$ $\overline{125}$ $\overline{140}$ $\overline{78}$ $\overline{128}$ $\overline{74}$

J. Goads (2 wds.)

$\overline{84}$ $\overline{19}$ $\overline{121}$ $\overline{99}$ $\overline{30}$ $\overline{68}$

K. Oscar nominee for *Schindler's List* (2 wds.)

$\overline{46}$ $\overline{3}$ $\overline{85}$ $\overline{77}$ $\overline{126}$ $\overline{106}$ $\overline{54}$ $\overline{79}$ $\overline{11}$ $\overline{41}$

L. Martini garnishes

$\overline{40}$ $\overline{8}$ $\overline{15}$ $\overline{62}$ $\overline{35}$ $\overline{100}$

M. Sometimes it's neither this (See clue N)

$\overline{55}$ $\overline{73}$ $\overline{26}$ $\overline{53}$

N. Nor this! (See clue M)

$\overline{83}$ $\overline{20}$ $\overline{133}$ $\overline{115}$

O. Sex appeal

$\overline{24}$ $\overline{109}$ $\overline{12}$ $\overline{104}$ $\overline{149}$

P. Cast readings after opening night

$\overline{23}$ $\overline{135}$ $\overline{2}$ $\overline{59}$ $\overline{32}$ $\overline{141}$ $\overline{132}$

Q. Setting for clue B (3 wds.)

$\overline{71}$ $\overline{44}$ $\overline{58}$ $\overline{33}$ $\overline{47}$ $\overline{94}$ $\overline{4}$ $\overline{154}$ $\overline{63}$

$\overline{18}$ $\overline{86}$

R. Belfast's province

$\overline{87}$ $\overline{95}$ $\overline{51}$ $\overline{21}$ $\overline{114}$ $\overline{136}$

S. Composer of *Air Music* and *Eagles* (2 wds.)

$\overline{139}$ $\overline{113}$ $\overline{28}$ $\overline{64}$ $\overline{123}$ $\overline{102}$ $\overline{37}$ $\overline{92}$

T. Song from the movie *Annie* (2 wds.)

$\overline{49}$ $\overline{103}$ $\overline{29}$ $\overline{98}$ $\overline{25}$ $\overline{43}$ $\overline{57}$ $\overline{89}$ $\overline{150}$ $\overline{144}$

ANSWER, PAGE 235

SLIGHTLY IRREGULAR READING

We've put an extra spin on a game that originated in the *Washington Post* and was brought to Uncle John fans in *Uncle John's Slightly Irregular Bathroom Reader*. Here's the spin: Add one letter to the beginning, middle, or end of each of the following words to give it the meaning described in its new definition.

Philanderer
He may hop from bed to bed, but he always washes the sheets.

Palindrome
Casanova von Asac, a legendary 18th-century seducer, later revealed to have gone both ways.

The Undead
Corpses who walk around at night with lampshades on their heads.

Guitar
A musical instrument whose strings are pulled by your mother.

Sitcom
Typical TV fare.

Siddhartha
A young Indian mystic who discovers the true meaning of life as a ferryman serving only the finest in freshly caught, hickory-grilled, and lightly lemon-seasoned fillets.

Iditarod
An annual Alaskan race in which morons pull huskies sitting on sleds.

Urinal
A guy who uses the one next to you even though all the others are occupied.

Hippopotamus
Love letters from Marlon Brando to Roseanne.

Rescue
Saving the attractive women, children, and puppies first.

ANSWER, PAGE 236

* * * * *

ALONE IN THE BIG CITY

If New York City was as densely populated as Alaska, how many people would live in Manhattan?

a. 14
b. 14,000

ANSWER, PAGE 236

YOUNGEST & OLDEST

Some people can overcome any obstacles to their careers—including age.

ACROSS

1 Kind of stew
6 Snow blown by the wind
11 Shout of triumph
15 Mine entrance
19 From that time
20 Stream transport
21 Andy's radio pal
22 À la ___ (pie order)
23 Youngest Emmy winner for acting, at 25
25 Very chic
27 Painful pleasure, briefly
28 Popular ISP
29 Frost work
30 Primp
31 Vitality
33 Understanding words
35 They live in the Orient
37 Lacking a musical key
39 The Charles' pooch
40 Skunk's defense
41 Badlands loc.
42 Oldest Major League baseball player, at 59
45 One of the Bushes
48 "On the contrary"
50 Sgt., e.g.
51 "That hurts!"
52 ___ further (stop)
53 Shaq's sch.
54 Oldest Emmy winner for acting, at 82
59 Name on many swimsuits
61 More ornery
63 U.S. Navy underwater habitat
65 Boutros-Ghali's U.N. successor
66 Buoyant thing
68 ___ Kan (Alpo rival)
69 On the way
71 Jargon

72 Iced tea brand
75 Bug's chest
76 Arab chieftains
78 Oldest pro hockey player, at 52
80 Bear's "embrace"
83 Primitive ski lift
84 "Now ___ this!"
86 Puppeteer Baird
87 Secret journal
89 Note after fa
90 Oldest Oscar-winning actress, at 80
95 Attach, but not permanently
96 Jazz of the '40s
97 Sore from the workout
98 Art studio props
100 French painter known for pointillism
102 Concerning
103 Tennis players Kournikova and Smashnova
104 Pile of hay
105 Kitchen finish?
107 Was on the ballot
109 Late times, in TV talk
112 *Sideways* implement
114 Youngest pro hockey player, at 16
117 Designer Klein
118 Syrian bread
119 More despicable
120 Singer Lopez
121 Worth a blue ribbon
122 Great server in tennis
123 Suppress
124 Big name in watches

DOWN

1 Doctrine's suffix
2 Social reformer Jacob

3 Ancient Peruvian
4 Dopey guys
5 Like a bad collision
6 Mid-seventh century date
7 Indian royal
8 Lowdown
9 Ill-advised
10 Cowboy's moniker
11 Lake out west
12 Friend of Françoise
13 Too opinionated
14 Volcanic powder
15 National rail system
16 Senior member
17 Runs in neutral
18 Mall rat
24 Poet Lazarus and actress Samms
26 Chiropractor's concern
29 Ring out
32 Big name in peanuts
34 Fr. religious figure
36 Contented or sad sounds
37 Bothersome situations
38 Youngest Oscar-winning actress, at 10
39 Slip ___ (blunder)
40 Spa room
41 Chevy Chase show, briefly
43 NEA mem.
44 Office betting pot
45 Youngest major league baseball player, at 15
46 Finish on
47 Debby or Daniel
49 Cicero was a great one
52 Salami selection
55 Article in *Le Monde*
56 Big role for Liam in 1993
57 Check your figures, perhaps
58 ___ Lama

60 Scored even on the links
62 Rarin' to go
64 Indebted (to)
66 Shoe style for tall girls
67 West Indies dance
70 ASAP
73 Let out ___ (show awe)
74 Actress Petty
75 "You can never be too rich or too ___"
77 Queen of ___ (Bible figure)
79 Online auction site
81 *Topaz* novelist

82 Swindle
85 Hard to understand
88 Sigourney Weaver movie (with *The*)
90 Sudden sharp pulls
91 Mason undertaking
92 Be a thespian
93 *Civil Disobedience* writer
94 New Age musician
96 Sand toy
99 ___ be (reportedly)
100 *Platoon* director
101 Works hard for

102 Fighting
103 Investor in a Broadway show
104 Sign of healing
106 Head of France?
108 Church recess
110 Author Wiesel
111 Audition for *American Idol*
113 Busy one in Apr.
114 Patio party, for short
115 WWW address initials
116 Actress Long

ANSWER, PAGE 236

FAR ABOVE PAR

By now you're either a golf fiend or sick and tired of hearing about it. Well, we don't care one way or the other, because we're puzzle folks and the most important thing is that golf has a nice vocabulary for us to play with. So after you fit all 49 golf terms into the grid, crossword-style, we'll meet you at the 19th hole.

3-letter words
Ace
Bag
Cup
Lie
Par
PGA
Pin
Tee

4-letter words
Away
Cart
Chip
Club
Fade
Fore

Grip
Hook
Iron
LPGA
Putt
USGA

5-letter words
Divot
Eagle
Glove
Green
Links
Rough
Round
Run-up
Swing

6-letter words
Birdie
Caddie
Course
Dimple
Dogleg
Hazard
Nassau
Stance
Stroke
Stymie

7-letter words
Address
Gallery
Scratch

8-letter words
Drop area
Foursome

9-letter words
Albatross
Hole-in-one

11-letter words
Play through
Sudden death

12-letter word
Driving range

THE NAME'S THE SAME

The people on both lists share the same famous name. Can you figure out the name and match the two?

1. One of the stars of Second City Television (SCTV)
2. The TV actor best known for his role as Mr. French on *Family Affair*
3. Reagan's Secretary of the Interior who infamously tried to ban the Beach Boys from performing in Washington because rock and roll encouraged drug use and attracted "the wrong element"
4. The Native American actor and Oscar nominee for his role in *Dances With Wolves*
5. The TV actor played patriarch Jock Ewing on *Dallas*
6. A late, far-from-great senator from Wisconsin
7. An American boxer at the beginning of his career
8. That same American boxer now

a. A 20th century shah of Persia
b. The manager of the New York Yankees from 1931 to 1946
c. The cartoonist who created Garfield the Cat
d. The 18th century inventor perfected steam engine
e. The British-born author of *Our Man In Havana*
f. The British-born son of the 16th century explorer/cartographer who was born "Giovanni Cabotine"
g. The founder of the Wendy's fast food chain
h. A 19th century American abolitionist

ANSWER, PAGE 236

* * * * *

MYSTERY PLATE II

Let's have some more G.I. grub. The column on the left lists the food; the right-hand column the G.I. nickname. BEANS would still be coded HREQP as on page 81, and the letter substitution remains constant throughout the list.

IRNWXFV	NZEQPDFPSGQ
CEVYR PBZFV	CEWXSQR GSY
CREN YGED	VNGCESQR PNREI
VEQWEIRP	ZFHHRZ VENWXRP
VGALRZRL CSYI	WXEYI
PEYN EQL VRVVRZ	PEQL EQL LSZN
PGFV	XGN AENRZ

ANSWER, PAGE 236

AND YOU CAN QUOTE ME!

But first you gotta catch me! Which of the following famous people uttered these utterances?

1. "I have remained consistently and nauseatingly adorable. In fact, I have been known to cause diabetes."

    a. Katie Couric
    b. Meg Ryan
    c. Hilary Duff

2. "I'm done with stupid movies. I want to be taken seriously again."

    a. Melanie Griffith
    b. Anthony Hopkins
    c. Jack Nicholson

3. "A nice pair of pumps, a skirt that goes to your knees, that Vargas-red-lipstick glamour—to me, that's what a girl is."

    a. Sarah Jessica Parker
    b. Isaac Mizrahi
    c. Charlize Theron

4. "I'm such a pussycat in real life."

    a. Christopher Walken
    b. Bill O'Reilly
    c. Arnold Schwarzenegger

5. "I think I came out of the womb loving makeup."

    a. Liv Tyler
    b. Catherine Zeta-Jones
    c. Minnie Driver

6. "I've been fortunate. I haven't had too many auditions. I've slept with all the right people."

    a. Nicollette Sheridan
    b. Pamela Anderson
    c. Mariah Carey

7. "I'm not obsessive, like I have to have the best abs or the best butt, but I like the idea of feeling strong and healthy."

    a. Jon Bon Jovi
    b. Tyra Banks
    c. Halle Berry

8. "As long as I can remember, I wanted to sleep late, stay up late, and do nothing in between."

    a. Robin Williams
    b. Jon Stewart
    c. Jon Favreau

9. "I love my curves and my softness and my breasts. I think they're beautiful, so I don't have a problem showing them."

    a. Jennifer Connelly
    b. Kim Cattrall
    c. Madonna

10. "I can't type. I can't write a letter. I'm absolutely ignorant in many ways that everybody takes for granted."

    a. Cher
    b. Martha Stewart
    c. Stockard Channing

11. "I'm like the friendly executioner. I think what I do is kinder than patronizing somebody with false hope."

    a. Donald Trump
    b. Simon Cowell
    c. Barbara Walters

12. "I was born to be a leader."

    a. Steven Seagal
    b. Tommy Lee Jones
    c. Arnold Schwarzenegger

13. "I bet on everything. I bet on the side that a train is going to come in on a platform."

    a. Brian Dennehy
    b. Robert De Niro
    c. Dame Judi Dench

14. "I used to think that famous people were so full of crap."

    a. Robert Downey Jr.
    b. Jamie Foxx
    c. Leonardo DiCaprio

15. "I don't think anyone's particularly shocked by anything anymore. Are they? We're all such old sluts now."

    a. Mia Farrow
    b. Diane Keaton
    c. Rupert Everett

16. "I live vicariously through my rumors."

    a. Calista Flockhart
    b. Jodie Foster
    c. Rosie O'Donnell

17. "In this day and age, if you sit up straight, chew with your mouth closed and have good manners, you're a snob."

    a. Oprah Winfrey
    b. Gwyneth Paltrow
    c. Prince Charles

18. "Sometimes it's good if people are afraid of you, especially men. I don't get the cheesy pickup lines."

    a. Keri Russell
    b. Denise Richards
    c. Pink

19. "Designers pay me not to wear their clothes."

    a. Wanda Sykes
    b. Ellen DeGeneres
    c. Michael Moore

20. "What I may be lacking in terms of my physical beauty, I make up for in personality and experience."

    a. Joan Rivers
    b. Wesley Snipes
    c. Martin Short

21. "People ask me if I went to film school. And I tell them no, I went to films."

    a. Martin Scorsese
    b. Quentin Tarantino
    c. Steven Spielberg

22. "Nothing wakes you up like running down a hallway a thousand times."

    a. Kiefer Sutherland
    b. Keanu Reeves
    c. Jennifer Garner

ANSWER, PAGE 236

* * * * *

BURIED TREASURE

What do these words and phrases have in common?

VALETUDINARIAN THE GRAPES OF WRATH
HAPPY ENDING CAFETERIA LINE
SAN FRANCISCO NEUROTIC

ANSWER, PAGE 236

OUCH!

No Uncle John book would be complete without a hand-picked selection of groaners. Sorry about that.

ACROSS

1 Aide, for short
5 Respond to a sneeze
10 Soda can features
14 ___ off the old block
19 Like most 78 recordings
20 Birdie beater
21 Remove unceremoniously
22 Valerie Harper title role
23 Chimney sweep's concern
24 What do witches put in their hair?
26 Like this year's model
27 Resettled
29 Eisenhower's W.W. II command
30 Worked on a manuscript
32 Eats
33 Provides the wedding dinner
36 Mélange
37 "Runaway" singer
39 What do you call a cow that just had a baby?
43 Where the Rhone and Saone meet
46 You can dig it
47 Dressing choice
48 Mod ending
49 Focal points
50 Have questions about
52 ___ Nicolaas (Santa in the Netherlands)
53 Yaks
55 Two in a deck
56 Serve with a Mickey Finn
57 What is it called when a fire follows an earthquake?
60 Tampa Bay footballer, briefly
61 Fireplace fallout
63 Indolent
64 Small ring of color

66 Leg bones
69 *Lorenzo's Oil* co-star
71 Lineup in a dorm bathroom
72 Ham
73 First name in architecture
74 Home hot spot
75 "Brother!"
76 What do you get when you cross a bear with a skunk?
80 The Coyote St.
84 Writer James and family
86 Scandinavian capital
87 Sign of a skunk
88 Do penance
89 Lanky
90 Dallas campus, for short
91 Where most people work
93 Legal Jane or John
94 Sports telecaster
95 What do you call a person who crunches his corn flakes?
98 Economics no.
99 Actress Negri
101 Cut out surgically
102 Throw a party for
104 Some party purchases
107 School org.
108 Praiseworthy
112 D.C. baseballers
113 What's a mosquito's favorite sport?
117 Move effortlessly
118 One of a heavenly dozen
119 Poi base
120 Social rank
121 Swiss abstract artist
122 "I beg to differ"
123 Seethe
124 Open the sneaks
125 Urban eyesore

DOWN

1 Radio type
2 Arias, for example
3 Get cozy
4 "___ is human..."
5 It's got the lowest odds
6 Close the sneaks
7 "Omigosh!"
8 Camera selection, briefly
9 Go out with
10 Dave Letterman's list
11 Disney's Sleeping Beauty
12 National youth grp.
13 Eye problem
14 Artificial fiber
15 Velvety fabric
16 What should you say when you meet a ghost?
17 *Tête* product
18 Tex's buddy
25 Seamstress' sleeve style
28 Sit in on, as a class
31 Style
33 Hoosegow
34 ___ worse than death
35 Funny Kaye of *Guys and Dolls*
37 Senator from Connecticut
38 Switch end
40 Redeems
41 Jennifer Garner's spy series
42 Schiaparelli of fashion
44 Supernatural
45 Daisy Duck's April, May, and June
51 Lulu
53 Small pest
54 Axlike tool
55 Origin (abbr.)
57 Puppeteer Lewis
58 Parcel out
59 Word in a Batman comic

62 Tons

65 Discharge, anatomically

66 Population subdivision

67 Pictures on a screen

68 What do skeletons say before they begin dining?

69 Diamond in music

70 Popular snack

71 Fatty chemical compound

73 Guarantee

74 Bobbin

77 Alaskan seaport

78 "Your taxi's here" signals

79 Legendary jockey Arcaro

81 Gym game

82 Auth. unknown

83 Hang on to

85 Makes a better person of

88 Comparable to a beet

90 "H"

91 Homer epic

92 Displaced person

96 Come to an end

97 Ad urging

100 Prop for Will Rogers

103 Assignments

104 ___ uproar

105 Dear, to Dante

106 Grounded Atl. fliers

108 Oskar Schindler had one

109 Opposed to

110 In ___ of (subbing for)

111 Kind of sch.

114 Kit ___

115 Post-op ward

116 Covert surveillance vehicle

ANSWER, PAGE 237

THE WHEEL THING

Like Sid Caesar said, "The guy who invented the first wheel was an idiot, the guy who invented the other three, he was a genius." Find the 58 wheeled things in the grid, reading across, down, and diagonally. When you're done, the leftover letters will reveal a comment made by *Wheel of Fortune* letter-turner Vanna White.

```
                  N A V I N I M
                I T R A C S T R O P S
              S R O T C A R T N P Y U G
            O R I C K S H A W T T E H L I B E
          M C O S Y T K C U R T L D I K R U N T
          O S T E L L F L H E L C T U Y G M W A
        L U P H R O L L E R C O A S T E R I P H J O A
        P R A O A B O I L D R A O B K C U B E E N R M
      E U E D P C G D T I T R E L L O R T S R E L E B A
      S L P D P X G H L B         B I C Y C L E T U I
      R L M Y I O O E I O         W U O S A B R S L R
      A E A W N C C M M M         R L S K R A B D E B
      E Y C A G D A S O O         H T E A C R M A T U
      H A C G C O R B U T         A N F T E R U O T S
      S R S O A A T E S U O B U G G Y D E E I O T R E N
        D M N R P B 1 I A 9 R 8 E 6 B E U S T W A D I
        D K O T O U L N H A V C H A R I O T N I A R T
          C S E T S E M I O O Y T K N O W L N A
          T A N H E H C A L Y S C O O T E R C E
            H A N D C A R T A O L F R A X
            T H H P A R T T H E E C O
              E G A I R R A C S E B
                I X A T R S R
```

AIRBUS	DRAY	PULLEY	STREETCAR
AMBULETTE	FLOAT	PUSHCART	STROLLER
AUTOMOBILE	GO-CART	RACER	SULKY
BICYCLE	GOLF CART	RICKSHAW	TAXI
BIG RIG	HACK	ROADSTER	TRACTOR
BOXCAR	HANDCART	ROLLER COASTER	TRAILER
BUCKBOARD	HANSOM	SCHOOL BUS	TRAIN
BUGGY	HEARSE	SCOOTER	TRAM
BUMPER CAR	LIMOUSINE	SEDAN	TRAP
CABLE CAR	MINIVAN	SEMI	TROLLEY
CAMPER	MOPED	SHOPPING CART	TRUCK
CARRIAGE	MOTORCYCLE	SHAY	TUMBREL
CHARIOT	OXCART	SKATES	WHEELBARROW
COUPE	PADDY WAGON	SPORTS CAR	
DOLLY	PEDICAB	STAGECOACH	

ANSWER, PAGE 237

THE UNKNOWN COMIC

Well, maybe not completely unknown. Mitch Hedberg had some guest spots on *Late Night With David Letterman* to his credit, and was famous among his fellow (and girl) stand-ups for lines like "I'm against picketing. But I don't know how to show it." Here are a few more Hedbergisms.

1.

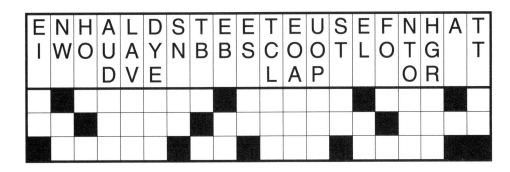

2.

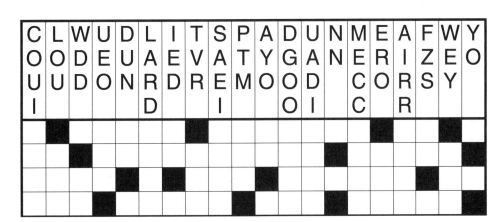

3.

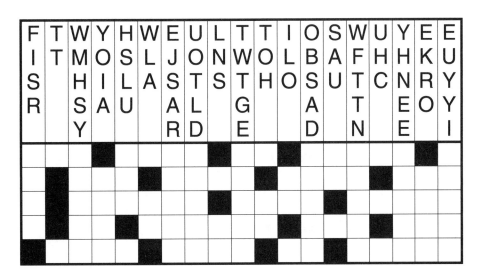

CELEBRITY FAVORITES

Knowing a celebrity's favorite food won't make your life any better, but it's fun to guess anyway.

1. Barbra Streisand's favorite food is:
    a. coffee ice cream
    b. bagels and cream cheese

2. Cameron Diaz's favorite food is:
    a. Twinkies
    b. French fries

3. Jennifer Love Hewitt loves:
    a. tofu burgers
    b. McDonald's cheeseburgers

4. Sandra Bullock's favorite movie is:
    a. *Rain Man*
    b. *The Wizard of Oz*

5. Ben Stein's favorite movie is:
    a. *Gone With the Wind*
    b. *Auntie Mame*

6. Leonardo DiCaprio's favorite hobby is:
    a. stamp collecting
    b. writing poetry

7. Brad Pitt's favorite hobby is:
    a. interior design
    b. crossword puzzles

8. Gloria Steinem's favorite book is:
    a. *The Second Sex* by Simone de Beauvoir
    b. *Little Women* by Louisa May Alcott

9. Woody Harrelson's favorite book is:
    a. *Uncle John's Bathroom Reader Plunges Into History*
    b. *A People's History of the United States* by Howard Zinn

10. Jeff Foxworthy's favorite book is:
    a. *Gone With the Wind*
    b. *You Might Be a Redneck if...* by Jeff Foxworthy

11. Roseanne Cash's favorite band is:
    a. the Beatles
    b. the Grateful Dead

12. Moby's favorite singer is:
    a. Connie Francis
    b. Donna Summer

13. If he could have another job, singer James Brown says he'd like to be a:
    a. big league pitcher
    b. riverboat gambler

14. Melanie Griffith says she'd like to be a:
    a. housewife
    b. brain surgeon

15. Roseanne would like to be a:
    a. teacher
    b. stripper

ANSWER, PAGE 237

* * * * *

STICKY SITUATION

Why doesn't Superglue stick to the inside of the bottle?

a. Because the bottle is treated with a light coat of solvent.

b. Because Superglue requires moisture to bond, and there isn't any inside the bottle.

c. Actually Superglue does stick to the inside of the bottle, but it's not a big deal; you're only losing a thin layer of glue.

ANSWER, PAGE 237

KIND OF KINKY

What do Bill Clinton and George W. Bush have in common? They're both fans of Texas novelist/songwriter/satirist Kinky Friedman, who has a lot to say on a lot of different subjects.

On the Creation

SU BSN XPIB FLG *DVKX TKGPFGX FLG LGPEGUB PUX FLG

GPKFL PUX PDD FLG OVUXGKB FLGKGSU. FLGKG PKG BVZG

VQ MB OLV QGGD FLPF *LG ZSHLF LPEG FPWGU YMBF P

DSFFDG ZVKG FSZG.

On Attitude

JI FQP DMCO BDO WDQJWO AOBEOOY DPGAHO MYU WQWLF,

KQ EJBD WQWLF. BDONO'Z MHEMFZ BJGO BQ AO DPGAHO

HMBON, QYWO FQP'CO AOOY VNQCOY DQNNOYUQPZHF,

JNNOCQWMAHF ENQYK.

On Patience

BD CGQ'TO WILBOKL IKP CGQ JIBL XGKN OKGQNU,

HGFOLUBKN JBXX QHQIXXC UIWWOK. IKP BL'XX QHQIXXC

YO HGFOLUBKN CGQ PGK'L XBVO.

On Rejection

CDXDWODDW ENVHLCJDQC QDBDTODG OJD AYWNCTQLEO,

YO KJLTJ OLAD *L IWDK *L JYG CPADOJLWZ EQDOOU JPO.

ANSWER, PAGE 237

LOONEY LAWS

Some awfully strange restrictions have made their way into the USA's legal codes. See if you can guess the missing part of each looney law.

ACROSS

1 Russian pancake
6 Film director's call
9 *The Lord of the Rings* baddies
13 Nissan model
19 It's illegal for barbers in Waterloo, Nebraska, to ___ between 7 A.M. and 7 P.M.
21 Impressive exploit
22 *Kinsey* star
23 It's against the law to ___ on a train passing through North Carolina
24 It's unlawful to tie a crocodile to a ___ in Detroit
26 Impudent back talk
27 Amber potation
28 It's passed from father to son
29 Sacrament
30 One-man sleds
32 In Garfield County, Montana, you can't draw funny faces on your ___
36 In Natoma, Kansas, it's illegal to throw knives at men wearing ___
40 Three on a sundial
41 Prop on a golf course
42 Gun-lobbying grp.
43 It's against the law to pawn your ___ in Delaware
49 Museum display
50 ___ de vivre
52 It's illegal to fish for ___ in any stream, river, or lake in Ohio
53 College walls clinger
54 "It's freezing in here!"
55 Pick up the check
57 Disturbed the peace, big time
58 Nobleman
59 Maine law states that you may not catch a lobster with ___
62 In Knoxville, Tennessee, it's illegal to ___ a fish
63 Harness strap
64 List-ending abbr.
65 British school founded in 1440

67 In Michigan, it's against the law to put a ___ in your boss' desk
70 In Portland, Oregon, it's illegal to shake a ___ in someone's face
76 Haughtiness
77 "Eediotic" cartoon cat
79 Markedly
80 Daiquiri ingredient
82 Frat party fixture
83 The law prohibits barbers in Omaha, Nebraska, from shaving the ___ of customers
84 *Candid Camera* creator
85 By way of
86 In Natchez, Mississippi, it's unlawful for ___ to drink beer
88 Maidenform purchase
89 ___ up (getting the smarts)
92 Holm of *The Lord of the Rings*
93 In California, it's illegal to ___ in your hotel room
96 You can't carry an ___ in your pocket in Lexington, Kentucky
102 Begat
103 Farmyard grunt
104 Backyard amenity
105 Bilko's rank (abbr.)
106 "When ___ Young" (The Animals song)
110 It's against the law to anchor your boat to the ___ in Jefferson City, Missouri
114 It's illegal to walk on a ___ in Winchester, Massachusetts (unless you're in church)
116 Retrieve, as files
117 Arkwright in Genesis
118 It's illegal to ride an ___ down the street in Wilbur, Washington
119 Old Persian provincial governor
120 Beauty pageant ID
121 Compass dir.
122 Drew to a close

DOWN

1 Hotel room pair
2 *Doctor Zhivago* heroine
3 "How sweet ___!"
4 Pebbled, as a bathtub's floor
5 Squid ejection
6 Ready to strike, as a snake
7 "___ I miss my guess…"
8 Disapproving sound
9 Light switch setting
10 Holds the throne
11 Was concerned
12 Courtroom employee
13 Even one
14 Was #1 in the rankings
15 Part of ATV
16 "Did you hear what ___?!"
17 Three-card ___
18 Pays to play
20 Mirrored
25 Hack down
31 ___ tree (in a tough spot)
32 Electrical cord
33 "Give ___ rest!"
34 Openly agreed (with)
35 Hurries
36 Use a shiv on
37 Bathrobe material
38 Like bell-bottoms and beehive hairdos
39 Form a coalition
43 "___ She Coo?" (R&B hit)
44 Quaker ___
45 Hispanic huzzah
46 Covers for someone, say
47 ___ *Bayou* (1997 indie film)
48 Lamb on pita sandwich
50 Playwright/director Cocteau
51 Galley ship's propeller
52 Cargo-hauling device
55 Long journey
56 Slugger's stat
57 Falling apart at the seams
58 Gasp for air
60 Fancy garden pots
61 Plenty
62 Call wrong in a coin toss
65 Shorten for TV, say

66 Egyptian king, for short
67 "For pity's ___!"
68 Richard who played Jaws in 007 films
69 Implore
70 Handmade object?
71 CPR experts
72 Sweetener in a blue packet
73 Try for a seat
74 Former North Carolina senator Sam
75 Feeling bad about
77 1953 western nominated for Best Picture
78 Richter scale maximum

81 Sorcerer
83 Burn around the edges
84 On the house
87 Harder to please
88 Golf legend Hogan
89 Deserving of merit
90 Neighbor of Scot.
91 Old-fashioned clothing press
93 Squeezebox songs
94 Give out, as homework
95 Criticize peevishly
96 Greek vowels
97 Approximately, in historic dates
98 Sign into law

99 Earth Day mo.
100 Haunted house sounds
101 Fireside drink
107 Scrabble formation
108 Cathedral section
109 Watermelon eater's annoyance
111 Org. involved in cryptanalysis
112 Recipe amt.
113 Librarian's admonition
114 Large cask
115 Widely seen article?

ANSWER, PAGE 238

THANKS A LOT!

Now you can mind your manners wherever you go!

ACROSS

1 Father figure
5 Said "Not guilty," maybe
9 *Chariots of Fire* climax
13 Poker night start-ups
18 Alda and King
20 Actress Taylor of *Six Feet Under*
21 ___ Bator, Mongolia
22 Down Under critter
23 "Obrigado" is "thank you" in ___
25 *Brave New World* drug
26 Rainbow-shaped
27 Not publish?
28 Is bogged down
31 Used a loom
32 NHL legend Gordie
34 ___ *generis* (unique)
35 Home hot spots
37 "Gracias" is "thank you" in ___
41 Month in Giverny
43 Tourist's interests
46 ___ Alto, California
47 Delicate state of affairs
53 "Old MacDonald" refrain
54 Fancy tie
56 Unemotional
57 Like some verbs, for short
58 *Frida* actress Hayek
59 "From This Moment" singer Twain
61 *"Ich bin ___ Berliner"*
62 *Let's Make ___*
64 Cub or Brave, for short
65 God of light
67 Letters in a bank window
69 In-flight guesstimates, briefly
71 "Dziekuje" is "thank you" in ___
73 Afr. nation

74 "Kamsa hamnida" is "thank you" in ___
77 Fifty percent, up front?
78 Horse halter
80 Sorry
82 "Dancing Queen" group
86 Features in an Al Hirschfeld drawing
88 Sushi bar staple
90 Jong et al.
92 Baker's dozen?
94 *End of Days* actor Kier
95 "Why? Because ___ so!"
97 Alabama city in '60s headlines
98 Houston athlete
99 Presbyterian groups
102 Grazing spots
103 Division
105 UFO crew
106 "Tack" is "thank you" in ___
108 Scandinavian "Cheers!"
111 Sighs of content
113 Maui instruments
114 Final Four org.
116 Evian container sealer
119 "Now!"
124 Writing paper in India
126 One-time Soviet ruler Andropov
127 "Ta" is "thank you" in ___
129 Big name in insurance
130 Sarah McLachlan hit song
131 Horse show on TV
132 ___ stone (not negotiable)
133 Like some tree trunks
134 City on the Rhone
135 Butter servings
136 Hackman of *Superman*

DOWN

1 *A Chorus Line* producer Joseph
2 Shaving cream additive

3 Young salmon
4 Against
5 More than one (abbr.)
6 Feudal figure
7 "That's something ___!"
8 Girth control plans
9 "Spasibo" is "thank you" in ___
10 Tons
11 *The Plague* author
12 Decree
13 "Wanted" poster letters
14 "Takk" is "thank you" in ___
15 Guacamole holder
16 Height (abbr.)
17 "Maureen" singer
19 Raw bar orders?
24 Haunted house resident
29 "Poison" shrub
30 Boxing stats
33 "___ On First?"
36 Contends
37 Fashionable resorts
38 Turkish authority
39 Creator of Jubilation T. Cornpone
40 *Teletubbies* name
42 "What ___ for Love"
44 Digital display
45 Fly high
48 Sporty truck, for short
49 Beehive or flip, e. g.
50 Obstructs
51 "Efharisto" is "thank you" in ___
52 Public speaker
55 Does groundbreaking work?
60 *Men in Black* creature
62 Most painful
63 Movie cowboy Lash
66 Heavy metal

68 Brooklyn add-on
70 Clairvoyants
72 "Sukria" is "thank you" in ___
75 Off the subject
76 Cores
79 Dear partner?
81 Tibetan priests
82 "Oh my!"
83 Anjou relative
84 Body Shop purchase
85 "Dankie" is "thank you" in ___

87 Best-rated
89 52, in old Rome
91 Obi, e.g.
93 Fair to middling
95 "___ Really Going Out With Him?" (Joe Jackson hit)
96 News anchor's work station
100 "Grazie" is "thank you" in ___
101 Use colorful language
104 Faerie queene of literature
107 "These," to Carlos
109 True blue
110 Hit the books

112 Rapscallion
113 Surprise at a tournament
114 Author/linguist Chomsky
115 Marc Antony's love, briefly
117 Jazz club ensemble
118 Saintly glow
120 Cassini of fashion
121 Nick at ___
122 Eve's child
123 Feminine suffix
125 Utter
128 Hula Bowl stats

ANSWER, PAGE 238

ANIMAL PLANET

The U.S. has its bald eagle and Canada has its beaver, but what about the rest of the world? We've rounded up 33 exotic creatures, all of which are the national symbols of their countries. See if you can fit them all in the grid, crossword-style, then check the answer section to see what nations they represent.

3-letter words
Cow
Elk

4-letter words
Bear
Kiwi
Oryx
Swan

5-letter words
Coqui
Horse
Llama
Takin
Tiger
Zebra

6-letter words
Condor
Garuda
Jaguar
Vicuña

7-letter words
Carabao
Markhor
Pelican
Quetzal
Rooster

8-letter words
Kangaroo
Sisserou

9-letter words
Bald eagle
Crocodile
Gyrfalcon
Red dragon
Springbok

10-letter words
Barbary ape
Doctorbird

11-letter words
Barn swallow
Hummingbird

15-letter word
Two-spot ladybird

ANSWER, PAGE 238

KIBBLE ME THIS

That bag of dry kibble in your pantry has quite the history behind it. Can you choose the truths about dog food from the choices in parentheses? If you get stuck, maybe Fido can lend a paw.

Over 2,000 years ago, a Roman poet and philosopher wrote the first farming manual, in which he advised giving farm dogs barley bread soaked in (**beer, salt water, milk**), as well as (**red wine to help tame them, the bones of dead sheep, goat meat**).

In medieval times, most dogs had to scrounge for what they could get. But royalty often employed "kennel cooks" who would make (**huge stews, oversized sandwiches, omelets**) for the hounds.

One notable dog owner from history was 19th-century empress Tzu Hsi of (**China, India, Mexico**). Her dogs ate better than most humans did, feasting regularly on (**quail breasts, antelope milk, Pekingese shark fins, all of the above**).

The dog food industry as we know it really began in the mid-1800s. While James Spratt was sailing to London, he noticed sailors throwing leftover (**hard biscuits, gruel, raw potatoes**) to the hungry dogs on the docks. This gave him the idea to create a similar product specifically for dogs, and in 1860, he introduced (**Spratt's Delicious Doggie Delights, Spratt's Semi-Digestable Food for the Dog of the Home, Spratt's Patent Meal Fibrine Dog Cakes**).

Despite their name, they became a hit in England and America, inspiring the inevitable imitators. A Boston veterinarian created the tasty-sounding (**Canine Quinine, Pupp-O Vitamin Snacks, Medicated Dog Bread**). In 1908, the F. H. Bennett Biscuit Company introduced a biscuit shaped like something dogs have a particular affinity for; when Nabisco bought the company, they renamed that product (**Snausages, Milkbones, Puppums**); it is still popular today.

The first canned dog food was introduced to the U.S. in 1922, made from (**Western buffalo, young calf, horse**) meat. It became so popular that the company was breeding and slaughtering (**5,000; 50,000; 500,000**) of those animals every year. Canned dog food had a 90 percent share of the market until World War II, when meat rationing made dry dog food popular again.

In the 1950s, food companies experimented with an "extruder" that cooked and "puffed up" (**Chex cereal, Three Musketeers bars, Swanson pot pies**) and came up with (**Purina Dog Chow, Alpo, Iams**), which quickly became—and still is—the best-selling dog food in America.

Advertising for packaged dog food took off in the 1950s and '60s. The Pet Food Institute bought radio spots that warned of "the dangers of (**the pantry, table scraps, no-name brands**)." Various pet food companies waged "beef wars" through TV ads, arguing about whose product had the most beef; one memorable spot involved (**Lorne Greene, Glenda Jackson, Laurence Olivier**) hawking Alpo while holding up a sirloin steak.

By 1975, there were already more than (**100; 400; 1,500**) dog foods on the market. Today, pet food takes in more than (**$700 million, $2 billion, $11 billion**) every year. That's a lotta kibble!

ANSWER, PAGE 238

WOODSTOCK: THE WORD SEARCH

Summer, 1969. Some 450,000 people gathered peacefully at Woodstock, New York, to hear the 32 people and/or groups like Mountain (hence the mountain-shaped grid) who performed or spoke on stage during the three-day festival. (The only two performers we couldn't fit in were Neil Young, who joined Crosby, Stills & Nash for a few songs, and the Paul Butterfield Blues Band. Whew!) First, circle all the performers in the grid; then read all the uncircled letters to reveal part of a speech made to the crowd and the name of the person who gave it.

```
                              I
                           T  H  I
                        S  I  N  N
                        K  W  Y  C  O
                     U  J  H  E  R  A
                  V  E  E  A  P  E  R  O
                  V  I  E  N  N  D  T  S
               O  M  R  E  T  H  I  I  W  N
               G  G  H  T  O  T  B  S  H  A
               E  R  W  T  Q  U  I  L  L  J  O  T
         R        L  A  D  T  U  H  A  T  E  Y  H  O  A  E
      L  F  A     T  M  I  L  G  L  I  O  S  A  N  K  P  Y  R
   H  S  I  F  E  H  T  &  E  O  J  Y  R  T  N  U  O  C  L  I
   D  S  C  F  A  E  N  G  E  L  T  T  O  R  D  G  E  T  T  I
   H  E  U  S  R  B  N  I  D  R  A  H  M  I  T  A  N  D  R  H  N
T  A  L  V  N  N  A  I  T  S  A  B  E  S  N  H  O  J  E  A  T  A
H  D  H  R  E  E  N  E  C  D  A  Y  S  O  G  E  F  F  U  H  M  N
N  E  J  A  N  V  D  D  A  M  U  S  I  C  A  B  F  N  D  H  F  O  A
A  W  O  A  R  A  K  N  A  H  S  I  V  A  R  A  A  V  E  N  E  U  N
D  O  H  A  J  O  H  N  N  Y  W  I  N  T  E  R  N  M  T  H  I  E  N  A
N  G  O  N  B  R  E  M  M  O  S  T  R  E  B  U  D  I  T  F  U  K  T  H  N
M  A  N  B  D  D  I  M  C  R  O  S  B  Y  S  T  I  L  L  S  &  N  A  S  H
E  U  S  A  H  I  H  C  G  O  D  B  R  U  G  S  A  Y  X  A  M  L  I  E  S
L  J  O  E  C  O  C  K  E  R  S  Y  R  E  T  F  A  S  R  A  E  Y  N  E  T
O  A  U  A  Z  A  L  I  A  D  N  A  N  I  D  A  H  C  T  A  S  I  M  A  W  S  L
S  A  N  T  A  N  A  S  R  A  E  T  &  T  A  E  W  S  D  O  O  L  B  M  A  X  Y  A
S  X  I  R  D  N  E  H  I  M  I  J  E  F  F  E  R  S  O  N  A  I  R  P  L  A  N  E
C  R  E  E  D  E  N  C  E  C  L  E  A  R  W  A  T  E  R  R  E  V  I  V  A  L  G  U  R
```

ARLO GUTHRIE
BERT SOMMER
BLOOD, SWEAT, & TEARS
CANNED HEAT
COUNTRY JOE & THE FISH
CREEDENCE CLEARWATER
　REVIVAL
CROSBY, STILLS, & NASH
GRATEFUL DEAD
[THE] INCREDIBLE STRING
　BAND
JANIS JOPLIN

JEFFERSON AIRPLANE
JIMI HENDRIX
JOAN BAEZ
JOE COCKER
JOHN SEBASTIAN
JOHNNY WINTER
KEEF HARTLY
MAX YASGUR
MELANIE
MOUNTAIN
QUILL
RAVI SHANKAR

RICHIE HAVENS
SANTANA
SHA NA NA
SLY AND THE FAMILY
　STONE
SWAMI SATCHADINANDA
SWEETWATER
TEN YEARS AFTER
THE BAND
THE WHO
TIM HARDIN

ANSWER, PAGE 239

HOPING FOR HIGHER MARKS?

In this puzzle, the acrostic—the first letters of the words in the word list—
finishes the quote. Complete directions for solving are on page 13.

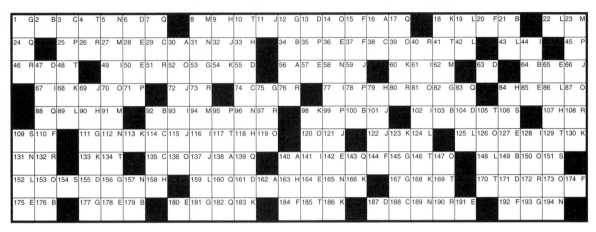

A. Is restless in bed
$\overline{16}\ \overline{30}\ \overline{56}\ \overline{140}\ \overline{162}\ \overline{138}$

B. Venue for equestrian events
$\overline{149}\ \overline{2}\ \overline{64}\ \overline{92}\ \overline{34}\ \overline{176}\ \overline{100}\ \overline{103}\ \overline{21}\ \overline{179}$

C. Put on public display
$\overline{38}\ \overline{3}\ \overline{29}\ \overline{114}\ \overline{135}\ \overline{188}\ \overline{74}$

D. Booker Prize novelist of *Life of Pi* (2 wds.)
$\overline{55}\ \overline{155}\ \overline{47}\ \overline{13}\ \overline{187}\ \overline{63}\ \overline{171}\ \overline{104}\ \overline{6}\ \overline{161}$

E. Get immediately serious (4 wds.)
$\overline{142}\ \overline{57}\ \overline{191}\ \overline{28}\ \overline{127}\ \overline{164}\ \overline{85}\ \overline{50}\ \overline{36}\ \overline{178}\ \overline{65}\ \overline{180}\ \overline{175}$

F. Franz Mesmer's specialty
$\overline{37}\ \overline{184}\ \overline{174}\ \overline{110}\ \overline{20}\ \overline{192}\ \overline{144}\ \overline{15}$

G. Site of the annual NFL Pro Bowl (2 wds.)
$\overline{193}\ \overline{156}\ \overline{145}\ \overline{75}\ \overline{53}\ \overline{1}\ \overline{177}\ \overline{167}\ \overline{82}\ \overline{12}\ \overline{181}\ \overline{111}$

H. A real nobody
$\overline{33}\ \overline{79}\ \overline{118}\ \overline{90}\ \overline{163}\ \overline{107}\ \overline{9}\ \overline{84}\ \overline{158}$

I. Bond (James Bond) nemesis
$\overline{49}\ \overline{61}\ \overline{93}\ \overline{128}\ \overline{44}\ \overline{116}\ \overline{102}\ \overline{77}\ \overline{141}\ \overline{67}$

J. Quadrennial U.S. event (2 wds.)
$\overline{32}\ \overline{11}\ \overline{101}\ \overline{115}\ \overline{122}\ \overline{69}\ \overline{72}\ \overline{121}\ \overline{59}\ \overline{137}\ \overline{66}$

K. Oscar winner for *Rain Man* (2 wds.)
$\overline{166}\ \overline{186}\ \overline{113}\ \overline{183}\ \overline{130}\ \overline{54}\ \overline{123}\ \overline{133}\ \overline{60}\ \overline{18}\ \overline{98}\ \overline{68}\ \overline{168}$

L. Classic book by Sun Tzu (4 wds.)
$\overline{22}\ \overline{89}\ \overline{124}\ \overline{86}\ \overline{159}\ \overline{148}\ \overline{43}\ \overline{152}\ \overline{125}\ \overline{42}\ \overline{19}$

M. Mary Chase play about a large rabbit
$\overline{23}\ \overline{94}\ \overline{62}\ \overline{8}\ \overline{27}\ \overline{91}$

N. Writer/star of the mockumentary *A Mighty Wind* (2 wds.)
$\overline{58}\ \overline{112}\ \overline{189}\ \overline{165}\ \overline{131}\ \overline{96}\ \overline{157}\ \overline{5}\ \overline{31}\ \overline{194}$

O. Picasso and Monet, e.g.
$\overline{120}\ \overline{52}\ \overline{173}\ \overline{136}\ \overline{150}\ \overline{70}\ \overline{119}\ \overline{14}\ \overline{126}$
$\overline{81}\ \overline{153}\ \overline{147}\ \overline{87}\ \overline{39}$

P. Theft
$\overline{78}\ \overline{99}\ \overline{25}\ \overline{45}\ \overline{71}\ \overline{35}\ \overline{95}$

Q. Irritability
$\overline{143}\ \overline{24}\ \overline{83}\ \overline{88}\ \overline{182}\ \overline{7}\ \overline{160}\ \overline{139}\ \overline{17}$

R. Where the power is, to a motor head (3 wds.)
$\overline{80}\ \overline{73}\ \overline{132}\ \overline{26}\ \overline{51}\ \overline{40}\ \overline{190}\ \overline{76}\ \overline{108}$
$\overline{46}\ \overline{172}\ \overline{97}$

S. Detractors' words
$\overline{154}\ \overline{109}\ \overline{151}\ \overline{106}$

T. Oscar nominee for *American History X* (2 wds.)
$\overline{105}\ \overline{170}\ \overline{129}\ \overline{117}\ \overline{41}\ \overline{169}\ \overline{146}\ \overline{185}\ \overline{134}$
$\overline{4}\ \overline{10}\ \overline{48}$

ANSWER, PAGE 239

DO GEESE SEE GOD?

When we told Otto and Ava that one of our writers had constructed
a crossword filled with palindromes, they said, "He did, eh?"

ACROSS

1 City in Florida
6 Driver's license and such
9 *Brave New World* drug
13 Third Greek letter
18 Golden Horde people
20 *The A-Team* cast member
21 Event calling for a limo
22 Small toiletry cases
23 Old typewriter key
24 **Result of a frat prank?**
27 Jackie's "O"
29 Old Soviet space station
30 "Too bad"
31 **Why Sasquatch had trouble at Payless?**
34 Be a vendor of
35 KO go-between
36 Yada, yada, yada
37 Chicago-based film critic
39 **TV season premiere?**
45 Serene
47 Showgirl's feathery scarf
50 Crazylegs Hirsch's real name
51 ___ glance
52 **Masseuse offering?**
56 Play part
57 Target alternative
59 Michaelmas daisies
60 Where cows get their munchies
61 Canapé topping
64 Cash register key
66 Neighbor of Okla.
67 **What a group of alarmed churchgoers say?**
70 Microwave
73 Novelist Lurie
75 "Food Glorious Food" musical

76 Half, for starters
77 *American Idol* judges look for this
79 West Point student
81 Sink
82 **Observation about an early drinker?**
85 Plasma TV maker
88 Elite group of invitees
89 Pester
90 Big role for Liz
91 **Reaction to some Hawaiian music?**
93 Actors Wyle and Beery
96 Conditions
99 Psychic gift
100 Habitual user
103 **Acrobat's perch?**
108 Bikini, say
111 Black tie affair garb
112 Miss an opportunity
115 **First job for a jury?**
118 ___ Dan (pop group)
119 Clear the tape
120 Paris airport
121 *The Name of the Rose* author Umberto
122 Less challenging
123 What the defense does
124 Starlet's goal
125 They cross aves.
126 Actress Zellweger

DOWN

1 Football great Graham
2 James of *Las Vegas*
3 Up on the diamond
4 Rope for Rogers (Will or Roy)
5 "You ___ Beautiful" (Joe Cocker hit)

6 Young rascal
7 Video store section
8 Marital discord
9 Mole, for one
10 Path for an astronaut
11 Debatable
12 Singer Tori
13 Yellowstone attraction
14 Besides
15 Bi-i-g picture
16 ___ *Vice*
17 Skier's mecca
19 Archie's order to Edith
25 Leisurely pace
26 Commanded
28 Latin dance
32 Letter-shaped bolt holder
33 Happen
37 Golfer Ernie
38 ASCAP rival
39 Inventor of alternating current
40 Stomach ache
41 "Good luck!" to a thespian
42 Centuries on end
43 Mixture "only her hair-dresser knows for sure"
44 "___ It to the Streets" (Doobie Brothers hit)
46 Christo's "Gates," to some
47 Finishes first effortlessly
48 ___ *Miss Brooks*
49 Sit-ups target
52 Timesaver for the cashier
53 Stun gun
54 "___ Her Again" (The Mamas & The Papas hit)
55 Letters on a Cards cap
58 *Juin* preceder
61 Jai alai equipment

62 Mil. address
63 Big wheels
64 Abbr. in U.S.N.A.
65 Unlock, to Longfellow
67 Some team statistics
68 ___ de la Cité
69 Glycerine opener
71 *Witness* folk
72 Spotted horse
74 Hula dancer's necklace
76 Radiant light
77 Half a score
78 One of Frank's exes
79 Middling grade

80 To have, in Le Havre
81 Good, to rappers
83 Acad.
84 French "they"
86 At the home of
87 Photographer Adams
92 Disagree with
93 Most agreeable
94 Pale yellows
95 "A-one and ___"
97 Lot
98 Outpourings from whales
100 Doubleday of baseball
101 *Mary* ___ (ill-fated ship)

102 Ladies of Lisbon
103 Ogre under a bridge
104 Precise
105 "Would you like to swing on ___?"
106 Jazzy Della
107 Front wheel alignment
109 Get an ___ effort
110 Prefix for American
113 Title role for Peter Fonda
114 *Pericles, Prince of* ___
116 Bakery order
117 Turndowns

OUI THE PEOPLE

While the French are trying to purge every English word and expression from their hotsy-totsy language, we're busy using French expressions every single day. And that includes you, mon ami. Let's show 'em a thing or two. Let's put all these fancy French words in their proper place…in the grid, crossword-style, that is.

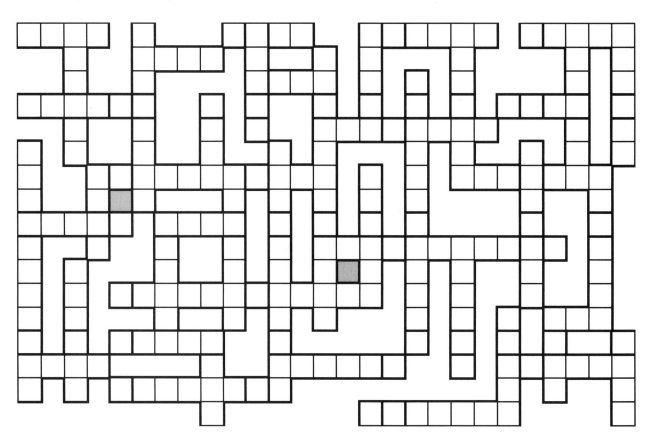

3-letter word
Née

4-letter words
Beau
Chef
Chic
Élan
Épée
Faux
Fête
Menu
Moue
Naif
Roué
RSVP

5-letter words
Adieu
Gaffe
Passé
Purée
Sauté
Suède

6-letter words
Au pair
Déjà vu
Exposé
Milieu
Petite
Risqué
Sachet

Séance
Soirée
Touché

7-letter words
Cuisine
En masse
En route
Faux pas
Gourmet
Maître d'
Protégé

8-letter words
À la carte
Apéritif
Critique

11-letter words
Coup de grâce
Raison d'être
Renaissance
Savoir-faire

12-letter words
Fait accompli
Laissez-faire
Ménage à trois

THE GREATEST

Muhammad Ali named himself "The Greatest" and you know what? We have to agree. Each saying has been translated by simple letter-substitution code. For further instructions and hints on how to solve, see page 7.

1. TLUP V ZVL JET RLTJB JEVK HK HB UHRX KT AX SXNXVKXS

OVL GXVOE STJL KT KEX ATKKTZ TN EHB BTIU VLS OTZX IF

JHKE KEX XWKGV TILOX TN FTJXG HK KVRXB KT JHL JEXL

KEX ZVKOE HB XYXL.

2. *U FY *FYTEUDF. *U FY KGT WFEK JCL HCI'K ETDCSIUOT.

XLK STK LNTM KC YT. XBFDP, DCIRUMTIK DCDPJ; YJ IFYT, ICK

JCLEN; YJ ETBUSUCI, ICK JCLEN; YJ SCFBN, YJ CHI; STK

LNTM KC YT.

3. *M PUCAK AGABR VMJICA TN CBUMJMJL, HIC *M XUMK,

"KTJ'C EIMC. XINNAB JTY UJK SMGA CPA BAXC TN RTIB SMNA

UX U ZPUVFMTJ."

ANSWER, PAGE 239

* * * * *

SECRET RECIPE MAN

The founder of Coca-Cola was once also:

    a. A Nobel Prize winner
    b. The mayor of Atlanta, Georgia
    c. The grower of a prize-winning pumpkin

ANSWER, PAGE 239

RENAISSANCE GUY

Leonardo da Vinci is most famous for paintings like the *Mona Lisa* and
The Last Supper, but painting was just something he did in his spare time.

ACROSS

1 Moisten the turkey
6 Snake's weapon
10 Quilting party
13 Means of escape
18 Inaptly titled 1991 Stallone flop
19 Logical lead-in
20 Granny
21 Be mad about
22 Leonardo invention #1
24 Leonardo invention #2
26 Topic in divinity sch.
27 Corp. partner of Time Warner
28 Shadows
30 Platters of the '60s
31 Dr. Seuss' Sam-___
32 Unheeding
34 Prevent violence, in a way
36 The enemy side
37 Part of a.m.
38 Piece of parsley
40 Leonardo inventions #3
44 Belief held by Thomas Jefferson
46 With 104 Down, legal order of prohibition
47 Speak with conviction
50 Conductor de Waart
53 Gain a lap?
54 Parts of the lymphatic system
58 Leonardo invention #4
61 Bawl out
64 Whirlpool
65 Like doing your taxes
66 Charles Lamb's pen name
67 Encl. with a submission
68 Make a choice, with "for"
69 Photo developing shop
70 Talk out of
72 Bad cholesterol (abbr.)

74 Grassland
75 Kings of France
77 Notable London art gallery
79 Road service org., familiarly
81 Periodic acct. deposit
82 "Cannonball" band, with "the"
84 Leonardo invention #5
86 More indignant
87 Salt Lake City athlete
89 Granola bit
90 Wise sayings
91 One who barely gets through life?
95 White heron
97 Leonardo invention #6
102 Tears
106 1982 film with ground-breaking special effects
107 "___ folly to be wise"
108 Lives, but just lives
110 Nair competitor
111 Show ___
112 It begins on the same day of the week every year as Apr.
113 *8 1/2* actress Aimée
115 Groove
117 *Boys' Life* org.
118 Leonardo invention #7
121 Leonardo invention #8
124 Five-pointed symbol used in wicca
125 The euro replaced it
126 *I Dream of Jeannie* star Barbara
127 Sibelius composition "___ Triste"
128 Decelerates
129 Rockets center ___ Ming
130 Snoop ___
131 Nifty ankle covers of the '20s

DOWN

1 College entrance exams
2 Napping
3 Having a series of steps
4 Cigarette ingredient
5 Humorist Bombeck
6 Finger snaps
7 Hubbub
8 Food of the gods
9 Kiddie vehicle
10 Galway and Monterey
11 Chang's conjoined twin
12 Place for a stud
13 Scenery chewers
14 Refreshing quaff
15 Bringing along
16 Be an artist
17 Greeks' name for Mercury
20 Where the Wild are
23 Boston specialty
25 *Otello*, for example
29 Apple product
33 Colleague of Che
35 *Three's Company* star
36 For a party
37 Extras
39 Pet rodent
41 Mamie's predecessor
42 China's Chou En-___
43 ___ uncertain terms
45 Repeat
47 Sucks up
48 Japanese beer brand
49 More gray and forbidding
51 Electron tube
52 A-Ha hit "Take ___"
55 Misnomer for using a touch-tone phone
56 Perfumer's extract
57 Sword covers
59 Jeff's *Life in Hell* companion

60 Succeed in irritating

62 Humdinger

63 Went to battle

66 *Traffic* actress Christensen

71 Mr. Rubik of cube fame

73 Pantry

76 "As ___ TV"

78 Yiddish word meaning "trouble"

80 Bernadette of Broadway

83 $1/_{16}$ ounce

84 Snafu

85 Downed

88 Twitch

92 Ryan's *Paper Moon* co-star

93 In a useful way

94 Cliff and Clair's son

96 It doesn't cover much

97 Denominator for calculating a baseballer's average

98 Main element of Duchamp's *Fountain*

99 *Code* ___ (Ken Follett thriller)

100 Oozed forth

101 Japanese martial art

103 Where a star is born?

104 See 46 Across

105 USA part

109 Phoenix hoopster

112 Writes down quickly

113 Flying prefix

114 Big D.C. lobby

116 Fast European trains, briefly

119 Do a lawn chore

120 ___ Maria liqueur

122 Relax, with "out"

123 Sucker

ANSWER, PAGE 240

TALES OF THE KING

Here are ten Elvis factoids presented in the form of a high-low quiz.
Decide for yourself whether the number presented is too high or too low.

	High	Low
1. Elvis had **22** Billboard #1 hits.	___	___
2. Elvis starred in **21** feature films.	___	___
3. Elvis made **38** television commercials.	___	___
4. The face value of the first Elvis Presley stamp was **33¢**.	___	___
5. **7** countries have issued Elvis Presley postage stamps.	___	___
6. On an average day, **2** people call Graceland and ask to speak to Elvis.	___	___
7. Elvis gave nearly **28,000** encores over the course of his career.	___	___
8. The hit song "Hound Dog" was written in about **30** minutes.	___	___
9. Elvis owned nearly **$10,000** worth of prescription sunglasses when he died.	___	___
10. The estimated value of a single pair of Elvis' underpants is **$4000**.	___	___

ANSWER, PAGE 240

* * * * *

JINGLE, JINGLE

Small crostic puzzles are solved just like the big ones (directions on page 13),
and the first letters of the fill-in words **do** spell out a message in this puzzle.

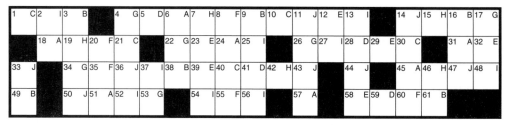

A. Edith Piaf, a.k.a. "The Little ___"

 24 51 57 6 45 18 31

B. Call upon the gods

 38 9 16 49 61 3

C. Sharply and stylishly attired

 30 40 10 1 21

D. Festive occasion

 28 59 41 5

E. Reddish-brown, as hair

 32 23 58 29 12 39

F. Oscar winner for *Two Women*

 20 55 35 8 60

G. Courtroom attorney's protesting cry

 34 26 22 17 4 53

H. Kathmandu's land

 19 15 7 46 42

I. Don't look this present in the mouth (2 wds.)

 37 48 54 25 2 52 56 13 27

J. 2004 movie for wine lovers

 50 36 47 11 14 44 43 33

ANSWER, PAGE 240

YOUR MOMENT OF ZEN

Three of the reasons why *The Daily Show With Jon Stewart* keeps winning those Emmys.

1.

E	R	S	S	H	D	I	N	G	I	T	O	N	H	U	R	S	N	N	H	E	C	E	T	M	W
P	N	E		I	O	S	N	G	T	V	U	S	M	A	A		N	O	W	U	I	N	C	A		R	D	H	E
A	R	E		G	E	E				B	E			A	P			O				N	A	R	H		H

2.

F	H	E	L	E	N	T	T	H	D	S	R	O	R	I	M	H	S	N	D	T	A	N	O	F	N	J
E	I	N	L	Y	U	U	A	A	T	E	O	W	O	M	H	I	A	E	B	I	O	T	W	R	N	L
I	V		S	O	D	W	H	R	I	S	W	H	O	O	I	A	S	S	E	O	R	Y		I	U	
O	N		R	I	D	S	R		C	A	P	P	L	N	A	A				N	L					

3.

Y	A	A	T	H	H	E	O	N	R	T	F	I	T	A	E	E	H	E	L	E	O	S	G	M	I	N
A	W	S	S	I	E	N	G	E	E	O	U	P	T	P	E	E	C	I	W	O	S	T	P	H	N	C
C	L	L	L	E	I	G	M			B	T	E	O	H	R	N	W	A	D	S	I	N	L	D	E	R
	O	S	T	R	H	A	R			S	H	O		F	I	T	S	I	L	I	N	R	T	A	O	T
	E	I		T	D	R	Y			O	R			H				A	L	N					T	

ANSWER, PAGE 240

MIXED-UP PEOPLE

We think it's weird and wonderful when the letters of people's names
scramble up into sayings that tell you something about them.

ACROSS

1 Showman called the Yankee Doodle Dandy
6 Sonic boomerang
10 Silents star Bow
15 Use a shiv on
19 Early adders
20 Memorable Gregory Peck role
21 Evinced amazement
22 Exxon competitor
23 "Understand?"
24 MADAM CURIE
26 Priest in a saffron robe
27 "Get the red out" stuff
29 Where Dr. J operated
30 Britain's Tony Award
32 Pesky sound (or person)
33 Ovum
37 Word with man or maiden
38 Graffiti writer
41 SALMAN RUSHDIE
45 Mine, in Marseilles
46 Varnish ingredients
48 Mideast gulf
49 Be in the red
50 Chili con ___
52 "Believe" singer
53 "___ Rebel" (Crystals hit)
55 Start of a Beatles title
57 Early second century date
58 U. S. GRANT, R. E. LEE
62 Ice cream brand known as Dreyer's in the West
63 Sane
65 Org. dealing with returns
66 *Damn Yankees* siren
68 Winter hazard
69 Low man on the army totem pole

73 Country spreads?
76 2004 AL MVP Guerrero, to fans
78 Penny face
79 Nonsense
82 Techno pioneer with the album *Hotel*
85 ALEC GUINNESS
89 Cool money?
90 Sign of the Ram
92 Hardly hirsute
93 Get prepared
94 School in Sèvres
96 "___ out!"
97 ___ arms (irate)
99 Soda's partner
101 "This is ___ for Superman!"
102 CLINT EASTWOOD
106 Ugly sight
108 Lamarr of *Ecstasy*
109 Showing bias
111 Jack of late-night fame
112 Shelter
115 *Wheel of Fortune* request
116 Seeming length of time in a waiting room?
120 *Été* month
121 GEORGE BUSH
125 ___-um (gnat)
126 Utz rival
127 Shake an Etch A Sketch
128 *The Joy of Cooking* author Rombauer
129 Big role for Madonna
130 Met, for one
131 Ate off the good china
132 Security slip
133 Actress Claire

DOWN

1 Bingo contraption
2 Comply with
3 ADOLF HITLER
4 Environmental hazard
5 Containing element #7
6 O.K. Corral name
7 Famous sequence in *The French Connection*
8 Snookered
9 Kimono closer
10 Searched high and low
11 Neighborhood people
12 "Gotcha!"
13 San ___ (Riviera resort)
14 Sweet girl of song
15 Rounds of fire
16 Large supply
17 High point
18 One charging on a safari?
25 *The Last of the Mohicans* Mohican
28 Tel. helper
31 Skater Slutskaya
34 Composer Edvard
35 Film noir, e.g.
36 ___ apso
38 Capital of Bangladesh
39 Modern correspondence
40 Come up again
42 Former congressman Mo
43 Off-kilter
44 They need to be taken
47 Dolly, for one
51 Merman of Broadway
53 Wife of Zeus
54 Once, once
56 Artichoke center
59 Prepare for another yard sale

60 1958 Oscar-winner David

61 Comfy spots

64 Zero originated this role

67 Expire

70 Gomez portrayer Julia

71 Footnote abbr.

72 Acclaim

74 JIM MORRISON

75 Sea dog

77 Kind of card

80 Knight's gear

81 West Point freshman

82 BLT condiment

83 Former Dodger Hershiser

84 Aviary

86 Grandmothers, to tots

87 Center of Florida

88 47 Down, for one

91 Desert boot material

95 Rake

98 Excited

99 Trig ratios

100 Hoopla

103 More drenched

104 Contract section

105 Made more pungent

107 Pulled down

110 Layer of skin

112 Hock

113 Disturb

114 Dustin's *Tootsie* co-star

117 Ship wood

118 Henri's head

119 Votes in favor

122 Prohibit

123 Hodges of the Dodgers

124 Neighbor of Wash.

ANSWER, PAGE 240

TAKE MY PUZZLE, PLEASE

Various grumbles and gripes from Henny Youngman, a.k.a. "The King of the One-Liners."

1.

H	E	Y	S	A	A	T	E	D	E	E	H	P	A	N	W	T	E	N	F	G	O	N	T
D	M		R	A		K	L	R	M	T		M	T	Y	U	H	P		E	R	G	O	T
I	E			O		O	H		E	E		A	I		U	U	E			I			R

2.

B	D	K	O	W	I	E	U	H	M	L	O	A	D	N	N	D	R	A	K	K	D	D	K
I	O	N	N	I	W	U	H	S	D	R	S	B	W	I	R	E	B	N	A	K	R	C	U
F	A	E		H	M	N	N	C	T	O	E	N	A	A	K	G	I	A	S	N	O	O	L
E	L	R		E	S	Y	Y		A	Y	Y	R	V	A	N		S		C	T	E		
O				N	H	T	T		E					A	S								

3.

O	N	U	I	S	C	O	U	E	L	W	E	N	K	E	E	Y	W	N	N	W	O	A	D	D	O
O	E		A	T	P	O	R	L	A	A	N	T	E	E	U	T	I	H	Y	T	H	W	V	O	W
E	M		I		R	U	O	P	T	K	I	T	H	O	Y	H	H	I	O	T	I	N		E	H
M	O		I		H	B	M	M	D	A	S	E	O	D	M		A	A		D	G	L		W	O
Y	R					O	T	L	H	H	S	E	D	E			E	E			E	E		R	

ANSWER, PAGE 240

PARALLEL HISTORY

In *Uncle John's Bathroom Reader Plunges Into History Again*, we pondered how some important events might have played out differently if just one letter had been changed. For example, a celebration ending World War I at which the Germans had to bring all the desserts would be THE TREATS OF VERSAILLES. Based on the new description of these famous historic events or eras, can you figure out which letter was changed?

WATERLOO – 1815
The real reason that Napoleon was defeated: His army got bogged down trying to cross a river in Belgium.

THE NORMAN CONQUEST – 1066
You've seen it before: your average, everyday overthrow of England by a bastard son of a duke.

THE STONE AGE – c. 2,000,000 years ago-c. 4,000 years ago.
The period of human history during which people learned to make wraps out of small furry creatures.

THE CIVIL WAR – 1861-1865
Conflict between Northern and Southern Japanese subcompact makers.

THE DARK AGES – 5th -14th centuries
Era during which everyone was sort of displeased.

THE HUNDRED YEARS' WAR – 14th-15th centuries
Long-term conflict among chain store outlets in Europe.

THE IDES OF MARCH – 44 B.C.
What Julius Caesar couldn't conceive of—until it was too late.

THE LONDON BLITZ – 1940s
Fashion trend (beaded jackets, gold lamé everything) adopted by Londoners as a way to keep up their spirits in those dark, dank, underground bomb shelters.

THE BATTLE OF THE BULGE – 1944
World War II event that gained the Allies a teensy bit of territory.

THE WARS OF THE ROSES – late 15th century
Cosmetic surgery was just coming into vogue when this violent rivalry between two families of plastic surgeons broke out.

THE GOLD RUSH – 1840s
In which thousands of hopefuls packed up and moved to California where they could play their favorite sport all year round.

THE LINCOLN-DOUGLAS DEBATES – 1858
Public meetings between two Senate hopefuls from Illinois; held in the good old days when you could get your money back if you weren't satisfied.

THE LONG MARCH – 1920s
Communist leader Mao Zedong couldn't talk anyone into going with him on his trek to northwestern China, so he did it all by himself.

ANSWER, PAGE 241

DON'T BE A LIRIPOOP!

"Liripoop" is an old word meaning "a silly creature." This crossword is filled with many real words
with similar unusual meanings. Solve this puzzle and your conversations will never be the same!

ACROSS

1 Enormous
5 Be like a sponge
11 Used a mop
18 Have ___ (live it up)
20 New Mexico city where Demi Moore was born
22 Colonnaded porch
23 A noisy or confused fight
25 Home to the Carter Center
26 ___ Kan dog food
27 ___ about (approximately)
28 Aspect
30 Encourage
31 Blue-veined cheese
33 A mineral such as toadstone or bufonite, said to have healing properties
37 Hood armament?
38 Vicinities
39 27, to 3
40 Degree description
43 Pulitzer category
45 Actress Van Devere
46 Drink heavily
47 Artsy area of NYC
48 Offered item on *The Bachelor*
49 Trigonometry function
50 Pertaining to waste matter
53 Signs a contract
54 Pays attention to
56 Response from the flock
57 Heartstrings' sounds?
58 Removes from text
60 Common hors d'oeuvre
62 Big name
63 Oscar winner Ameche
64 Having a long narrow nose
68 Toll road (abbr.)
71 Director Craven

72 One of Michael Jackson's brothers
73 In progress
75 Get clean
78 Ticket sales
80 Move slowly
82 They may be put on
83 A great-grandfather's grandmother's sister
86 Not e'en once
87 ___ *fixe*
88 Gravy holder
89 Go off-course
90 Dianne of *Bullets Over Broadway*
92 Venomous viper
93 Dancer Miller
94 Has-___
95 "Occupant needed"
96 Grope around
97 Hit with a fish
99 Actress Tia of *Wayne's World*
102 Reason for some medals
105 Ending for stink
106 Auel heroine
107 Blood type description (abbr.)
108 In an angry manner
110 Having the upper and lower teeth unlike
115 Steve Winwood hit
116 Went back
117 Chew the scenery
118 Piles up
119 Judo instructor
120 Word on a store door

DOWN

1 Cab drivers
2 W.W. II vessel
3 Baggy trousers
4 Capital of Latvia?

5 Pyromaniac's crime
6 Physicist Niels
7 Card-issuing grp.
8 Acknowledge
9 Gas option (abbr.)
10 They float above stadiums
11 Use as a step stool
12 Kind of suit or blanket
13 *What's My Line?* panelist Francis
14 She played the Spider Woman in *Kiss of the Spider Woman*
15 Firecracker's sound
16 Outer (prefix)
17 Watergate figure
19 *GoodFellas* star
21 Carrie Fisher role
24 Baseball legend Slaughter
29 Make a cryptogram
32 Most ineffectual
33 Betrayed grief
34 Matter for the courts
35 Sounds during a massage
36 "___ your pardon!"
38 CNN war correspondent Peter
40 Morning's end
41 Hired goon
42 *Bonanza* character
43 Like some flower arrangements
44 Instrumental composition
45 Restrain
46 *In the Bedroom* actress
47 Impertinent girl
49 Pumps and such
51 It evokes pity
52 Online periodical
55 More nimble
59 Winter forecast, sometimes
61 Part of MoMA
62 Skywalker's father

65 Fish-eating mammal
66 Most exposed
67 River recess
68 An effeminate-looking man
69 "Gay" city
70 Orchestra leader Kay
71 "Could you repeat that?"
74 Oakland athlete
75 Rum-soaked dessert
76 Very much
77 Eliot Ness, for one
78 They could symbolize jealousy

79 *Lend Me* ___ (1989 Broadway play)
81 "___ You Now" (#1 hit for Eddie Fisher)
84 At any point
85 Off base?
91 Land in *la mer*
92 Add bubbles to
94 Hole-making tools
95 Certain steaks
96 FDR's pooch
97 Pigeon homes
98 Male guinea pig

99 Pop singer Lauper
100 Way to go
101 Germany's eighth-largest city
102 Brawny competitor
103 Composer Khachaturian
104 Sounds after tra
106 Screenwriter James
109 Be mendacious
111 Hockey surface
112 Capitol Hill figure (abbr.)
113 "___ bodkins!"
114 Type of insurance plan

ANSWER, PAGE 241

REDUNDANT AND REPETITIOUS

This puzzle contains 22 two-word phrases, each of which contains a redundancy. One such example could be CIRCLE AROUND, which is what you'll want to do with all the hidden phrases in the grid. The word list gives you the first word in each phrase and the blanks show you the number of letters in the second word of each phrase. If you can find the first word in the grid, the second word will follow. (Note: There are two phrases that each start with the words NEW and OLD. Don't think we're just being redundant.) After you've circled all 22 phrases, the leftover letters in the grid will spell out a sentence that contains five additional redundancies. If you need some help—or assistance—turn to the complete word list on page 241.

```
              A R E P U S F O
            C S S F P A I W A L N C
          O S L M I A S T I O D A N A
        J N U T O R C T E V W F H C O W
      A O W I S A S S E M E N O O T Y E K
      V I O L E N T E X P L O S I O N B C
  L D N D L G F P L P E A E S E Z U A E
  R F T D E I U R U E R R E I L A T T B B
  H E O N G S T I F R T O H L A L D W T F
  U T G E A T U O S I A U X U R E E O C P
  O T E C L I R R S E N N D I E X C L E N
  T R T S P U E I E N T D E I M T A L L L
  F I H E O R P T C C R F K H E I E O F C
  O U E D A C L Y C E U L A D D N T H E C
    I R R C E A C U L M E N A R C O Y R
    U N D H R N T S H E A E E A T R T H
      F O I W S R H I S F R E L I L O
        W N E C O L D A D A G E O O
          G N I N N I G E B W E N
            U N T R Y M E N
```

AND _ _ _.	NEW _ _ _ _ _ _ _ _
BABY _ _ _ _	NEW _ _ _ _ _ _ _
BARE _ _ _ _ _	OLD _ _ _ _ _
CLOSE _ _ _ _ _ _ _ _ _	OLD _ _ _ _ _ _
DESCEND _ _ _ _	PAST _ _ _ _ _ _ _ _ _
FIRST _ _ _ _ _ _ _	REFLECT _ _ _ _
FREE _ _ _ _	SUCCESSFUL _ _ _ _ _ _
FUTURE _ _ _ _ _	SWIVEL _ _ _ _ _ _
HOLLOW _ _ _ _	TEMPER _ _ _ _ _ _ _
ILLEGAL _ _ _ _ _ _ _ _	TOTAL _ _ _ _ _ _ _ _ _
JOIN _ _ _ _ _ _ _ _	VIOLENT _ _ _ _ _ _ _ _

ANSWER, PAGE 241

YE GODS!

It's been a lot of work, but we've finally finished our pantheon to the ancient gods and goddesses listed below. Blessings upon you if you can fit all 51 of them into their proper places in the grid, crossword-style.

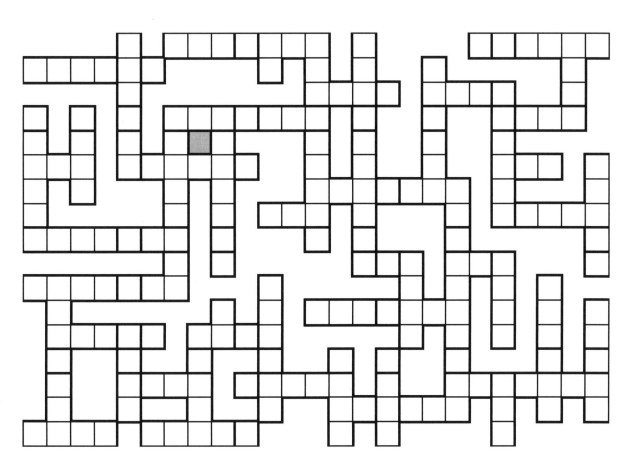

2-letter words
Ku
Ra

3-letter words
Eos
Hel
Nut
Pan
Sol
Ull

4-letter words
Ares
Eros
Gaia

Hera
Isis
Juno
Kane
Lofn
Loki
Odin
Pele
Seti
Thor

5-letter words
Ceres
Hades
Janus
Njord

Pluto
Thoth
Vesta

6-letter words
Anubis
Apollo
Athena
Baldur
Frigga
Ostara
Saturn
Selene
Snotra
Uranus

7-letter words
Artemis
Astrila
Bacchus
Demeter
Imhotep
Jupiter
Mercury
Minerva
Neptune

8-letter word
Dionysus

9-letter word
Aphrodite

10-letter words
Persephone
Proserpina

ANSWER, PAGE 242

GARDEN OF EATIN'

Dedicated to food fetishists everywhere—those among us
who know that food is more that just something to eat.

ACROSS

1 Family men?
6 Repeated jazz theme
10 Not exact
17 On one's toes
18 Signs up
22 More effusive
23 Foodie who invests her calories in frozen assets?
25 All together
26 Egyptologist's interest
27 Sent out of the country
29 Cheep joint?
30 KLM competitor
31 Derek and Jackson
32 "___ that you can…"
33 "For shame!"
35 Average on the course
36 Three, in Pisa
38 Hayes of *Will & Grace*
40 Slight push
44 Ms. Lewinsky
47 Lean and sinewy
49 Sharon Stone played one in an Albert Brooks film
51 Hot stuff from a politico?
52 Extreme edge
53 Foodie who practically lives in Chinatown?
57 *Laugh-In* comedian Johnson
58 Ending of some store names
59 Cavaliers' sch.
60 First try, to a film director
61 Phoenix-to-Tucson dir.
62 Chinese, in combos
63 6 Down's co-host
65 Construction worker's supply
66 Foodie whose preference is perfectly clear?
70 Slow down

73 Manner
74 Julie's *Doctor Zhivago* co-star
75 Rapping Dr.
78 A look that may inflict harm
80 Lucy of *Ally McBeal*
81 Confident reply
82 Carrot, to Frosty
83 Foodie who's always on the hunt for his favorite meal?
86 Intense
87 A bit of work
88 *The Godfather* author Mario
89 Catch of the day, perhaps
90 Really pester
91 Misinform
93 Shoppe sign word
96 Year, in Madrid
97 "___ tree falls in the forest…"
98 Deli scale stats
100 Hitting the roof
102 '70s radical grp.
103 Form 1040 issuer
106 Purple shade
109 Drove by
111 Region of northeast Spain
114 Footwear fixer
116 Foodie who's sweet on sweets?
118 Nourish
119 Athlete's no-no
120 It runs through Carnegie Hall
121 Prickly weed
122 Jillian and Landers
123 Take the wheel

DOWN

1 Throws (off)
2 Hawaiian greeting
3 Shimon ___ (former Israeli prime minister)

4 Planets
5 "Give me some room, will you?"
6 First name in morning TV
7 Party to
8 Continuous change
9 Christmas tree, often
10 1958 Pulitzer winner James
11 Cake sale cake
12 Doctrine
13 Alanis Morissette song
14 Chantilly's river
15 *Daniel Boone* star Parker
16 Guitar feature
19 *Peter Pan* pirate
20 Lone Star State
21 Subway gate
24 Actress Birch of *American Beauty*
28 Camel's kin
32 *Wozzeck* composer
34 More underhanded
35 Evergreen tree
36 Like some brownstone apartments
37 Knee-slapper
39 Night, in Normandy
41 *The Aviator* actor Willem
42 Big guy
43 Gray sea eagles
44 CFOs' degrees
45 Benjamin and Bobby
46 Prime time, informally
48 "That's crazy!"
50 Austere
53 A dog is ___ best friend
54 Poet of ancient Rome
55 Amazed look
56 *Scream* actress Campbell
58 "Let me add…"

62 Achilles heel
64 Guacamole ingredient
66 Colombian metropolis
67 ___ *18* (Leon Uris novel)
68 Golda ___ (former Israeli prime minister)
69 Land on the Arabian Sea
70 Merrymaking
71 "If ___ should leave you…"
72 Touch of color
75 McClure of *The Virginian*
76 Alphabetical quartet
77 Extra-large shoe width

79 Auto mogul Ferrari
81 "No man ___ island"
82 March Madness org.
84 Voting venues
85 "If ___ my druthers…"
86 They can make hay?
90 Seasoned rice dish
92 Sounds from a bird bath
94 Computer inserts
95 Tennis legend Chris
99 Go bad
101 Paris brainstorm
102 Virile guys

103 Occupied
104 Army weapon
105 Less dangerous
106 "Do you want to hear a secret?"
107 "Forget it!"
108 ___ *fan tutte* (Mozart opera)
110 Best-rated
111 "Let's go!"
112 Neat as ___
113 Life story?
115 Gangster's gun
117 Coach Parseghian

ANSWER, PAGE 243

NICE HOUSE...NOBODY HOME

We've taken 20 of our favorite ways to say someone's stupid, and left out two key words or phrases in each. Then we've hidden those items in the duck-shaped grid below. For example, in the first saying, "A few F _ _ _ _ _ _ _ short of a whole D _ _ _," the fill-ins are FEATHERS and DUCK. Notice that we've given you the first letters of each. After you've found all 40 words and phrases in the grid, the leftover letters will reveal two more ways of saying someone's stupid. The complete list is on the answer page.

```
              G  R  U  N  T
              B  R  S  L  I  O  P
           R  M  A  T  T  E  L  P  E
        A  R  T  I  F  I  C  I  A  L
     I  D     I  N  N  S  T  S  O  O
  N  T        H  E  E  T  O  G  E
              M  P  U  A
              S  I  N  N
              E  S  R  T
           P  S  L  O  O  E  L  R
        O  N  E  L  P  W  N  P  E  E
        S  W  N  H  F  E  W  N  N  X  A  H
     L  O  N  E  L  Y  O  T  A  H  S  E  G  S
  E  L  A  L  O  I  F  B  E  L  T  R  E  G  U  I
  C  H  U  O  A  I  R  J  D  S  R  E  H  T  A  E  F
  C  W  R  E  M  O  T  E  C  O  N  T  R  O  L  A  W  K
  R  I  A  H  C  I  R  C  U  S  S  S  N  E  O  H  P  C  T
  W  E  A  S  N  O  T  T  U  B  B  M  V  E  E  K  O  U  T  C  H
     I  C  A  B  N  G  S  R  R  A  A  R  E  B  M  U  D
     N  E  A  D  A  I  A  A  T  H  L  R  S  S  C
        L  I  H  A  N  R  O  M  S  P  T  A  S  H
        T  V  C  M  R  A  M  S  N  D  A  R
        H  E  I  H  A  S  A  N  I  Q
        R                 P
        R                 U
        O                 T
  B  L  E  R        D  O  G  S
```

1. A few F _ _ _ _ _ _ _ short of a whole D _ _ _.
2. His B _ _ _ doesn't go through all the L _ _ _ _ _.
3. Missing a few B _ _ _ _ _ _ on her R _ _ _ _ _ _ _ _ _ _ _.
4. His E _ _ _ _ _ _ _ doesn't go all the way to the T _ _ _ _ _ _.
5. Couldn't pour W _ _ _ _ out of a boot with I _ _ _ _ _ _ _ _ _ _ on the heel.
6. The W _ _ _ _'_ spinning, but the H _ _ _ _ _ _'_ dead.
7. If he had another B _ _ _ _, it would be L _ _ _ _ _.
8. Warning: O _ _ _ _ _ _ _ _ _ _ _ _ _ _ are D _ _ _ _ _ than they appear.
9. Her A _ _ _ _ _ _ doesn't pick up all the C _ _ _ _ _ _ _.
10. H _ _ _ _ _ _ of 2, but it takes 3 to G _ _ _ _.
11. Body by F _ _ _ _ _, brains by M _ _ _ _ _.
12. His R _ _ _ _ _ _ _ is off the H _ _ _.
13. He fell out of the S _ _ _ _ _ _ _ _ _ and hit every B _ _ _ _ _ on the way down.
14. A few C _ _ _ _ _ short of a C _ _ _ _ _.
15. Doesn't have all his D _ _ _ on one L _ _ _ _.
16. No G _ _ _ _ in the S _ _ _.
17. Several N _ _ _ short of a full P _ _ _ _.
18. Doesn't know much but leads the L _ _ _ _ _ _ in nostril H _ _ _.
19. An E _ _ _ _ _ _ _ _ _ in A _ _ _ _ _ _ _ _ _ Stupidity.
20. As S _ _ _ _ as B _ _ _.

ANSWER, PAGE 245

HERE'S JOHNNY!

The late, great Johnny Carson gave us countless hours of late-night entertainment, including the three pure-Carson jokes below. Choose a letter from each column and drop it into its proper place in the grid.

1.

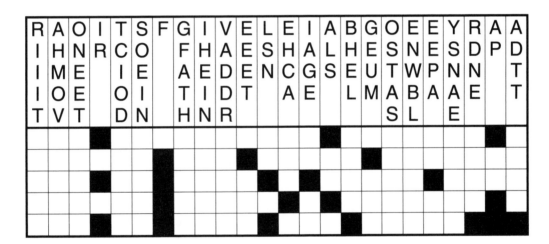

2.

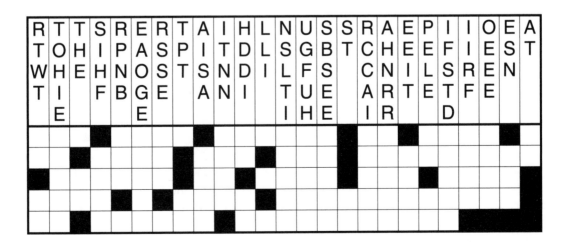

3.

ANSWER, PAGE 241

"THE WHO?"

According to legend, a rock band called The High Numbers was looking for a new name. Every time someone came up with an idea, they jokingly asked, "The who?" Finally a friend suggested they just call themselves "The Who." Here are a few more stories…

ACROSS

1 Knocks to the canvas
6 Bear Bryant's school, for short
10 Actress/author Fannie
15 Lejeune or Pendleton
19 Jerk
20 Former Ugandan dictator
21 Stretchy stuff
22 Brown-and-white snack
23 Band that got its name from a Ouija board when they asked it what they'd be having for dinner
25 Where an acolyte serves
26 School grps.
27 Sadness
28 Band named for something Ralph Kramden said on *The Honeymooners*
31 Line of work
34 Comedian Philips
35 Overseer of parishes
36 *The Ice Storm* director Lee
39 Boss Tweed caricaturist
41 Forever ___ day
44 Mimic
45 Band that got its name from World War II pilot slang for UFOs
49 Mentalist Geller
51 Pluck
55 Topic for Hoyle
56 Composer Schifrin
57 Lively Highland dance
59 Scottish isle
60 Burning
62 Band whose name is an anagram of "Cully Stout Beer"
65 Bust agent
67 Seaweed product
68 Archbishop Desmond of South Africa

69 Bigfoot's shoe width?
70 Flatter
74 Charlemagne's kingdom, briefly
75 Ribbons worn on sleeves
77 Verse start?
78 Angelina's *Tomb Raider* role
79 Actress Swenson
81 Arrests
82 Band named after the slang term for the capillaries in your face that burst because of excessive drinking
86 Put the nacho to the salsa
90 Yugoslavian unifier
91 ___ *of a Salesman*
92 Pianist Gilels
94 Feature of a Weight Watchers salon
95 Ghost
97 Jane Tennison's rank on *Prime Suspect*
98 Band that named itself after a friend's cat, the Latin for "beyond all things"
100 One of a timely doz.
102 Hockey great Phil, familiarly
104 Actress Campbell
105 "Hold On Tight" grp.
106 Ice Capades stars
110 Likely
112 Allocates (with "out")
115 Band whose name is a cross between a movie star and the head of a murderous gang
119 What cheerleaders try to be in?
123 City on Utah Lake
124 "Get to the ___ already!"
125 Band named for the favorite song of its guitarist's grandmother
128 *Taxi* co-star Carol
129 ___ *With Love* (Poitier film)
130 The U.S.

131 Cracks a book
132 Letters from Athens?
133 Cold-hearted
134 Oxen neckwear
135 ___ Park, Colorado

DOWN

1 Mil. decorations
2 Alpine retort?
3 "Dark Lady" singer
4 S.S. Kresge, today
5 State of deep sleep
6 Cheers is one
7 Henri's pal
8 Flaky mineral
9 Bracelet locale, sometimes
10 Perfume bottle
11 Singer Lovett
12 Broadway opening?
13 Piano size
14 Grateful Dead head
15 Fine, in old slang
16 Chef Bucco on *The Sopranos*
17 Stands for
18 Wild West chasers
24 Nashville sound?
29 " ___ corny as..."
30 Beer ingredient
32 *James and the Giant Peach* author
33 Founding-date abbr.
36 Bushy top
37 Sentence subject, usually
38 Tiger's game
40 "I cannot ___ lie"
42 In an authorized manner
43 Whitney Houston's record company
46 Fencing ploy
47 Mideast native
48 Rather bumpy
50 One after another

52 French cathedral city
53 Leaderless
54 Aussie buddies
57 One who precedes another
58 Hit the roof
61 Go-fer's job
63 Is deserving of
64 Poppycock
66 Reined in
70 Smoking section leavings
71 Not with it
72 Connect with
73 Fairy tale setting
76 Critters' rights org.

80 Deity of ancient Egypt
83 CBS sitcom of the '70s
84 Man of Mayberry
85 "Attack, Rover!"
87 Prepare an apple
88 Month in the Jewish calendar
89 Sample from the band
93 Tennis score term
96 Fall (over)
98 Boston ___ Orchestra
99 Abate
101 Mummy sites
103 Kitchen storage
106 Cure, as meat

107 Jeweler's measure
108 Sphere of action
109 Schnozzola
111 Early TV fare
113 Get used (to)
114 Horse farm papas
116 Japanese soup
117 Have ___ (know someone)
118 *Nautilus* skipper
120 Disagreement
121 Ye ___ Shoppe
122 Capone nemesis
126 " ___! A mouse!"
127 Before (prefix)

ANSWER, PAGE 243

SQUIFFY AND SWACKED

No, that's not the name of a new comic strip—it's a pair of words that both mean "drunk." Below are 37 other words and phrases that mean the same thing. Can you—*hic!*—fit them all into the grid before the room starts swimming?

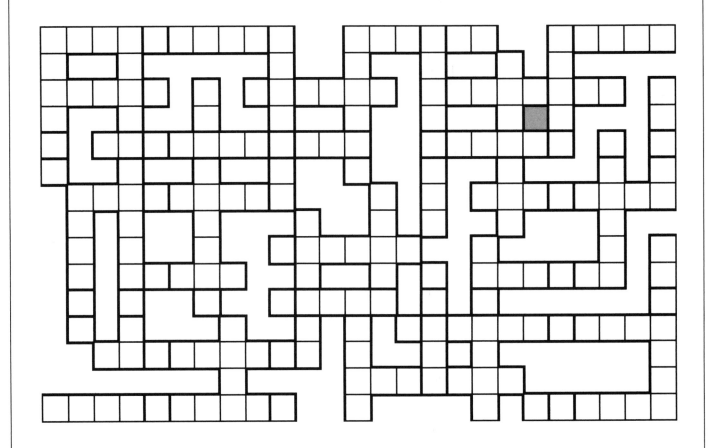

4-letter word
Bent

5-letter words
Beery
Blind
Boxed
Fried
Fuzzy
Oiled
Piped
Stiff
Tipsy

6-letter words
Buried
Busted
Hooted
Juiced
Potted
Primed
Rum-dum
Slewed
Soused
Tanked
Zonked

7-letter words
Drunken
Fuddled
Pickled
Raddled
Spiffed

8-letter words
Besotted
Ossified
Whoozled

9-letter words
Jug-bitten
Plastered
Snockered

10-letter words
Half-shaved
Lubricated

11-letter words
High as a kite
Pifflicated

13-letter word
Feeling no pain

ANSWER, PAGE 244

WOULD WE LIE ONE MORE TIME?

Oh, yeah. In this quiz, we explain some odd phenomena that may have long puzzled you. The only trouble is, once again, we're offering too many explanations. Can you find the one true answer in each set?

1. Why does paper defeat rock, according to the World Rock Paper Scissors Society?
   a. The idea is that a rock loses its crushing power if it's wrapped in a lot of paper. The Society helpfully suggests envisioning "a baseball-sized rock wrapped in a volleyball-sized wad of paper."
   b. The explanation comes from ancient China. When petitions were given to the emperor for approval, he could either signal acceptance by placing the document under a rock, or signal denial by draping it over a rock. Paper covering rock came to be associated with defeat.
   c. Actually, even the society has no official explanation of why paper defeats rock. Their standard response: "It's just the way the game is played."

2. Why does orange juice taste so bad after you brush your teeth?
   a. Most toothpastes are flavored with mint, which combines very badly with the taste of orange. (I mean, really: how many "orange & mint" candies have you seen?)
   b. Most toothpastes contain a detergent which temporarily modifies your taste system. Specifically, it reduces your ability to taste sweetness and saltiness, and makes sour foods—like orange juice, for instance—intensely bitter.
   c. Actually, if you drank fresh-squeezed orange juice shortly after brushing your teeth, it wouldn't taste unusual (apart from the fact that you'd be mixing it with mint flavor). It's the preservatives in commercially sold orange juice that combine with the standard chemicals in toothpaste to produce the yucky taste.

3. Where did Mussolini get that raised-hand salute of his?
   a. He picked it up from his father, who worked as a blacksmith and frequently ordered young Benito around while holding a hammer in his upraised hand.
   b. Mussolini adopted the salute after seeing the German army goose-stepping in formation, a sight that greatly impressed him. The new salute deliberately mimicked the goose-stepping motion of a leg.
   c. Actually, the unusual salute was adopted to avoid shaking hands as much as possible. Mussolini had a deep-seated handshaking phobia.

4. Where did the custom of garnishing a meal with a sprig of parsley come from?
   a. Parsley is a natural breath freshener. The ancient Greeks served it with meals to mask garlic breath.
   b. Parsley is a natural purgative. Elizabethans served it with meals to avoid constipation.
   c. A sprig of parsley was typically used in ancient Rome to tickle the back of one's throat and induce vomiting, thus allowing gluttonous diners to eat still more. (Very wealthy Romans used ostrich feathers for this purpose, but parsley was a much cheaper alternative.)

5. America's area codes seem randomly assigned. What's the logic behind them?
   a. They were assigned sequentially to phone districts as soon as the borders of those districts were decided—but since these decisions were often held up by dealmaking and bickering, the resulting assignments look pretty random.
   b. The codes were based on the size of the city. Bigger cities got codes with lower digits because those numbers could be dialed (remember dialing?) faster on dial telephones, saving the phone company money. (That's why the Big Apple got 212.)
   c. The only criterion when assigning area codes was to make neighboring area codes as different as possible, in order to avoid wrong numbers. Apart from that, they really are random.

ANSWER, PAGE 242

CLOWN ALLEY

We know you've been planning to run off and join the circus—it's a good thing we got here in time. This puzzle is filled with circus slang that you'd better commit to memory before you go, otherwise they'll think you're a 123 Across.

ACROSS

1 Squash or pumpkin
6 "No ___ traffic"
10 Shoe seller Thom ___
14 Doesn't ignore
19 Cop ___
20 Park the yacht
21 Tops
22 Large combo
23 Circus master of ceremonies
25 Circus concessionaire who sells toys and souvenirs
27 Steppe, say
28 The "U" in I.C.U.
30 White of the eye
31 Salad topping
32 Charles who was a 97-lb. weakling
34 1996 title role played by Gwyneth Paltrow
36 Embarrassed
37 Really went for, man
40 Hair goop
42 Circus workers who set up the big tents
45 Head of Harpo Productions, Inc.
47 Plastic ___ Band
49 Occupied
50 Jostle
54 Circus laborers
57 Worth a blue ribbon
59 Woody's boy
60 Oft-replaced joint
61 Transform
62 Final Commandment
63 Plaintiff in court
64 Low bow
66 "You Won't ___" (1970s hit song)
68 "You said it!"

70 Last show of the circus season
74 Like a country road
78 1970s hot spot
79 "Scram!"
84 Actress Miles
85 Linda Ronstadt's "___ Easy"
88 Register
90 Solitary
91 Devil's work
92 Just ___, skip, and jump
93 Circus food stand
95 Summary
97 ___ year (annually)
99 Radio settings
100 Swiss mathematician
101 Circus musician
104 Frequently, to poets
106 Mrs., abroad
107 Hosp. hookups
110 Popular card
111 Myanmar's former name
113 Home of the Braves (abbr.)
115 Idea
117 Art Deco designer
118 It borders Djibouti
123 Circus rookie
126 Circus aerial act performed on a loop of rope suspended from the top of the tent
128 Florida city
129 Approximately
130 The Volunteer St.
131 Kukla's pal
132 Turn away
133 Horrible (with "the")
134 Former Wrigley Field slugger
135 Turndowns from Putin

DOWN

1 Fishing hook
2 Iridescent gem

3 Radius neighbor
4 Right-hand page
5 Opening, for a fullback
6 Govt. agent
7 Accord maker
8 Go bad
9 Sci-fi writer Le Guin
10 Memorable Dolley
11 Harold portrayer Bud, in *Harold and Maude*
12 Some
13 Lincoln loc.
14 Denny's selection
15 "To everything there is a season" source (abbr.)
16 It can put you out
17 Big name in farm equipment
18 Valuable strings
24 Wan
26 Mil. branch
29 Allies' foe
33 Companies
34 *Barnaby Jones* star
35 Eminent conductor, generically
37 Nerds
38 "When you wish ___ star..."
39 Thin porridge
41 Timber wolf
43 Gullible one
44 Cut drastically
46 Sailing
48 From Oslo
51 Champagne option
52 Stick on the table?
53 Showing signs of age
55 Cleaning compound
56 Group in *Tommy*
58 Darner's finger guard
62 High school kid
65 Cry of surprise
67 ___ *culpa*

69 "Whaddya know!"
71 Ways to work
72 Turntable component
73 Walker of whiskey fame
74 Radio transmission word
75 Actress Campbell
76 Idle of the Pythons
77 Steven Bochco show
80 Noted baseball family name
81 Works
82 Personal
83 Aquarium fish
86 Skating star Henie

87 Animal rights grp.
89 ___ buco
93 Full range
94 Toss overboard
96 Key
98 Organisms at an early stage
102 El ___
103 Puts up
105 Saudi leader
107 About to experience
108 A Juilliard study
109 Bra band
112 Very long times

114 Not at all noble
116 Capri, for one
117 Bridge seat
119 Bumble Bee product
120 Carpet quality
121 Monogram pt.
122 "Rock of ___"
124 Dandy
125 CAT scan relative
127 Zodiac "zoo" member

ANSWER, PAGE 243

MY OTHER CAR IS...

The first bumper stickers were business advertisements. And when you think about it, we're carrying on the tradition by advertising our political preferences, our hopes for a better world, and the basic human need to insult people from a safe distance.

Here's an opportunity to read 36 bumper stickers without having to inch up too close to that crazy-looking guy in the pickup truck. Of course, we couldn't make it that easy on you; you'll have to complete each bumper sticker saying (1-36) by filling in the blanks with one of the words or phrases (a-jj) on the opposite page.

1. Why Are You ___ At My Bumper, You Pervert!
2. I'm ___: I Can Talk And Annoy You At The Same Time
3. You Are Depriving Some Poor ___ Of Its Idiot
4. I May Be Slow But I'm ___ Of You
5. Do ___ Have 18 Half-Lives?
6. A Bartender Is Just A ___ With A Limited Inventory
7. Everyone Has A Photographic Memory, Some Just Don't Have ___
8. I'll Bet You A New Car I Can ___ Than You Can!
9. If I Throw A Stick, Will You ___?
10. Jesus Is Coming: Everybody Look ___
11. ___ and Drive!
12. Keep Honking: I'm ___
13. Do Molecular Biologists Wear ___?
14. Try Not To Let Your Mind Wander—It's Too Small To Be ___
15. ___, No Donut
16. I Love Defenseless Animals—Especially In A ___
17. Boycott Shampoo! Demand ___!
18. My ___ Keeps Complaining That I Never Listen To Her...Or Something Like That
19. Don't Piss Me Off! I'm Running Out Of Places To Hide The ___
20. Everyone Has The Right To Be Stupid; Some Just ___
21. I Drive Way Too Fast To Worry About ___
22. Politicians and ___ Need To Be Changed...Often For The Same Reason
23. Warning: I Have An ___ And I Know How To Use It
24. Gravity: It's Not Just A Good Idea, It's ___
25. Whose Cruel Idea Was It For The Word ___ To Have An S In It?
26. If You Don't Like The Way I Drive, ___ The Sidewalk
27. Meandering To A Different ___
28. Where Am I Going, And Why Am I In This ___?
29. Therapy Is Expensive; Popping Bubble Wrap Is ___! You Choose.
30. Vegetarian: Indian Word For ___
31. I'm Not A Complete Idiot—Some ___ Are Missing
32. Friction Can Be A ___
33. Consciousness: That Annoying Time Between ___
34. Don't Make Me ___ You
35. Rehab Is For ___
36. As Long As There Are Tests, There Will Be Prayer In ___

ANSWER, PAGE 244

...A WORD SEARCH PUZZLE

Now see if you can find all 36 words and phrases in the word list hidden in the car-shaped grid. When you're done, the leftover letters will reveal two more complete bumper sticker sayings.

```
              G O O D G R A V Y B
              H O T F G E R N V O P B
          B M Q R L H O A S K D I R U R
        A B U S E T H E P R I V I L E G E
        A I L S E N W A L E D G A T L T N L
      C D T F T L Y T E K S A B D N A H A S A O
    H C T F I I O I H R F I N W G E E R I G A H A M O
  N O E L Y S T L C K C H O L E S T E R O L E F Y D D R
I P R V B P H A R M A C I S T A Y O F F G S R E P A I D I
N S G T P U B L I C S C H O O L S L I I R E A L P O O N K E
T D R U M M E R E D U T I T T A H I D W S T G N I R A T S G O
L O U S Y H U N T E R P I R A D I O A C T I V E C A T S S
        P A R T S S                 E V A E L S
        A Y E O                     H U O F
        N D                         A F
```

a.	ABUSE THE PRIVILEGE	m.	FILM	y.	PHARMACIST
b.	AHEAD	n.	GOOD GRAVY	z.	PUBLIC SCHOOLS
c.	ATTITUDE	o.	HANDBASKET	aa.	QUITTERS
d.	BAD COP	p.	HANG UP	bb.	RADIOACTIVE CATS
e.	BODIES	q.	KILL	cc.	REAL POO
f.	BUSY	r.	LEAVE	dd.	RELOADING
g.	CHEAP	s.	LISP	ee.	STARING
h.	CHOLESTEROL	t.	LOUSY HUNTER	ff.	STAY OFF
i.	DESIGNER GENES	u.	MULTI-TALENTED	gg.	STOP FASTER
j.	DIAPERS	v.	NAPS	hh.	THE LAW
k.	DRAG	w.	OUT BY ITSELF	ii.	VILLAGE
l.	DRUMMER	x.	PARTS	jj.	WIFE

REALITY TV WATCHING

Congratulations! Because of your dedication to reality TV, you've been selected to be a contestant on *Surviving the Amazing Reality TV Show*. Let's see how well you can do on these five challenges.

ACROSS

1 Queen ___ lace
6 Eyed Idaho item
10 Did really well, as on a test
14 Prison fence-top snaggers
19 Like an unshaven face
20 Carryall
21 Domesticated
22 "___ you" (confrontational phrase)
23 South of the border friend
24 Times to remember
25 Lake fed by a pair of falls
26 Frank Lloyd Wright's ___ House
27 CHALLENGE #1
31 Caste member
32 Kitchen suffix
33 Stockholm residents
34 Oscar, Tony, Emmy, and Grammy winner Rita
37 Gear used often in a driveway
40 Tablelands
42 Autobahn make
43 Emit
46 Long.'s perpendicular counterpart
47 State lic. plate bureau
50 CHALLENGE #2
55 Double curve
56 Vegetarian's dietary restriction
57 Bordeaux maker
58 Hearty shade plant
59 Agree
60 Large workhorse's weight
62 Word after mai and before chi
65 Traditional garb in India
66 CHALLENGE #3
73 Introductory med. course
74 Voice vote
75 Personal history, for short
76 Longtime Yugoslavian leader
77 Fragrant compound
79 Size on a 97 Down tag (abbr.)
82 The capybara is the largest one
84 Tanning lotion letters
87 CHALLENGE #4
92 Direct or invent add-on
93 Wrestling victory
94 From far away
95 Common noun ending
96 Neck tie
98 Part of B.A.
99 Nickelodeon inspector
101 Attack with a vicious review
104 Police unit of last resort
107 Phrase on some Chinese menus
109 CHALLENGE #5
116 Follow
117 Yesterday, to Yves
118 Promgoer's rental
119 Scarlett of fiction
120 Discharge
121 Art Deco designer
122 Away from the wind
123 Fancy Beverly Hills drive
124 Chats
125 Ultimate degrees
126 Eliot of *The Untouchables*
127 "Criminy!"

DOWN

1 Limp as ___
2 City in Alaska
3 Night in Normandy
4 First thing a newborn chick pecks at
5 Sure thing
6 War-horse
7 Critter with spines on its spine
8 Northwestern state in the Four Corners
9 Lucy's husband
10 Bomb trial, briefly
11 Jewel's weight, perhaps
12 A.k.a. Marshall Mathers
13 Monopoly card
14 Check out the grackles, grouses, and grebes
15 Thinks the world of
16 Foaming at the mouth
17 It's the salt in saltwater
18 Doesn't hide, in a kid's game
28 Three after L
29 Type of tea
30 Determine the value of, as gold
34 Sport a long face
35 Number, in music
36 Fam. reunion invitees
38 Pilot a plane
39 Manse resident
41 Northerner with curly-toed shoes?
43 Sexual cell
44 AM/FM regulator
45 Dedication starter
47 African warrior
48 In ___ (kind of fertilization)
49 Bathtub exit
51 Watt or pound, e.g.
52 Cajun sandwich
53 Best-in-show wannabe
54 Must
59 New York Yankees' #2
61 Penpoint
63 Ship propeller's location

64 "I'd do ___ heartbeat"
66 Karate-like aerobics system
67 Racing's Bobby, Al, or Al Jr.
68 Dressed to the nines
69 What 50 U.S. senators represent
70 Construction beam
71 Hit the road, on foot
72 Important memo header
78 Perps' records
80 Electronic picture format
81 Skeleton prefix
83 Fifi, Rex, and Benji

84 Part of a hit parade
85 Color that even sounds ugly
86 Worry
88 Not nearly so nasty
89 Tin oxide
90 Muse of poetry
91 Sonic of video game fame, for example
96 When the sun is setting
97 See 79 Across
99 Truck co.
100 Back on land
101 Like Frosted Flakes

102 Type of line at many weddings
103 Nature photographer Adams
105 *Christina's World* artist Andrew
106 Actor Lew
108 Western Indians
110 At what date
111 Bator or Ule preceder
112 ___ E. Coyote
113 Arp art
114 Mad
115 New Mexico city

ANSWER, PAGE 243

NOT THE WORLD'S HARDEST CROSSWORD PUZZLE

This crossword is distinctive in a couple of ways. For one thing, look at all that white space in the middle. We're sure it's some kind of Puzzleville record. For another thing, the puzzle was constructed by Frank Longo, who wrote "The World's Hardest Crossword Puzzle" for our contest in 2004. You'll probably find this one a lot easier—but maybe not *all* that easy.

ACROSS

1 Flea market eateries
11 It has a spin-off set in Miami
14 Capital of Tanzania
20 Film featuring Sally Bowles
21 Did a Columbus
23 Monkeyshine?
24 Dirtbag
25 Fork you don't eat with
26 Loaded
28 Stray from the straight path
29 Title girl in a Left Banke hit
30 Go aboard
32 "Read Across America" org.
33 Cubist Fernand
34 Fail to notice
37 Lair
38 Short date?
40 Swerve
42 Old anesthetic
44 Place pinpointer
46 Blue moon
47 Ran up
51 Chunk of change
53 "...oh, oh, oh what ___!"
55 *Wait Wait...Don't Tell Me!* airer
56 "Way" to Lao-Tzu
57 Club sandwich's shorter cousin
58 Joe the Bartender's portrayer
63 Lact- or malt- suffix
64 Biblical land
66 Good choice for a sugar-and-caffeine double-whammy
67 Some colonists
68 Cooperstown's Sandberg
69 Frankest

70 "Move it!"
71 Fictional circumnavigator
72 Where your vestibule is
73 Look for gold dust
74 Rap's OutKast, e.g.
75 Scoops
77 London's ___ Gardens
78 "Rhythm ___ Dancer" (1993 pop hit)
79 Electronic drug in William Shatner novels
80 Character actor Roscoe
81 Hoedown move
83 Very big things
85 Old English letter
86 Charged swimmer
89 One getting off the fence
90 Pt. of NASCAR
91 It's on the Rhone
93 It may be hair-raising
95 Snow in the country field
96 Raccoon in *Pocahontas*
99 Parrot ___ (Turks and Caicos resort)
101 Heaven on earth
104 *Ben-Hur: ___ of the Christ*
105 Singer Stewart and others
106 Big name in Swiss watches
107 Must
111 Many an Internet game
114 He played Proximo in *Gladiator*
116 Matter and energy can flow out of one
117 Getting one's teeth around
118 M&Ms scare of 1976 to 1985
119 Moe Berg's org.
120 Fairy tale meanie

DOWN

1 Sock deliverer
2 Royal Hawaiian island
3 Dark sky, say
4 1977 NBA All-Star
5 Negligible
6 Gave zest
7 Québecois comrade
8 Cocktail of sweet vermouth, gin, and bitters
9 Creator of an eddy
10 Private places
11 Bank investments, briefly
12 What "hymn" and "damn" have in common
13 Val d'___
14 Amt. in a Krispy Kreme box
15 Study to a fault
16 Big name in diamond mining
17 It's rare for an adult one to ever touch the ground
18 Big scuffle
19 *How to Read a Difficult Book* author Mortimer J.
22 Desert inn
27 Wish, in a kind of desperate way
31 Candy brand
34 Statement on a bank sign
35 Gloating declaration
36 It's often blocked
39 Work like a bee
41 Licensed
43 New Delhi's ___ Path
45 Put oils to canvas
48 Two-time Lady Byng Trophy winner

49 Literary classic set in Salinas Valley
50 Is retired
52 Bad acting
54 Prepares oneself
59 Old West hats for hunters
60 Finnish president Juho ___ Paasikivi
61 Surround
62 Doe chaser?
65 PC unit
67 Elec. coolers
75 Linda Ronstadt hit
76 He played Fong in *Flower Drum Song*
82 *Wayne's World* director Penelope
84 Jerry Brown is its mayor
85 Champs ___
87 Part of the French Revolution motto
88 Went first
92 "Nattering" big shots
94 Some are in the closet
96 Foremost
97 ___ du Tour (cycling event)
98 Overhung, as a roof
100 ___ the good
102 Turned on again
103 Bruguera of tennis
108 Dimple, really
109 *Crâne* container
110 Nitrogen doesn't have one
112 Newbery winner *Ginger* ___
113 Abbrs. that follow Scrabble
115 Somebody special

ANSWER, PAGE 245

ANYTHING GOES

Before you pick up that pencil, there's something you should know. Most (but not all) of the answer phrases in this puzzle are nonsensical—in fact, downright illegal. For example, the clue "Special at the Red Planet diner" might turn out to be MARTIAN MENU ITEM. Or the clue "Lawrence of Arabia star felt rushed" might be O'TOOLE HURRIED. See what we mean? So take the clues very literally, keep that eraser handy, and enjoy!

ACROSS

1 Film fawn's refuse
11 Heavy alloy
16 Female fliers of W.W. II
20 A coward cries
22 "What's ___ for me?"
23 Dramas set among Bunsen burners
24 World's longest river
25 Person who's been bamboozled
26 Tree that shades the whole neighborhood
27 ___ fatale
28 "Do we breathe the same ___ does?"
29 Tug-of-war, for one
31 Two-way highway exit
32 "If you find the ___ great, why buy a GTO?"
33 Palatine pickle
34 Last morning (abbr.)
35 Tampa NFLer, for short
36 Wall art over a four-poster
37 At 70, you might keep working, ___ instead
38 Cheer for Sampras
40 Little horse opera star
42 Against Fontanne's hubby
44 Ameche and Braga, together
45 Auto-racing org. label
47 Language-peculiarity snafus
48 Where you'll see old-timers rocking on screen someday?
50 He spins "Haldeman Rag" and "Liddy Lullaby"
54 Sign that a soft metal is chilly

59 Melted marmalade/muenster mix
61 Wherein you may find an ASPCA pimiento
62 Movie about a dog star's marriage
64 2 Live Crew to-do
65 Anti-Skelton Act result
66 Downed a bundt
68 ___ de France
69 Set dried fruit on fire
70 It hides Physician's Potbelly
71 ___, WV, DE (states that border MD)
72 Hen product expected
73 Freebies at Dad's Diner
74 Doled out
75 Patellas' places
76 Zeus hated to see ___ from the flu
77 The second vowels in "steal" and "roam"
78 Actress Skye
79 Dull sampler
82 Used a trucker's radio
83 Where Munchkins go to dance
84 Hershey product
85 En ___ (as a group)
86 The alien needs a drink

DOWN

1 Cereal made from an evergreen tree
2 How Tennessee Williams dressed for the Lizards' Ball
3 Soup orders under the Moscow arches

4 Exclude Costello's first baseman
5 make cummings mad
6 Not "dose"
7 Middle of order
8 Topless Spanish painter
9 Obtain with difficulty
10 Moses' staff, e.g.
11 *Memoirs of a Central Hollywood Square* ___
12 Goof off again
13 Just like Pacino does it
14 The 11th secret agent
15 Draft card issuer: Abbr.
16 Two Chiantis for you :: one Bordeaux for me, etc.
17 Muskrat Manor and the Hippo Hotel
18 Shoot Gale Storm character
19 Hard-to-climb flattops
21 Punny Steinway review
27 "What do you think your partner will do to win this trick?" "___"
29 Spitting on mousetraps, pulling cats' tails, etc.
30 Extended mantra sound
31 Delivery-room slip-up
33 Campaign-button slogan of 2004
34 Zeta Beta Bauxite and Rho Gamma Galena
36 Mental giant in an exclusive L.A. suburb
37 Big shot from Dayton
39 Photo
41 "There's many a slip ___..."
43 Sea-dog tattled

46 Actress Davis

49 Puts a woodcutter's tool in commercials

50 Rockette's unsteady movement

51 ___-Wan Kenobi (charge *Star Wars* sage)

52 Adulterate the DNA

53 The Z file at the Real Estate Archives

55 They, in French

56 Mar Mensa measures

57 Dr. Carver's nightmare

58 Enjoys author Josephine again

60 "Old MacDonald had a palindrome, ___!"

63 Don't annoy the ___ he inform the countess

67 450, to Brutus

70 Cuomo and Puzo

71 Naysaying president

73 Le Pew and Le Moko

74 Two Greek letters

76 Laugh-track sound

77 Crystal ____ (she's on drugs)

79 Video channel on the rise?

80 ___ the abbreviation for our capital

81 Mrs. Pillar-of-salt's husband

ANSWERS

1 FREE ADVICE

J	A	W	S		L	A	N	A		E	M	A	I	L
A	V	I	A		A	N	O	N		M	A	D	L	Y
M	A	R	K	T	W	A	I	N		B	R	A	I	N
E	I	E	I	O		D	R	A	W	L		M	E	X
S	L	R		L	E	E		R	H	E	O			
			E	R	M	A	B	O	M	B	E	C	K	
I	N	S	I	D	E		N	O	M		E	A	R	N
C	O	N	D	O		A	G	R		I	S	S	U	E
E	L	I	A		I	L	L		S	N	E	E	Z	E
S	O	P	H	I	A	L	O	R	E	N				
	O	N	M	E		E	L	I		C	P	U		
A	A	A		A	S	Y	L	A		N	O	H	I	T
J	C	R	E	W		C	A	R	Y	G	R	A	N	T
A	R	E	N	A		A	C	M	E		E	R	T	E
R	E	A	D	Y		T	E	S	T		O	D	O	R

3 MONSTERS, INC.
The leftovers letters spell: They froze it and dropped it at the North Pole. Back then, no one figured on global warming.

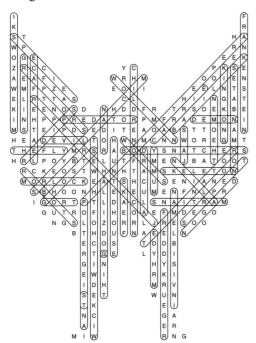

FYI: Gort was the robot in *The Day the Earth Stood Still*, Mike Wazowski was the one-eyed hero of *Monsters, Inc.*, and Morlocks were a subterranean race in H. G. Wells' *The Time Machine*. Those nasty worms were featured in *Dune* and *Tremors*.

2 NUMEROLOGY
1. At any given time, there are **366,144** people traveling in airplanes.
2. A person swallows **295** times during an average meal.
3. Kareem Abdul-Jabbar scored **38,387** points over his entire career.
4. A healthy slug can travel **50** yards a day.
5. A pelican can hold **25** pounds of fish in his beak.
6. In 2003, **164,848** people in Germany were arrested for "offensive gestures."
7. If the elevators were broken in the Empire State Building you'd have to climb **1,860** steps to get to the top.
8. As of 2004, Japan had **350,000** industrial robots at work.
9. There are **17** species of penguin.
10. About 100 people die every minute; the number of people who are born in the same time span is about **200**.
11. The number of calories a person consumes during a one-hour phone call is **71**.
12. There are **17,508** islands in the Indonesian archipelago.

2 RELAX, ALREADY!
2.6 days (that's two days and about fourteen and a half hours).

4 LOONEY LAWS: THE QUIZ
1 – a ("oh, boy!")
2 – b (high-heeled shoes)
3 – c ("exceedingly ugly")
4 – b (bear gallbladder)
5 – b (knowing where you're going)
6 – a (a bathtub)
7 – c ("unusual haircuts")
8 – a (bite a dog)
9 – a (scowl at)
10 – b (you're a licensed electrician)

5 WILDE ABOUT OSCAR
1. Life is much too important a thing ever to talk seriously about it. (from *Vera, or The Nihilists*)
2. One should never give a woman anything she can't wear in the evening. (from *An Ideal Husband*)
3. When one is in town one amuses one's self. When one is in the country one amuses other people. (from *The Importance of Being Earnest*)

6 CELEBRITY RUMORS

1. **FALSE**. When Siskel died in February 1999, his lawyer was quoted in a UPI story as saying, "Gene wanted to be remembered as a Thumbs-Up kind of guy." But the story about him wanting to being buried with a thumb up was proven false when reporters checked out a copy of Siskel's will.

2. **FALSE**. The rumor was based on an old joke that had been applied to a lot of "actresses," including Pia Zadora. Vanna White never played Anne Frank on stage, on TV, in the movies, or anywhere else.

3. **FALSE**. Cher never had the procedure done—and neither did other rumored celebs like Jane Fonda, Janet Jackson, or even Marilyn Manson—because no such procedure exists. Cher got so fed up with the rumor that she sued the French magazine *Paris Match* that had started the rumor (they retracted the story). She even hired a physician to examine her and release his findings to the public.

4. **FALSE**. The stars were marketing codes—*Playboy* was published in several different regional editions, and the company used different numbers of stars to identify the different editions.

5. **TRUE**. Cody was born Espero DeCorti to Italian immigrant parents, in Kaplan, Louisiana. He'd assumed the native American identity in the 1920s to get acting work in Hollywood westerns.

6. **TRUE**. The papers, published in the 1880s, extolled the virtues of cocaine. But contrary to that other rumor, Freud never became addicted to the stuff. He preferred cigars.

7. **FALSE**. Hoover was a homosexual, but the stories of his cross-dressing were the invention of Susan Rosenstiel, a woman who was trying to get revenge because she believed that Hoover had put FBI agents on her tail to help her husband during their divorce.

8. **FALSE**. While it's true that the numbers 66 + 73 + 76 + 76 + 71 + 65 + 84 + 69 + 83 = 663, neither 3 nor III has the ASCII value 3, to arrive at 666.

9. **TRUE**. Wayne had four kids to support, which was his public reason. But it's generally believed that he stayed out of the armed forces to save his career—he thought he'd be washed up by the time he returned from the war. So instead he made war-themed movies like *Flying Tigers* and *Back to Bataan*. By the time the war was over, he was a superstar.

10. **TRUE**. When Garcia was four years old, he and his brother, Tiff, were splitting wood and playing "chicken" with the ax. Jerry mistimed removing his finger from the block, and Tiff accidentally chopped Jerry's finger off.

7 THE QUOTABLE JOHN

"I" Am Not a Camera
The name "Kodak" has no meaning. Founder George Eastman explained, "The letter K has been a favorite with me. It seems a strong, incisive sort of letter."

Something Completely Different
At first, Monty Python was on so late that it could only attract a cult following, which meant, according to the Pythons, "insomniacs, intellectuals, and burglars."

When in Rome
Slaves awarded to Roman soldiers for bravery in battle were known as "addicts." Eventually, the term came to mean a person who was a slave to anything.

8 I LOVE A PARADE

St. Patrick's Day Parade, 1766
Mardi Gras Parade, 1837
Ticker-Tape Parade, 1886
Rose Parade, 1890
Mummers Parade, 1901
Santa Claus Parade, 1905
Macy's Thanksgiving Day Parade, 1924
Chinese New Year Parade, 1958

10 R.I.P.

A	J	E	T		Q	A	N	D	A		Z	A	P	S
B	A	Y	H		U	N	C	A	S		E	D	I	E
A	G	E	E		I	T	A	L	Y		N	U	N	N
		T	H	A	T	S	A	L	L	F	O	L	K	S
I	C	E	U	P			A	A	A		T	I	E	
T	H	E	B	E	S	T	I	S		V	A	S	E	S
S	E	T		H	E	N		P	R	E				
	T	H	E	B	E	A	T	G	O	E	S	O	N	
	O	L	D		H	M	S			D	E	F		
P	H	A	S	E		Y	E	T	T	O	C	O	M	E
A	O	L		S	C	I			P	H	N	O	M	
T	O	G	E	T	H	E	R	A	G	A	I	N		
A	T	O	Z		A	L	O	N	E		N	E	W	T
K	E	R	R		I	D	O	N	T		U	L	E	E
I	D	E	A		M	S	D	O	S		P	L	E	X

9 YOU'RE INVITED TO A POTTY

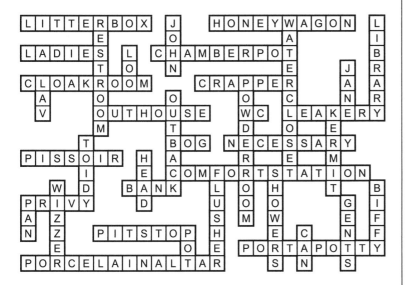

12 IT'S LIKE...A SIMILE

1 – a ("Alimony is like…buying oats for a dead horse."—Arthur "Bugs" Baer)

2 – g ("Dressing a pool player in a tuxedo is like…putting whipped cream on a hot dog."—Minnesota Fats)

3 – d ("Eating responsibly at McDonald's is like…going to a strip club for the iced tea."—Roger Ebert)

4 – c ("Giving money and power to government is like…giving whiskey and car keys to teenage boys."—P.J. O'Rourke)

5 – h ("Hubert Humphrey talks so fast that listening to him is like…trying to read *Playboy* with your wife turning the pages."—Barry Goldwater)

6 – e ("Naming a national forest after Ronald Reagan is like… naming a day-care center after W C. Fields."—Bob Hattoy)

7 – f ("Sex at 90 is like…playing pool with a rope."—Camille Paglia)

8 – i ("Trying to get the presidency to work is like…trying to sew buttons on a custard pie."—James D. Barber)

9 – j ("Trying to sneak a fastball past Hank Aaron is like…trying to sneak the sunrise past a rooster."—Joe Adcock)

10 – b ("Writing about music is like…dancing about architecture."—Elvis Costello)

12 UNCLE OSCAR'S BIG NIGHT # 1

1 – e (JANE FONDA, *COMING HOME*)

2 – a (CLARK GABLE, *IT HAPPENED ONE NIGHT*)

3 – d (HELEN HUNT, *AS GOOD AS IT GETS*)

4 – c (PETER FINCH, *NETWORK*)

5 – b (SALLY FIELD, *PLACES IN THE HEART*)

15 FRANKENSTEIN'S GREAT-AUNT TILLIE

The phonies are *My Brother, Frankenstein* and *Frankenstein of the Future*.

11 WOULD YOU RATHER LIVE IN...

1. Sun; Moon
2. War; Peace
3. Rock; Roll
4. Duet; Solo
5. Papa; Mummie
6. Start; Stop
7. Straight; Gay
8. Boring; Rapture
9. Devil Town; Angel
10. Liberty; Justice
11. Paradise; Hell
12. Hungry Horse; Fuller

13 DEPP PERCEPTION

The acrostic: You're the inspiration

The quote: Johnny Depp based his character Captain Jack Sparrow in *Pirates of the Caribbean* on a mix of Rolling Stones guitarist Keith Richards and the amorous cartoon skunk, Pepe LePew.

The clue answers:
A. YACHT
B. OHIO STATE
C. UPSETS
D. RIPOFFS
E. ELAND
F. THE PAJAMA GAME
G. HITCHCOCK
H. ERIK LARSON
I. INJUNCTION
J. NEWSPAPER
K. SPONGEBOB
L. PAPRIKA
M. INSURE
N. RON HOWARD
O. ALEXANDER
P. TRICKS
Q. ITHACA
R. ORBIT
S. NERDS

18 RHYMES WITH TICKLES

1. Some day you'll go far…and I hope you stay there.
2. There's a train leaving in half an hour. Be under it.
3. I looked high and low for you. I didn't look low enough.

18 A KISS IS JUST A KISS?

b. An English kiss

14 THE CAT'S PAJAMAS

The leftover letters spell: "Once in a dirty while" means "From time to time." A "sharpshooter" is a young man who spends a lot and dresses well. A "struggle buggy" is the back seat of a car.

BEARCAT: A hot-blooded girl

BIG SIX: A strong man (from the new, powerful six-cylinder engines)

BILLBOARD: A flashy man or woman

BREEZER: A convertible

BRILLO: Someone who lives fast and spends money freely

BUTT ME: Give me a cigarette

BUTTON SHINING: Close dancing

CAKE-EATER: A ladies' man

CHARLIE: A man with a moustache

CHOICE BIT OF CALICO: An attractive female

CORN SHREDDER: A man who's an awkward dancer

DOG JOCK: A man who walks his wife's dogs

FACE STRETCHER: An older woman trying to look young

FATHER TIME: Any man older than 30

FIG LEAF: A one-piece bathing suit

FIRE ALARM: A divorced woman

FIRE EXTINGUISHER: A chaperone

GOOFY: In love, attracted to

HIGH HAT: A snob

JACK: Money

KILLJOY: Anyone who's too solemn

NIFTY: Good

OLIVER TWIST: A good dancer

PANTHER SWEAT: Whiskey

PETTING PANTRY: A movie theater

PIPE DOWN: Keep quiet

PRUNE PIT: Anything that's old-fashioned

SHEBA: A woman with sex appeal

SHEIK: A man with sex appeal

SUGAR DADDY: An older boyfriend

SWANKY: Elegant

TEN MINUTES: An exceptionally tough (hard-boiled) man

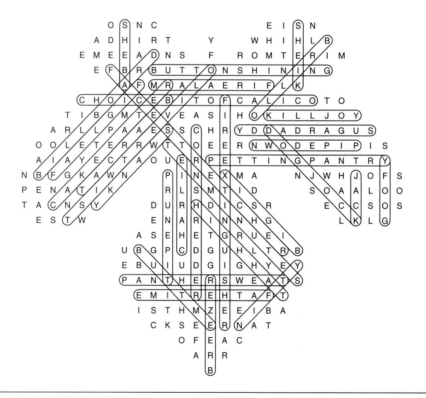

16 GIVE 'EM HELL, HARRY

1. All the president is is a glorified public relations man who spends his time flattering, kissing, and kicking people to get them to do what they are supposed to do anyway.

2. A pessimist is one who makes difficulties of his opportunities and an optimist is one who makes opportunities of his difficulties.

3. A politician is a man who understands government. A statesman is a politician who's been dead for fifteen years.

4. Three things can ruin a man—money, power, and women. I never had any money, I never wanted power, and the only woman in my life is up at the house right now.

17 DOUBLE TIME

20 RED ALL OVER

19 FILL IN THE LIMERICKS

1. calm; shark; Psalm
2. granny; there; fanny
3. sank her; two; anchor
4. drearier; yell; Superior
5. higher; throat; choir
6. blue; cool; stew
7. wheel; ground; meal
8. glee; craft; see
9. abhorrence; missed; torrents
10. died; another; side-by-side

21 CRAZY EIGHTS

The leftover letters spell: Presidents from Virginia are Washington, Jefferson, Madison, Monroe, William Henry Harrison, Tyler, Taylor, and Wilson.

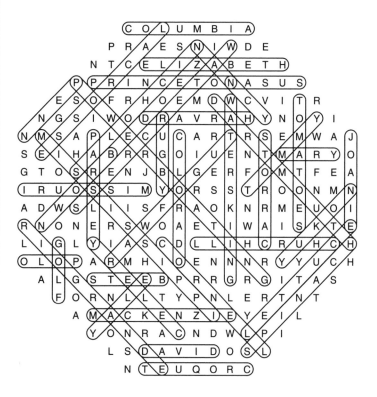

23 ALABAMA KLEENEX

1 – j (Alabama Kleenex: toilet paper)
2 – c (Arizona nightingale: a burro)
3 – g (Arkansas wedding cake: cornbread)
4 – d (Boston strawberries: baked beans)
5 – f (Colorado Kool-Aid: Coors beer)
6 – a (Full Cleveland: a '70s-style leisure outfit: loud pants and shirt, white belt, white loafers)
7 – b (Michigan bankroll: a big wad of small-denomination bills with a big bill on the outside)
8 – i (Missouri featherbed: a straw mattress)
9 – h (Tennessee toothpick: a raccoon bone)
10 – e (West Virginia coleslaw: chewing tobacco)

25 IS IT HOT IN HERE?

Hawaii.

26 INCENTIVE TO WIN?

True.

22 THEY ALMOST GOT THE ROLE

P	E	P	S	■	C	H	E	E	K	■	A	B	I	T
U	N	U	M	■	H	A	U	T	E	■	J	A	D	E
B	I	L	L	M	U	R	R	A	Y	■	A	C	E	S
L	G	S	■	A	T	P	■	T	W	A	■	H	A	T
I	M	A	G	I	N	E	S	■	E	T	R	E	■	■
C	A	R	L	■	E	R	I	C	S	T	O	L	T	Z
■	■	I	V	Y	■	E	A	T	A	L	O	N	E	■
A	S	K	M	E	■	L	S	D	■	C	A	R	T	E
C	H	I	P	S	H	O	T	■	S	K	I	■	■	■
R	O	D	S	T	E	W	A	R	T	■	D	I	S	C
■	S	E	R	A	■	S	A	R	A	S	O	T	A	■
B	A	T	■	Y	R	S	■	V	A	L	■	D	O	R
E	Q	U	I	■	K	E	V	I	N	K	L	I	N	E
T	U	F	T	■	E	M	E	N	D	■	O	N	E	S
S	A	F	E	■	N	I	X	E	S	■	B	E	D	S

The Rod Stewart story is especially interesting since Elton John, after convincing Stewart not to take the role, ended up playing the Pinball Wizard himself. He'd wanted the role all along and purposely talked Stewart, the producers' first choice, out of taking it.

24 CREATURE FEATURE

The acrostic: Talk about odd couples
The quote: Actor Andy Serkis provided the voice and movements for Gollum in the *Lord of the Rings* films. He based the voice on the sound of his cat coughing up a hairball. Special effects artists modeled Gollum's bony frame on punk rocker Iggy Pop.
The clue answers:
A. THE EDGE OF NIGHT
B. APOLOGISTS
C. LINCOLN LOGS
D. KEANU REEVES
E. ASHTON KUTCHER
F. BIG DADDY
G. OFF-THE-RECORD
H. UNFOLDING
I. TONY KUSHNER
J. OLMECS
K. DIMMEST
L. DOVETAILS
M. COLOR
N. OH PROMISE ME
O. UP FOR GRABS
P. PATRICIA MCBRIDE
Q. LAYOFFS
R. EVANOVICH
S. STEPHANIE PLUM

23 ALL YOU NEED IS LOVE...

JOHN
JOIN
LOIN
LAIN
PAIN
PAIL
PAUL

The six-step solution:
NEED
PEED (there's that word we warned you about)
PEND
POND
PONE
LONE
LOVE

Here's an example of a seven-step solution:
NEED
FEED
FEND
BEND
BOND
BONE
LONE
LOVE

25 DUMB JOCKS

Don King: Some of the great Oedipuses in the world have been built by Donald Trump.
George Steinbrenner: David Cone is in a class by himself with three or four other players.
Joe Theismann: He'll take your head off at the blink of a hat.
Jerry Coleman: Next up is Fernando Gonzalez, who isn't playing tonight.
Jack Kraft: That was the nail that broke the coffin's back.
Mike Greenwell: I'm a four-wheel-drive-pickup type of guy and so is my wife.
Danny Ozark: Even Napoleon had his Watergate.
Larry Anderson: If a guy is a good fastball hitter, does that mean I should throw him a bad fastball?

31 THE EYE HAS IT

b. "Private eye" comes from Pinkerton's logo.

26 I DON'T GET IT

1. Why can't a bicycle stand alone? Because it is two-tired.
2. What's the definition of a will? A dead giveaway.
3. Time flies like an arrow… Fruit flies like a banana.
4. What's the definition of acupuncture? A jab well done.
5. In democracy it's your vote that counts. In feudalism it's your count that votes.
6. Did you hear about the man who fell into an upholstery machine? He's fully recovered.
7. She had a boyfriend with a wooden leg. But she broke it off.
8. When you've seen one shopping center… You've seen a mall.
9. Practice safe eating. Always use condiments.
10. What's the definition of a shotgun wedding? A case of wife or death.

29 HO, HO, HO!

The leftover letters spell: Many historians think Jesus was born in April.

Here's the story: The birthday of Mithras, a Persian deity, was traditionally celebrated at the winter solstice in late December. Mithraism and Christianity were both becoming popular in the Mediterranean region at about the same time, and the Christians were determined to prevail, so they co-opted the December date as their own. By the third or fourth century A.D., the already popular day was entrenched as the Nativity.

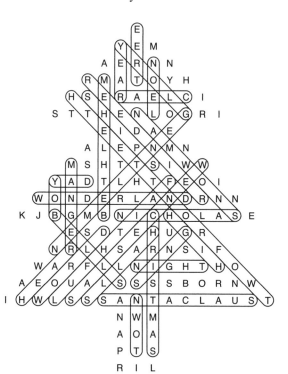

27 THE SUSPENSE IS KILLING ME!

The famous person is ALFRED HITCHCOCK (39 Across) and the six films are: *SUSPICION* (18 Across), *THE BIRDS* (20 Across), *FRENZY* (28 Across), *PSYCHO* (46 Across), *LIFEBOAT* (61 Across), and *NOTORIOUS* (63 Across).

All I Want for Christmas Is My TWO FRONT TEETH
Angels From the Realm of GLORY
Angels We Have Heard on HIGH
Away in a MANGER
Deck the HALLS
Do You Hear What I HEAR
The First NOEL
Frosty the SNOW MAN
God Rest Ye Merry, GENTLEMEN
Good King WENCESLAS
Hark! The Herald Angels SING
Have Yourself a Merry Little CHRISTMAS
I Heard the Bells on Christmas DAY
I Saw Mommy Kissing SANTA CLAUS
I Saw Three SHIPS
It Came Upon the Midnight CLEAR
It's the Most Wonderful Time of the YEAR
Jingle BELLS
Jolly Old Saint NICHOLAS
Joy to the WORLD
The Little Drummer BOY
O Come, All Ye FAITHFUL
O Little Town of BETHLEHEM
Rocking Around the Christmas TREE
Rudolph the Red-Nosed REINDEER
Santa Claus Is Coming to TOWN
Silent NIGHT
Winter WONDERLAND

28 BANANARAMA

1. Americans eat an average of **75** bananas a year per person.
2. The **banana split** was invented by Dr. David Strickler.
3. Technically, the banana is **a berry**.
4. A banana has about **110** calories.
5. The banana has **never** been Fruit of the Month.
6. **True.** The Charleston was danced on banana peel-covered floors. But probably not for long.
7. The jingle was once played on the radio **376** times in one day.

---

28 AND MUDDY WATERS?

The quote: A "bo diddley" is an African single-string guitar.
The clue answers:
  A. FADES
  B. LABRADOR
  C. INDIGNITY
  D. CURIE
  E. GIANTS
  F. SIGNAL

---

32 CAPITAL IDEA!

1. ROME (Italy)
2. OSLO (Norway)
3. BERN (Switzerland)
4. TUNIS (Tunisia)
5. LIMA (Peru)
6. MALE (Maldives)

30 THAT'S DR. PRESIDENT TO YOU, BUDDY!

---

32 PROVERBIAL WISDOM

China: The palest ink is better than the best memory.
Germany: Let your head be more than a funnel to your stomach.
Niger: Hold a true friend with both hands.
Zimbabwe: If you can walk you can dance. If you can talk you can sing.
Spain: Don't give me advice, give me money.
Greece: Distrust the advice of the interested.
Japan: Fall seven times, stand up eight.
Wales: Be honorable yourself if you want to associate with honorable people.
France: If only the young knew; if only the old could.
Italy: The best way to get praise is to die.

---

31 LUCKY AT CARDS...

1. Bad (Being dealt the four of clubs; if it happens in the first hand, get up and leave the game)
2. Good (Blowing or spitting on the cards; preferably when no one is looking, but don't make a mess)
3. Bad (Dropping a black ace on the floor; if you do, leave the game immediately)
4. Bad (If you're a man, playing in a room where there's a woman present unless she's playing with you. And vice versa if you're a woman)
5. Bad (Lending another player money during a game; don't borrow it either)
6. Bad (Letting someone put their foot on the rung of your chair; on the other hand if you want to give someone else bad luck, put your foot on a rung of their chair)
7. Bad (Picking up your cards before they've all been dealt)

8. Playing cards:
   a. Bad (in a room with a dog in it)
   b. Bad (on a bare table)
   c. Bad (with a cross-eyed person; this dates back to the days when people thought a cross-eyed person could see the cards of the person sitting next to them)
9. Good (Seeing a hunchback on your way to the game; but don't touch the hump, just seeing is enough)
10. Bad (Singing or whistling during a game)
11. Good (Sitting on a handkerchief; especially if you're losing and you want to change your luck)
12. Bad (Sitting with your legs crossed; you're literally crossing out your luck)
13. Good (Wearing a pin in your lapel)
14. Good (Wearing an article of dirty clothing; the theory is that the dirt keeps evil at bay)

33 MIX-UP AT THE HONKY-TONK

1. "Get Your TONGUE Outta My Mouth 'Cause I'm Kissing You GOODBYE"
2. "I Would Have Wrote You a LETTER, But I Couldn't Spell YUCK!"
3. "I'd Rather Have a BOTTLE in Front of Me Than a Frontal LOBOTOMY"
4. "She Got the Gold MINE and I Got the SHAFT"
5. "Tennis Must Be Your RACKET 'Cause Love Means NOTHIN' to You"
6. "Thank GOD and GREYHOUND She's Gone"
7. "When the Phone Don't RING, Baby, You'll Know It's ME"
8. "We Used to Just KISS on the Lips But Now It's All OVER"
9. "You Were Only a SPLINTER as I Slid Down the BANISTER of Life"
10. "You're the Reason Our KIDS Are So UGLY"

33 HOLD ON TO YOUR HAT!

1. Texas
2. Oklahoma
3. Kansas
4. Florida
5. Nebraska
6. Iowa
7. Illinois
8. Missouri
9. Colorado
10. Louisiana

36 BAD HAIR DAYS

The fake stories are Model Behavior and Coming Out Ahead.

34 THEY NEVER WON A GRAMMY

35 WOULD WE LIE TO YOU?

1 – a (Someone who's "not up to snuff" is a poor judge of tobacco.)
2 – c (The phrase refers to Sing Sing, "up the river" from New York City.)
3 – a (The "knot" is that of a bride's girdle in ancient Rome.)
4 – b (To "lay an egg" is to score no runs in cricket.)
5 – b (The original phrase was "happy as a clam at high tide.")

37 WHAT'S YOUR SIGN?

The leftover letters spell: The thirteenth is called Ophiuchus, the serpent bearer.

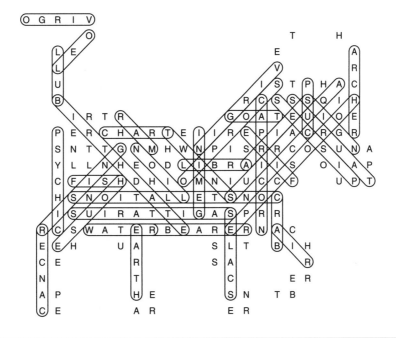

38 QUOTATIONARY

Animal: Something invented by plants to move seeds around. (Terrence McKenna)

Camel: A horse designed by committee. (Alec Issigonis)

Comedy: A funny way of being serious. (Peter Ustinov)

Cheese: Milk that you chew. (Chandler, on Friends)

Gossip: When you hear something you like about someone you don't. (Earl Wilson)

Guilt: The gift that keeps on giving. (Erma Bombeck)

Laughter: The shortest distance between two people. (Victor Borge)

Playboy: A man who believes in wine, women, and so long. (John Travolta)

Stock Market: A weapon that destroys people but leaves buildings still standing. (Jay Leno)

Sweater: A garment worn by a child when his mother feels chilly. (Alma Denny)

Tact: The ability to describe others as they see themselves. (Abraham Lincoln)

39 CIRCULAR REASONING

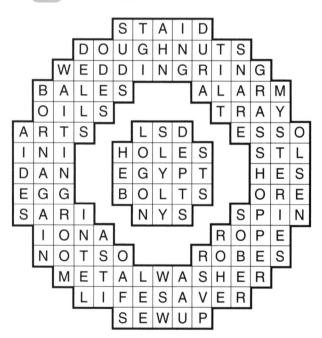

40 YEAH, WRIGHT

1. I put instant coffee in a microwave and almost went back in time.

2. He asked me if I knew what time it was. I said, yes, but not right now.

3. I had some eyeglasses. I was walking down the street when suddenly the prescription ran out.

41 TOM SWIFTIES

1 – c ("But I don't know how to start a Model-T Ford," Tom said crankily.)

2 – a ("I can't help thinking about the people who aren't here," Tom said absentmindedly.)

3 – e ("I'll have a martini, minus the vermouth," Tom said dryly.)

4 – i ("I'm waiting for my magazine to arrive," Tom said periodically.)

5 – j ("I've never had a car accident," Tom said recklessly.)

6 – d ("My grandfather's buried over there," Tom said cryptically.)

7 – h ("The doctors removed my left ventricle," Tom said half-heartedly.)

8 – b ("This seafood platter doesn't taste fresh to me," Tom said crabbily.)

9 – g ("Three Mile Island? I used to live there," Tom said glowingly.)

10 – f ("Yes, we have no bananas," Tom said fruitlessly.)

41 THAT SINKING FEELING

The quote: "If at first you don't succeed, your sky-diving days are over."—Milton Berle

The clue answers:

A. MUTES
B. IVY LEAGUE
C. TURIN
D. CADDIES
E. OFFICERS
F. ROYALTY
G. DONNYBROOK
H. STRIVED

42 FINAL NOTICE

43 PERFECT 10 #1

Worldwide, the average woman is **5** inches shorter than the average man.

The Danube River flows through **8** European countries.

A full moon is **9** times brighter than a half-moon.

There are **7** holes in a Ritz cracker.

A human eyeball weighs **1** ounce.

A "Big Band" is any band with **10** or more musicians.

A regulation hole in golf is no less than **4** inches deep.

Giant sequoia bark can be **2** feet thick.

According to criminal law, **3** people are necessary for a disturbance to be called a riot.

The average yawn lasts **6** seconds.

43 DON'T LEAVE EARTH WITHOUT IT

The quote: The Klingon Dictionary has sold over two hundred and fifty thousand copies to date.

The clue answers:

A. CURVE
B. DENTIST
C. TEASE
D. LAUNDRY
E. NOTIFY
F. DONDI
G. FASHION PLATE
H. DOCTOR
I. SHADOW
J. KNIGHTHOOD

44 YOU BET YOUR SWEET PATOOTIE!

The leftover letters spell: "That's one for Ripley" refers to "Ripley's Believe It or Not!" cartoons. It means anything strange or bizarre.

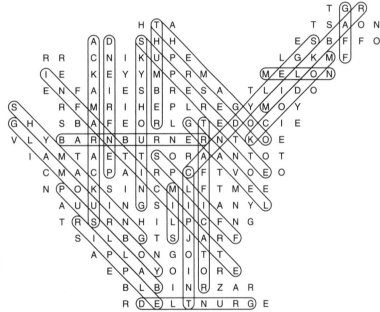

ACKAMARACKUS: Nonsense

BALLS-UP: Messed up, ruined, confused, or disordered

BARNBURNER: A riotous party

CANDY LEGS: A rich and popular young man

CLIP JOINT: A bar that charges outrageously high prices

GAFF: A building or a house

GLAMOUR BOY: Like a pretty boy but more masculine

GRAVEL: Sugar

GRUNTLED: Happy. The word was created by dropping the dis- from disgruntled

INFANTICIPATE: Pregnant or expecting; hence, anticipating an infant

MELON: A financial windfall

MILK BAR: Like a regular bar except that the drinks are made with milk, not alcohol. The milkshake is one of the few such drinks that survives today.

MODOCK: A man who becomes a military pilot to be glamorous and have sex appeal

PEN-FRIEND: What a pen pal used to be called

RIPPLE: Ice cream with a colorful syrup stirred in, giving it flavor and a rippled appearance

SHY-MAKING: Embarrassing

SKY-SHOUTING: Skywriters write messages in the sky with trails of smoke; sky-shouters broadcast messages to the ground via loudspeakers

SLIM: Lose weight by dieting

SPLIFF: A marijuana cigarette

SUPERETTE: A small supermarket, something about the size of a modern 7-Eleven

THE MAGOO: Sex appeal

THUMBER: A hitchhiker

TRAFFICATOR: What some 1930's cars had instead of blinkers—"arms" on either side of the car that could be raised when the driver wanted to indicate a turn

45 FLUBBED HEADLINES

1. HILLARY CLINTON ON WELFARE
2. MILK DRINKERS ARE TURNING TO POWDER
3. MAN SHOOTS NEIGHBOR WITH MACHETE
4. RETIRED PRIEST TO MARRY SPRINGSTEEN
5. DEFENDANT'S SPEECH ENDS IN LONG SENTENCE
6. NINETEEN FEET BROKEN IN POLE VAULT
7. LARGE CHURCH PLANS COLLAPSE
8. OFFICIAL: ONLY RAIN WILL CURE DROUGHT
9. BRITAIN INCHES GRUDGINGLY TOWARDS METRIC SYSTEM
10. OLD SCHOOL PILLARS ARE REPLACED BY ALUMNI

47 PLEASE PASS THE CORN

50 HONEST ABE

46 GEEKSPEAK

1 – f (Ant farms: Giant multiscreen movie complexes found in shopping malls.)
2 – a (Anus envy: A common condition among fans of Howard Stern or Rush Limbaugh who try to imitate their heroes.)
3 – h (Batmobiling: Putting up protective emotional shields just as a relationship enters an intimate, vulnerable stage.)
4 – c (Begathon: A TV or radio fundraiser.)
5 – g (Body Nazis: Hardcore fitness fanatics who look down on anyone who doesn't exercise obsessively.)
6 – i (Deboning: The act of removing subscription cards and perfume ads from a magazine before reading it.)
7 – d (Height technology: Computer-geek for "ladder.")
8 – e (Meatspace: Computer-geek for the physical world (as opposed to cyber-space); also known as the carbon community or RW (Real World).)
9 – j (Prairie dogging: When someone raises a commotion in a *cube farm*, and everyone else's heads pop over the walls to get a look.)
10 – b (Um friend: A sexual relation of dubious standing.)

46 WHAT'S SO FUNNY?

c. To "put someone in stitches" is to make them laugh so hard it hurts.

48 CELEBRITY SUPERSTITIONS

The Bill Clinton superstition is the phony. But the same superstition can be applied to President Woodrow Wilson who, in fact, ordered a ship to slow down so he'd arrive in Europe on the 13th.

48 THAT HEAVY TRUNK, TOO

The quote: The ears of an African elephant can weigh up to one hundred ten pounds each.
The clue answers:
A. NEPTUNE
B. AFFECTIONATE
C. RENOWNED
D. POURED
E. HANNAH
F. UNISPHERE
G. GALAHAD
H. SCOTCH

49 CHICKEN À LA RING

The acrostic: The worst matador going
The quote: Raphael "El Gallo" Ortega employed a technique called the "sudden flight" that was unique in the history of professional bullfighting. When the bull entered the ring, he panicked, dropped his cape, and ran away.
The clue answers:
A. THE SHINING
B. HAPPENED
C. ELOQUENCE
D. WALLFLOWERS
E. ON THE QT
F. REPUTE
G. SHIPSHAPE
H. THE THIRD DEGREE
I. MUFFLE
J. ADENOIDS
K. THE SEAGULL
L. ANDY RODDICK
M. DUENNA
N. OUT-OF-THE-WAY
O. RABBLE
P. GALLANTRY
Q. OPHELIA
R. ILLICIT
S. NAPHTHA
T. GRACING

52 LISTOGRAMS

5 Greatest American Generals (according to a Gallup poll in 2002):
GEORGE PATTON
DWIGHT EISENHOWER
DOUGLAS MACARTHUR
COLIN POWELL
GEORGE WASHINGTON

The 5 Most Germ-Ridden Places at Work:
PHONE
DESKTOP
WATER FOUNTAIN
MICROWAVE DOOR
KEYBOARD

52 THE NEW ECONOMY

The quote: "The most embarrassing thing is that the salad dressing is outgrossing my films." —Paul Newman.
The clue answers:
A. HOMONYMS
B. LITTER
C. EGGHEADS
D. SMARTS
E. INSTITUTE
F. ALMONDS
G. WRISTS
H. AMPHIBIANS
I. LAUGHING GAS
J. FERNS

51 TWO LADIES IN A SHOE STORE

1. ABC: A-2-3
2. Ajax: A-J
3. American Airlines: A-A
4. Assault Rifle: A-K-4-7
5. Mongrel: K-9
6. Cowboys: K-K
7. Dolly Parton: 9-5
8. Fred & Ethel: Q-J
9. Heinz: 5-7
10. Hockey Sticks: 7-7
11. Huey, Dewey, and Louie: 2-2-2
12. Jack Benny: 3-9
13. Jackson Five: J-J-5-5
14. Jesse James: 4-5
15. Kojak: K-J
16. Lucy & Ricky: K-Q
17. Lumberman's Hand: 2-4
18. Oldsmobile: 9-8
19. Quinine: Q-9
20. Sail Boats: 4-4
21. Snowmen: 8-8
22. Thirty Miles: 10-10-10
23. Washington Monument: 5-5-5 (because it's 555 feet high)
24. Woolworth: 5-10

51 WHO'S THE BOSS?
Verizon Communications.

54 WELL, I NEVER!

Billy Wilder: You have Van Gogh's ear for music.
Golda Meir: Don't be humble. You're not that great.
George Bernard Shaw: She had lost the art of conversation, but not, unfortunately, the power of speech.
Milton Berle: I'm old? When you were young, the Dead Sea was only sick!
Samuel Johnson: Your manuscript is both good and original, but the part that is good is not original, and the part that is original is not good.
Redd Foxx: She was so ugly that one time she tried to enter an ugly contest. They told her, "Sorry, no professionals allowed."

53 LOOK BOTH WAYS

The leftover letters spell out three palindromes: BORROW OR ROB; NO PINOT NOIR ON ORION TO NIP ON; MARGE LETS NORAH SEE SHARON'S TELEGRAM.

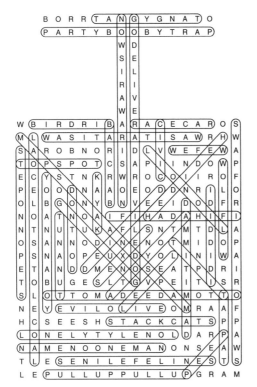

55 FROM A TO Z

54 CAUGHT IN THE MIDDLE

1 – c (Spencer Bonaventure Tracy)
2 – a (Walter Elias Disney)
3 – f (John Ernst Steinbeck)
4 – b (James Eugene Carrey)
5 – d (Richard Evelyn Byrd)
6 – e (Donald Fauntleroy Duck)

57 YOU'RE (NOT) THE TOPS

1 - b (Angioplasty)
2 - a (Candy)
3 - c (Cockatoo)
4 - b (Vegetable beef)
5 - d (Being naked in public)
6 - d (Orange)
7 - c (Leo)
8 - a (Power tools)
9 - c (Current relationship status)
10 - b (Nitrogen)

57 COLORFUL QUESTION

b. Dusty

56 HARD AS NAILS

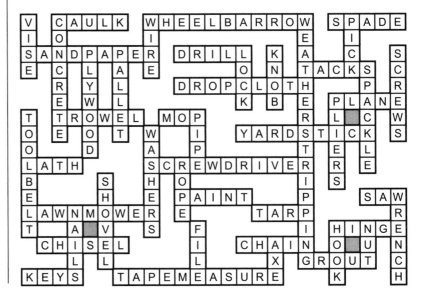

58 FLOWER POWER

D	R	A	N	G		S	O	B	A		A	T	A	D
O	N	I	O	N		R	T	E	S		L	O	V	E
C	A	R	N	A	T	I	O	N	S		I	M	I	N
	B	E	T	H	L	E	H	E	M		M	A	N	
O	E	R		S	E	A		U	T	I	L	I	T	Y
A	R	U	T		E	N	T	R		S	A	X	E	S
F	I	S	H	C	A	K	E		T	T	Y			
	C	H	R	Y	S	A	N	T	H	E	M	U	M	
		O	C	T		S	E	R	R	A	N	O	S	
S	H	A	W	L		H	E	R	O		N	I	L	E
M	O	S	S	I	M	O		R	U	N		O	D	E
I	M	P		C	O	M	E	A	G	A	I	N		
L	A	O	S		D	E	L	P	H	I	N	I	U	M
E	G	O	S		A	L	L	I		A	S	S	A	I
S	E	R	A		L	Y	O	N		D	O	T	E	S

59 INSIDE HOLLYWOOD

1. *Jaws* (1975)
2. *When Harry Met Sally* (1989). The faked-orgasm scene was suggested by star Meg Ryan, who also suggested shooting it in a restaurant.
3. *GoodFellas* (1990)
4. *Singin' in the Rain* (1952). The "feverish" star was Gene Kelly, of course.
5. *The Great Escape* (1963). For the tunneling scenes, Charles Bronson advised director John Sturges on effective earth-moving techniques.
6. *Almost Famous* (2000). Brad Pitt's role went to Billy Crudup.
7. *Fargo* (1996)
8. *The Dirty Dozen* (1967)
9. *Pulp Fiction* (1994).
10. *From Here to Eternity* (1953)

60 MARRIED-GO-ROUND

1. "Why can't someone invent something for us to marry besides women?"
2. "There is so little difference between husbands, you might as well keep the first."
3. "Never get married in the morning; you never know who you might meet that night."

61 FRUIT SALAD

The leftover letters spell: (7 Things Invented) by Canadians are the snowmobile, paint roller, plastic garbage bag, washing machine, electric range, zipper, and foghorn.

62 UNCLE OSCAR'S BIG NIGHT #2

1 – d (MERYL STREEP, *SOPHIE'S CHOICE*)
2 – c (ANTHONY HOPKINS, *THE SILENCE OF THE LAMBS*)
3 – a (HENRY FONDA, *ON GOLDEN POND*)
4 – e (JACK NICHOLSON, *ONE FLEW OVER THE CUCKOO'S NEST*)
5 – b (HILARY SWANK, *MILLION DOLLAR BABY*)

62 SHARK ATTACKS PUZZLE EXPERTS

1 – g (ASTRONAUT TAKES BLAME FOR GAS IN SPACECRAFT)
2 – f (CALIFORNIA GOVERNOR MAKES STAND ON DIRTY TOILETS)
3 – l (CRITICS SAY SUNKEN SHIPS NOT SEAWORTHY)
4 – i (ECUADOREAN PRESIDENT DECLARES HE'S NOT DEAD)
5 – d (MOORPARK RESIDENTS ENJOY A COMMUNAL DUMP)
6 – j (NUDE SCENE DONE TASTEFULLY IN RADIO PLAY)
7 – h (REASON FOR MORE BEAR SIGHTINGS: MORE BEARS)
8 – c (SAFETY EXPERTS SAY SCHOOL BUS PASSENGERS SHOULD BE BELTED)
9 – b (STORM DELAYED BY BAD WEATHER)
10 – k (SUMMER SCHOOLS BOOST SCRORES)
11 – a (THANKS TO PRESIDENT CLINTON, STAFF SGT. FRUER NOW HAS A SON)
12 – e (WOMAN NOT INJURED BY COOKIE)

64 IT'S ALL YOUR FAULT

The acrostic: Lily Tomlin punch line
The quote: Ninety-eight percent of the adults in this country are decent, hard-working, honest citizens. It's the other two percent that get all the publicity. But then, we elected them.
The clue answers:
A. LECTERN
B. I KID YOU NOT
C. LIGHTWEIGHT
D. YEAST
E. TRENT
F. OTTER
G. MOTHER SHIP
H. LUNGED
I. IN THE FLESH
J. NEWHART
K. PETTY
L. UTTER
M. NEW HEBRIDES
N. COTTON STATE
O. HICCUP
P. LET IT BE
Q. INCHED
R. NATCHEZ
S. ENACT

63 TWISTED TITLES

W	I	D	T	H		S	L	A	B		T	A	T	I
I	N	A	W	E		L	O	L	A		E	W	A	N
N	A	B	O	B		I	N	O	N		N	I	T	E
		F	R	I	D	G	E	T	O	O	F	A	R	
	P	L	E	A	D			A	R	R	E	S	T	
P	A	T	R	I	O	T	D	A	M	E	S		
E	S	C		C	L	O	W	N		L	A	B	O	R
E	C	O	L		S	W	A	G	S		X	R	A	Y
P	O	L	A	R		E	R	I	C	S		O	S	U
		C	O	L	D	F	O	U	N	T	A	I	N	
S	T	E	E	L	E			L	O	A	D	S		
M	Y	L	I	F	E	A	S	A	L	O	G		
O	P	E	N		W	I	L	L		Z	O	N	K	S
L	E	N	T		A	W	O	L		E	U	B	I	E
T	R	I	O		Y	A	P	S		S	T	A	T	E

66 WHAT'S THE WORD?

Y	A	M	S		S	W	A	P		B	A	C	O	N
A	B	E	L		P	O	G	O		A	B	O	V	E
C	H	A	U	F	F	E	U	R		R	A	M	I	E
H	O	T	E	L		F	A	K	I	R		A	D	D
T	R	Y		O	S	U		Y	V	E	S			
		L	O	L	L	A	P	A	L	O	O	Z	A	
S	L	E	A	Z	Y		V	I	N		R	U	I	N
A	U	T	R	Y		J	O	G		I	T	S	N	O
S	N	A	G		D	E	W		S	M	I	T	E	S
K	A	L	E	I	D	O	S	C	O	P	E			
		S	N	A	P		A	D	A		P	T	A	
B	M	I		H	Y	A	T	T		L	U	R	I	D
A	R	O	M	A		R	I	G	M	A	R	O	L	E
J	E	W	E	L		D	R	U	M		A	X	E	L
A	D	A	G	E		Y	E	T	I		L	Y	R	E

67 DANGER! MAD SCIENTIST AT WORK

1. Tesla could produce lightning bolts, sparks running across the ground, and ghostly blue glows in the air. In fact, all those wild-eyed men in white coats in Hollywood pictures are based on him.
2. The electricity flashing around Dr. Frankenstein's castle? A direct copy of real-life conditions in Tesla's lab. *Frankenstein* was the first of many movies to use real Tesla coils to get those weird arcs of artificial lightning.
3. He was a classic obsessive-compulsive who loved pigeons, the dark, and the number three, and was terrified of dirt, germs, and round objects, especially pearls. He sometimes signed his letters "G.I." for Great Inventor. Other than that he was fine.

65 THE LANGUAGE OF LOVE

The leftover letters spell: A man who chases other women during the first month after his wife has given birth; a lecture given by a wife at bedtime; to kiss. (The definitions are for GANDERMOONER, CURTAIN-SERMON, and SMICK, respectively.)

ACHARNE: To thirst for blood
AMORET: A loving look, glance
BABIES-IN-THE-EYES: The reflection of oneself in a beloved's pupils
BESPAWLED: Covered with spittle and saliva
BRIDELOPE: Wedding
CHICHEVACHE: A thin, ugly face
CLARTY-PAPS: A slovenly, dirty wife
CURTAIN-SERMON: [see the hidden message]
DELUMBATE: To sexually maim
ENTERBATHE: To bathe together; literally, to mix tears
FAIRHEAD: A beauty
FARDRY: To paint the face with white make-up for cosmetic benefit
FLESH-SHAMBLES: A dirty, ill-reputed brothel
FRIKE: Lusty, bawdy
FRIM: Fleshy, vigorous
FUCUS: A kind of rouge made from lichen
FULYEAR: A man who dishonors women
GANDERMOONER: [see the hidden message]
GRANDGORE: Infectious disease
GREADE: A woman's bosom
HALCH: To embrace tightly
HALF-MARROW: A husband or wife
LAVOLT: A lively dance
LIBS: Castrates
LOVESHIP: Act of love-making
MODESTY-PIECE: A lace cloth that covers a woman's chest
MORMALS: Inflamed sores
MUSKIN: A term of endearment for a woman; sweetheart
RAVALRY: A fit of passion
RUSH RING: To "wed" without a ring; to convince a woman that a false marriage was legal
SMICK: [see the hidden message]
STEWED PRUNE: Madam in a brothel
WINCHESTER GOOSE: A sexually transmitted disease

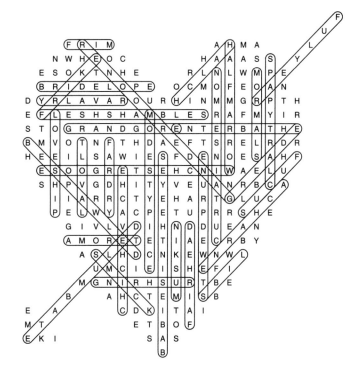

68 LET ME WRITE SIGN— I SPEAK ENGLISH

On the grass in a Paris park:
PLEASE DO NOT BE A DOG
Outside a Hong Kong dress shop:
LADIES HAVE FITS UPSTAIRS
On a menu in Nepal:
COMPLIMENTARY GLASS OF WINE OR BEAR
In a Rome hotel room:
PLEASE DIAL 7 TO RETRIEVE YOUR AUTO FROM THE GARBAGE
On a menu in China:
COLD SHREDDED CHILDREN AND SEA BLUBBER IN SPICY SAUCE
At a Seoul hotel desk:
CHOOSE TWIN BED OR MARRIAGE SIZE; WE REGRET NO KING KONG SIZE

68 IT SOUNDS WORSE THAN IT IS

1 – a (Bilateral perorbital hematoma: black eye)
2 – i (Epistaxisis: nosebleed)
3 – b (Eructation: burp)
4 – e (Horripilation: goosebumps)
5 – d (Otalgia: earache
6 – l (Pandiculation: yawn)
7 – h (Punctuate pruritis: itchy spot)
8 – f (Singultus: hiccup)
9 – g (Spheno pulatine ganglio neuralgia: ice cream headache)
10 – j (Sternutation: sneeze)
11 – k (Verruca vulgaris: wart)
12 – c (Xeroderma: dry skin)

69 PERFECT 10 #2

The first Apple computer in 1976 had **8** bytes of RAM.

A married man is **4** times more likely to die during sex if his partner isn't his wife.

Etiquette experts claim you should hang up if no one answers your call after **6** rings.

After 84 days in Skylab, astronauts found they were **2** inches taller.

The average Briton brews about **9** pounds of tea a year.

One ton of iron can turn into **3** tons of rust.

In the average film, male actors utter **10** times as many profanities as female actors.

The element astatine accounts for about **1** ounce—total—of the Earth's crust.

Shirley Temple won an honorary Oscar in 1934, when she was only **5** years old.

The average Ph.D. candidate spends **7** years on his/her dissertation.

70 THE TEXICON

1. A common greeting in Texas, as in "Mornin', darlin', **hair yew** today?"
2. A dish served in an Italian restaurant, as in "Ahl have the meatballs and **sketty**."
3. A question about a person's previous meal, as in "Hey, **jeet** yet? Ahm hungry."
4. Almost, as in "Ah was so tard ah **putnear** fell asleep."
5. Intending to, as in "Ahm **fixinta** go to the movies."
6. Large or extreme, as in "He's nothin' but a **biggo** drunk."
7. Personal concern, as in "It's none-a yer goldam **binness** where Ahm goin'!"
8. Someone who's not too sharp, as in "That boy's an **idjit**!"
9. The next number in the sequence: "…four, fahve, six, seb'n, **ite**…"
10. What makes a car run, as in "You got enough **gace** in yer truck to git there?"

71 MISNOMERS

M	A	R	A		L	I	K	E	N		H	A	N	S
A	M	E	N		I	N	A	W	E		E	X	I	T
D	O	U	G	L	A	S	F	I	R		A	L	L	Y
C	E	N	S	O	R		K	N	O	R	R			
A	B	E	T	S		T	A	G		A	T	L	A	S
P	A	D		E	K	E			R	E	B	A	T	E
		G	R	E	N	A	D	E		U	R	A	L	
	H	O	R	S	E	S	H	O	E	C	R	A	B	
M	E	T	A		L	E	A	D	S	I	N			
S	A	T	Y	R	S		G	E	N		P	A	S	
G	R	O	W	N		S	H	E		E	V	E	N	T
	H	A	S	T	O		E	M	E	R	G	E		
A	Q	U	A		C	A	S	P	I	A	N	S	E	A
C	U	R	L		A	L	T	E	R		D	I	L	L
T	O	N	E		B	L	A	Z	E		S	A	S	S

69 GROUNDED FOREVER

The quote: In her witchcraft trial, Joan of Arc was also charged with disobeying her parents.

The clue answers:

A. CALAIS
B. ROTATION
C. FLOWER
D. THATCHER
E. ARCHERY
F. GANDHI
G. BENJI
H. SWEAT
I. CARPING
J. SWORDFISH

70 A.K.A. HIS NIBS

a. "High muck-a-muck" comes from the Chinook phrase for "plenty to eat."

73 SEX-CESS STORIES

1. Women need a reason to have sex. Men just need a place.
2. It's been so long since I've had sex, I've forgotten who ties up whom.
3. It isn't premarital sex if you have no intention of getting married.

75 I LOVE THE '80s!

1988
1985
1981
1986
1982
1989
1987
1984
1980
1983

72 SHOW ME THE MONEY

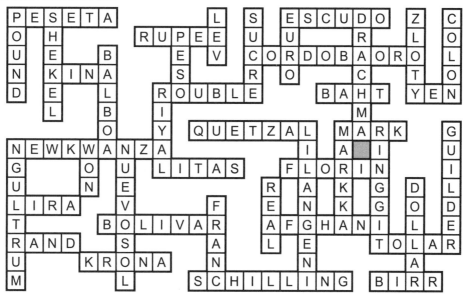

Afghani (Afghanistan)
Baht (Thailand)
Balboa (Panama)
Birr (Ethiopia)
Bolivar (Venezuela)
Colon (Costa Rica, El Salvador)
Cordoba Oro (Nicaragua)
Dollar (USA, Canada, Fiji, and
    lots of other places)
Drachma (Greece)
Escudo (Portugal)
Euro (European Union)
Florin (Aruba)
Franc (France)
Guilder (Netherlands, Netherland
    Antilles, Suriname)

Kina (New Guinea)
Krona (Iceland, Sweden)
Lev (Bulgaria)
Lilangeni (Swaziland)
Lira (Italy, Turkey)
Litas (Lithuania)
Mark (Germany)
Markka (Finland)
New kwanza (Angola)
Ngultrum (Bhutan)
Nuevo sol (Peru)
Peseta (Spain)
Peso (Mexico, Cuba and more)
Pound (Britain, Egypt, Lebanon,
    and more)
Quetzal (Guatemala)

Rand (South Africa)
Real (Brazil)
Ringgit (Malaysia)
Riyal (Saudi Arabia)
Rouble (Russia)
Rupee (India, Pakistan, Nepal)
Schilling (Austria)
Shekel (Israel)
Sucre (Ecuador)
Tolar (Slovenia)
Won (North and South Korea)
Yen (Japan)
Zloty (Poland)

74 HOMONYMICAL MARRIAGE

78 PARLEZ-VOUS DOUBLESPEAK?

1. Sliced
2. Girdle
3. Janitor
4. Dry cleaner
5. Toilet paper
6. Car mechanic
7. Toothpick
8. Checkout clerk
9. Dogcatcher
10. Greeting cards
11. Gravedigger
12. Stock market crash
13. Newspaper deliverer
14. Repairman

76 GET A JOB

The leftover letters spell: Dog-Food Dough Mixer, Soiled Linen Distributor, Subassembly Assembler, Fish Flipper, and Pantyhose-Crotch-Closing Machine Operator.

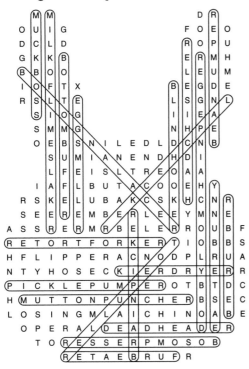

77 IS DE WIDDLE FELLA HUNGWY?

The acrostic: Is dinner ready yet, Mom?

The quote: Baby blue whale calves drink mother's milk—and how! A baby blue whale is the fastest-growing organism on earth, putting on a staggering two hundred twenty pounds per day in its first weeks of life.

The answer words:

A. IGGY POP
B. SILAGE
C. DE BRUNHOFF
D. IN THE BUFF
E. NAGGED
F. NAIL-BITER
G. ERNEST TUBB
H. ROWAN
I. ROBERT ALTMAN
J. EVENTIDE
K. AT WIT'S END
L. DAWDLES
M. YOUNGSTOWN
N. YELLOWISH
O. ERIC KNIGHT
P. TARAWA
Q. MISTAKES
R. OSHKOSH
S. MURPHY'S LAW

79 IN THE TRENCHES

C	A	L	C	■	H	I	M	O	M	■	A	D	A	R
O	M	A	R	■	U	S	O	F	A	■	S	E	M	I
N	O	M	A	N	S	L	A	N	D	■	I	S	B	N
T	R	E	B	E	K	■	T	O	E	N	A	I	L	S
■	■	B	A	S	K	■	T	H	Y	■	G	E	E	■
J	A	P	E	■	I	D	E	A	M	A	N	■	■	■
I	T	O	■	A	B	E	E	■	S	P	L	A	T	S
G	O	I	N	G	O	V	E	R	T	H	E	T	O	P
S	I	N	N	E	R	■	R	U	E	S	■	E	R	A
■	T	W	I	N	B	E	D	■	■	A	D	I	N	■
A	R	B	■	S	L	O	■	E	M	I	R	■	■	■
F	U	L	L	M	O	O	N	■	I	T	C	H	E	S
T	R	A	P	■	S	H	E	L	L	S	H	O	C	K
R	A	N	G	■	E	O	S	I	N	■	E	L	H	I
A	L	K	A	■	R	O	S	I	E	■	R	O	O	T

80 BACK TO THE TRENCHES

E	T	H	■	C	L	A	I	R	■	M	A	C	R	O
M	O	I	■	P	I	N	T	O	■	O	C	H	E	R
B	O	T	T	L	E	D	S	U	N	S	H	I	N	E
E	L	M	O	■	■	■	G	E	T	I	N	T	O	■
D	E	E	P	K	I	M	C	H	I	■	L	A	S	S
■	■	■	S	A	R	A	H	■	L	I	L	■	■	■
A	L	L	■	B	O	X	E	D	■	C	E	D	A	R
R	E	D	Z	O	N	E	■	E	P	I	S	O	D	E
C	E	L	E	B	■	D	A	F	O	E	■	T	E	X
■	■	P	S	I	■	P	O	S	S	E	■	■	■	■
C	C	U	P	■	B	O	U	G	H	T	G	U	T	S
R	O	P	E	D	I	N	■	■	■	■	O	P	A	L
A	P	P	L	E	S	A	U	C	E	E	N	E	M	A
S	T	E	I	N	■	I	T	A	L	Y	■	N	E	T
H	O	R	N	S	■	R	E	T	I	E	■	D	R	Y

81 ELEPHANTS PLEASE STAY IN YOUR CAR

1 – f (At a convalescent home: For the Sick and Tired of the Episcopal Church)
2 – a (At a drycleaner: 38 Years on the Same Spot)
3 – i (At a McDonald's: Parking for Drive-Thru Service Only)
4 – c (In a department store: Bargain Basement Upstairs)
5 – h (In a hospital maternity ward: No Children Allowed)
6 – d (In a safari park: Elephants Please Stay in Your Car)
7 – b (In the offices of a loan company: Ask About Our Plans for Owning Your Home)
8 – j (Next to a traffic light: This Light Never Turns Green)
9 – e (Outside a house: For Sale Buy Owner)
10 – g (Outside a photographer's studio: Have the Kids Shot for Dad From $24.95)

82 MORE SEX-CESS STORIES

1. Bisexuality immediately doubles your chances for a date on Saturday night.
2. Women might be able to fake orgasms, but men can fake a whole relationship.
3. Sex is one of the most wholesome, beautiful, and natural experiences money can buy.

83 I FOUND IT ON eBAY

Grandma: $1,000,300
Meaning of Life: $3.26
Melrose Place Pool Water: $7.99
Woodstock Air: $9,999,999
Crackers: $0.05
One Dollar: $0.67
Justin's French Toast: $3,154
My Dignity: $10.50

81 MYSTERY PLATE

Beans
Bread
Coffee
Crackers
Grape Nuts
Ammunition
Gun wadding
Battery acid
Dog biscuits
Shrapnel

85 GAMES PEOPLE PLAY

The leftover letters spell: To alter the run of the cards, you'll have to turn your chair around three times and walk around it three times.

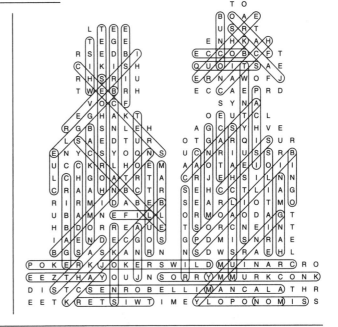

84 GRAVE HUMOR

P	H	A	S	E		S	H	I	N		N	O	A	H
R	E	R	U	N		T	O	N	E		E	L	M	O
O	N	C	E	I	W	A	S	N	T		L	I	N	T
			G	O	R	E		S	A	L	V	E	S	
S	L	A	M	M	E	R		T	A	D		E	S	P
A	E	N	E	A	S		C	O	L	D		R	I	O
L	E	I	S		R	O	D	E	O		T	A	T	
	T	H	E	N	I	W	A	S	N	O	W			
T	E	A		D	O	G	E	Y		M	I	L	O	
R	U	B		U	S	E	R		P	R	I	S	O	N
A	R	R		C	E	L		S	E	A	T	T	L	E
P	A	Y	M	E	R		F	I	L	M				
E	S	A	U		I	A	I	N	T	A	G	A	I	N
Z	I	N	G		N	I	L	E		D	A	N	C	E
E	A	T	S		G	R	E	W		A	G	N	E	W

87 THE HUMAN ZOO

G	U	T	S		B	R	A		E	F	L	A	T
E	P	E	E		E	U	R		P	O	O	L	E	D
E	L	E	P	H	A	N	T		I	L	L	I	N	I
S	I	T	T	I	N	G	D	U	C	K		S	S	A
E	T	H		R	I	S	E	N		T	O	T	E	M
			E	E	E		C	I	G	A	R			
K	I	E	V		T	O	T	A	L	P	I	G	S
A	T	P	E	A	C	E		E	Y	E	H	O	L	E
L	Y	I	N	G	R	A	T	S		A	N	O	X
		L	E	T	B	E		D	O	N				
F	L	O	Y	D		A	A	R	O	N		R	S	A
L	Y	S		B	I	G	C	H	I	C	K	E	N	S
U	S	O	P	E	N		H	O	N	E	Y	B	E	E
B	O	L	T	E	D		E	N	G		L	A	V	A
	L	E	A	F	Y		R	E	S		E	R	A	T

86 DANCELY POPULATED

The Time Warp is danced in *The Rocky Horror Picture Show*: "…let's do the Time Warp again!"

88 BLONDE AMBITION

1. I was looking up at the big sign that says Hollywood, and I thought, "Wouldn't it be great if someday I could jerk that big ol' H down and put a D there to make it Dollywood?"
2. I feel good and I don't look bad for my age. I look like a cartoon anyway, so what difference does it make? I'm always gonna look like Dolly, like a freak. But I'm the best freak I've ever been.
3. I know myself and what I want, and what I don't want is to go out to pasture. I have agreed to pose nude for *Penthouse* on my one hundredth birthday.
4. Bluegrass is the music I would have been doing all along if I could have made a living at it. It's like I had to get rich in order to sing like I was poor.

89 TOM SWIFT AND HIS AMAZING MENAGERIE

1 – a ("Get back here with that tennis ball!" Tom barked.)
2 – i ("Hey, don't get too close to that turtle!" Tom snapped.)
3 – g ("How many times have I told you not to ride that horse?" Tom nagged.)
4 – b ("I feel so sorry for that poor beached whale," Tom blubbered.)
5 – e ("I hate going bird-hunting," Tom groused.)
6 – c ("I much prefer bird-watching," Tom chirped.)
7 – h ("I warned you not to tease the lions!" Tom roared.)
8 – d ("I've been just as busy as a bee," Tom droned.)
9 – f ("My dad's name is Billy and my mother's name is Nanny," Tom kidded.)
10 – j ("There are all sorts of beasts of burden, you know. In Peru, they've got their llamas, and in Tibet…" Tom yakked.)

89 THE SAME OLD MATH

The quote: "As long as there is algebra, there will be prayer in school."—Larry Miller
The clue answers:
A. ALLENTOWN
B. THRILLER
C. LEGREE
D. ORRIS
E. SHARPIE
F. LARAMIE
G. SCROLL
H. GABBY HAYES

97 ROTTEN TO THE CORPS?

The quote: A group of frogs is called an army; a group of army officers is called a mess.
The clue answers:
A. GLORIOUS
B. MACRAME
C. SPINOFFS
D. MORSEL
E. PARAGUAY
F. SCARCELY
G. FORAGE
H. DAFFODILS

90 FLUGIE & FRIENDS

"Gobbledygook," a close relative of "bafflegab" and "Pentagonese," was coined by Representative Maury Maverick in 1944 while he was chairman of the Smaller War Plant Committee in Congress. He later explained that he was thinking of the gobbling of turkeys while they strutted pompously.

91 SCRABBLE BABBLE

1 – o (AA: Rough, cindery lava)
2 – m AE: One)
3 – s (AI: A three-toed sloth)
4 – e (AL: An East Indian tree)
5 – d (BA: The eternal soul in Egyptian mythology)
6 – q (JO: A sweetheart)
7 – p (KA: The spiritual self of a human being in Egyptian religion)
8 – c (LI: A Chinese unit of distance)
9 – b (NE: Born with the name of)
10 – h (OD: A hypothetical force of natural power)
11 – t (OE: A whirlwind off the Faeroe Islands)
12 – r (OP: A style of abstract art)
13 – a (OS: A bone)
14 – k (UT: The old name for the first tone "do" in the scale sequence do, re, mi, fa, etc.)
15 – j (XU: A monetary unit of Vietnam)
16 – n (ID: A part of the psyche)
17 – l (NA: No; not)
18 – i (OM: A mantra used in contemplation of ultimate reality)
19 – g (PE: A Hebrew letter)
20 – f (XI: A Greek letter)

91 UNCLE OSCAR'S BIG NIGHT #3

1 – c (SEAN PENN, *MYSTIC RIVER*)
2 – d (KATHARINE HEPBURN, *THE LION IN WINTER*)
3 – e (ROD STEIGER, *IN THE HEAT OF THE NIGHT*)
4 – b (INGRID BERGMAN, *GASLIGHT*)
5 – a (GLENDA JACKSON, *A TOUCH OF CLASS*)

95 *JEOPARDY!*

How It Came to Be
Merv and Juliann Griffin invented the show. Says Merv, "I mentioned how much I liked the old quiz shows, but reminded her of the scandals. 'Why not give them the answers to start with?' she kidded." The *Jeopardy!* format was born.

How It Got Its Name
We called the game *What's the Question?* but a network executive commented, "The game needs more 'jeopardies'," situations where the player risks losing it all. Goodbye, *What's the Question?*, hello *Jeopardy!*

Are You *Jeopardy!* Material?
Every year, two hundred fifty thousand people apply for an audition. Only fifteen thousand are chosen for the initial screening exam, and only fifteen hundred qualify to become contestants. Then, only five hundred actually make it on the air.

92 THAT'S ABOUT THE SIZE OF IT

94 TAKE A LODE OFF

The acrostic: Rich—and getting richer
The quote: The first U.S. Gold Rush wasn't in California. Surprisingly, it was North Carolina. It started when a boy found a seventeen-pound nugget on his father's farm. The lode supplied all the gold for the nation's mint for the next twenty-six years.
The clue answers:
A. RIN TIN TIN
B. IMPORTANT
C. CHIEF OF STAFF
D. HOWARD HUGHES
E. ANITA SHREVE
F. NULLIFY
G. DALLAS TEXAS
H. GETTYSBURG
I. ESTATE TAX
J. TWO-SPOTS
K. TORONTO
L. INSINUATION
M. NEWLYWEDS
N. GRIDS
O. RUFF AND REDDY
P. INTERPRETS
Q. CHARLIE SHEEN
R. HOPALONG
S. ELIHU THOMSON
T. RUNNEL

93 **TRULY DROOLY**

The leftover letters spell: "Slide your jive" means "to talk freely." "Gas" means "to engage in idle conversation."

Word List:

AQUARIUM: A house or apartment

BAGPIPE: Someone who talks too much

BEAGLE: A hot dog

BEAT: Broke

BEEFBURGER: Another name for hamburger, which was considered misleading

BOOGIEMAN: A jivester

BRIGHTY: Very smart

BRUSH: A moustache

BUZZ: To kiss

COGS: Sunglasses

CRAZY: Wonderful

DATE BAIT: A good-looking girl

DEAD PRESIDENTS: Money

DEUCE OF HAIRCUTS: Two weeks

FALL: To be convicted of a crime

GOBBLEDYGOOK: Inflated, unintelligible language

HARDWARE: Glitzy jewelry

HERD: A pack of Camels

HINGES: Elbows

IVORY-DOME: An intellectual

JACKSON: A form of address like "Buddy" or "Mac"

JUMP: To dance to swing music

PEEK-A-BOO: A woman's hairstyle in which the hair falls over one eye, but not the other

ROBOMB: Short for "robot bomb," the name given to German V-1 rockets before such weapons became known as "guided missiles"

ROLLING: Wealthy

ROOST: A house or apartment

SHORTIE: A prefix for extra-short garments—shortie skirts, shortie pajamas, etc. It was eventually replaced by "mini."

SLIMLINE: Sleek styling of consumer products such as radios and televisions, inspired by streamlined trains and planes

SQUILLION: An unspecified, very large number, like zillion

SQUIRREL FEVER: A romantic urge

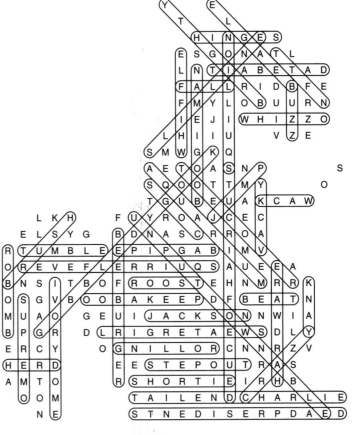

STEP OUT: To parachute from an airplane

SUPREMO: The highest military officer in the land, kind of like "generalissimo"

SWEATER GIRL: A movie starlet who wears tight sweaters to call attention to her bust

TAIL-END CHARLIE: The person who mans the gun in the tail end of a World War II bomber

TOECOVER: A cheap, useless item given as a gift

TTFN: Good-bye (short for "Ta-ta for now!")

TUMBLE: To dance

UNPUTDOWNABLE: Just what it sounds like—a book or magazine article that's so good you can't put it down

VACKY: An evacuee. During World War II, British women and children moved from the cities to the safer countryside.

WACK: An eccentric person

WHIFFLE: A crew cut

WHIZZO: Wonderful

YANK: A dentist

---

97 **ALABAMA KLEENEX REDUX**

1 – b (Arkansas fire extinguisher: a chamber pot)

2 – d (California collar: a hangman's noose)

3 – e (Cincinnati oysters: pickled pigs' feet)

4 – j (Kansas sheep dip: whiskey)

5 – h (Kentucky breakfast: steak and bourbon—and a dog to eat the steak)

6 – c (Mississippi marbles: dice)

7 – f (Oklahoma rain: a sandstorm)

8 – a (Texas turkey: an armadillo)

9 – g (Tucson bed: sleeping on the ground without cover)

10 – i (Vermont charity: sympathy, but little else)

98 BRITISH SPOKEN HERE

The leftover letters spell: "That was a bloody Masonic handshake, you sly old wog," on meeting His Holiness Pope John Paul II at the Vatican in 1988.

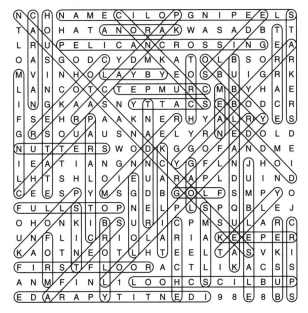

AFTERS (dessert)
ANORAK (parka)
ARGY-BARGY (heated argument)
BROLLY (umbrella)
BUBBLE AND SQUEAK (cabbage/potato dish)
BUSKER (street performer)
CARAVAN (motor home)
CHAT UP (chat flirtatiously)
CLING FILM (plastic wrap)
CONKERS (horse chestnuts)
COOKER (oven)
CRECHE (day-care center)
CRISPS (potato chips)
CRUMPET (attractive woman)
DODDLE (easy task)
FIRST FLOOR (second floor)
FLOG (sell)

FORM (grade in school)
FULL STOP (period)
GAFFER (boss)
GAOL (jail)
HOUSING ESTATE (tenement)
IDENTITY PARADE (lineup)
JUMBLE SALE (yard sale)
KEEPER (curator)
LAY-BY (rest stop)
LOLLIPOP LADY (crossing guard)
LOUNGE (living room)
MEAN (stingy)
MINDER (bodyguard)
NAUGHTS AND CROSSES (tic-tac-toe)
NUTTERS (kooks)
PANDA CAR (police car)
PARALYTIC (drunk)

PELICAN CROSSING (pedestrian crossing)
PLONK (cheap wine)
PUBLIC SCHOOL (private school)
REDUNDANT (newly unemployed)
SCATTY (scatterbrained)
SKINT (broke)
SLEEPING POLICEMAN (speed bump)
SLIDE (barrette)
SMALLS (underwear)
STARKERS (naked)
TAILBACK (traffic jam)
TELLY (television)
TERRACE (bleachers)
TORCH (flashlight)
YOBBO (hooligan)

96 TOUR DE FRANCE

103 G WHIZ

a. Gorelick

99 SIX OF ONE...

Nobel Prize Categories: Economics
Wives of Henry VIII: Jane Seymour
Rodeo Contests: Bull riding
Parts of the Circulatory System: Capillaries
Categories of Dog Breeds: Terrier
Layers of the Earth: Outer core
Branches of the U.S. Armed Forces: National Guard
Grades of Meat: Choice
Hockey Positions: Center
Sinister Six (Spider-Man's Enemies): Dr. Octopus
Main Vocal Ranges of the Human Voice: Baritone
Six Flags Over Texas: Texas

102 LOOPY LEXICON

1 – f (To give up all hope of ever having a flat stomach)
2 – b (A missing golf peg)
3 – j (Where Noah kept his bees)
4 – e (The person upon whom someone coughs)
5 – d (Appalled over how much weight you have gained)
6 – g (What a guy in a boat does)
7 – c (A person who sprinkles his conversation with Yiddish expressions)
8 – i (What you see from the top of the Eiffel Tower)
9 – a (A Jamaican proctologist)
10 – h (What trees do in the spring)

100 HAIL TO THE CHIEFS

1 – c (No one.)
2 – c (He had laryngitis.)
3 – b (Ronald Reagan)
4 – a (He was a stray; she found him at a gas station.)
5 – b (Lincoln)
6 – b (Jefferson)
7 – c (Saw them holding hands.)
8. John F. Kennedy, Lyndon Johnson, Richard Nixon, Gerald Ford, Jimmy Carter, George H.W. Bush
9 – b (Roosevelt was scheduled to meet with a Methodist minister who was working as a missionary in Rome and speaking out against the papacy. Vatican officials insisted that T.R. at least meet with the pope first, but Roosevelt refused, saying that the pope did not have the right to dictate the itinerary of an American citizen.)
10. 1-c; 2-a; 3-b
11. John Quincy Adams
12. Woodrow Wilson
13. Dwight Eisenhower
14. Abraham Lincoln
15. Lyndon Johnson
16. George Washington
17. Benjamin Harrison
18. Jimmy Carter
19. Harry Truman
20. Dwight Eisenhower
21. Franklin Roosevelt
22. Richard Nixon
23. Ronald Reagan
24. Andrew Johnson
25. The Johnsons: Lyndon Baines, Lady Bird, Lynda Bird, and Luci Baines Johnson
26. Harry Truman
27. Betty Ford
28. Jackie Kennedy
29. Herbert and Lou Hoover
30. Jimmy and Rosalynn Carter

105 WOULD WE LIE TO YOU AGAIN?

1 – c (The name derives from the candy being "scotched" into squares.)
2 – b (The original dumbbell was an exercise machine that mimicked the bell-ringing device.)
3 – b (It's an anglicized form of vlie market.)
4 – a (It derives from panch, meaning five.)
5 – c (It derives from fawney rig, an old con game.)

102 YOU MEAN LIKE THIS ONE?

The quote: A study by the Department of Veterans Affairs Medical Center in Vermont found that studies are often misleading.
The clue answers:
A. MUTANT
B. EMBARRASSMENT
C. DELIGHTFUL
D. UNDERSTATED
E. NOVICE
F. DETERMINATION
G. AFFIDAVIT
H. TANNERS
I. COFFEE SHOP
J. YESTERDAY

103 THE TALENTED MISS AMERICA

The fakes are 1970 (Miss California) and 1982 (Miss Hawaii).

104 CAN WE TALK?

1. I wish I had a twin so I could know what I would look like without plastic surgery.
2. I hate housework. You make the beds, you wash the dishes, and six months later you have to start all over again.
3. My parents hated me. They said to me, "Why can't you be like the girl next door?" We lived next door to a cemetery.

106 OLD-FASHIONED GIRLS

The leftover letters spell: Never lend your car to anyone to whom you have given birth. (Erma Bombeck)

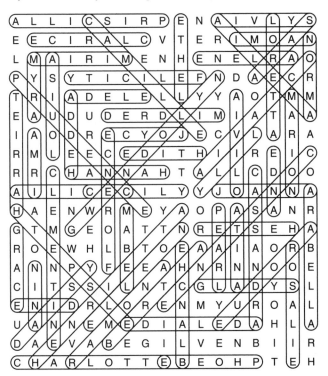

107 OLD-FASHIONED BOYS

The leftover letters spell: Insanity is hereditary. You can get it from your children. (Sam Levenson)

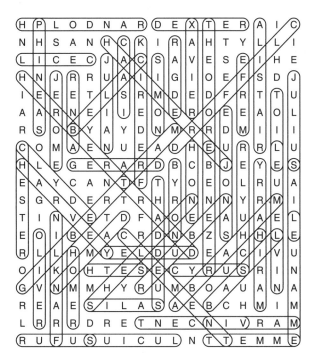

108 WHERE AM I?

26 Across is Concord, New Hampshire; 85 Across is Lincoln, Nebraska.

110 GOING TO EXTREMES

c. "Bitter end" is an old sailing term.

110 IT'S OIL IN THE WAY YOU SAY IT

1 – f (Boll weevil: An oilfield newbie who is given a hard time—and the worst jobs to do.)
2 – j (Bulldog: A tool used to fetch broken pipe out of the hole.)
3 – e (Christmas tree: A tall and cluttered setup of valves, fittings, spools, gauges, and so on that's often painted green.)
4 – c (Doghouse: A little shack at the drill site that typically doubles as an office, supply closet, and place to hang provocative calendars of girls in bikinis holding oilfield tools.)
5 – d (Doodlebug: A person or device (like a divining rod) supposedly able to sniff out oil, gas, or precious minerals.)
6 – i (Monkeyboard: A small oil rig platform a derrick hand stands on when handling pipe.)
7 – b (Mousehole: A hole in the rig floor though which drilling pipe is fed.)
8 – h (Pebble pup: A field geologist's assistant; also a kid who collects rocks.)
9 – a (Rockhound: A field geologist.)
10 – g (Roughneck: Any member of a drilling crew.)

112 THAT'S WHY THEY CALL IT TRIVIA

1. c. Woods' ethnic background includes African-American, Thai, Chinese, and Indian.
2. They're all true.
3. b. a is true for Quentin Tarantino, and c is true for Bruce Springsteen.
4. True.
5. c. Audio Science is the son of Shannyn Sossamon and Dallas Clayton. Elijah Bob Patricius Guggi Q is the name of Bono's son. Geoffrey Crayon and Launcelot Wagstaffe were pseudonyms used by Washington Irving.
6. c.
7. b.
8. a and b are true.
9. b.
10. b.
11. b.
12. a.
13. c.
14. a. Lowe appeared in Super 8 movies made by classmates Penn and Sheen.
15. They're all true.
16. b.

111 LOCATION, LOCATION, LOCATION

Grand Fenwick (country in *The Mouse That Roared*)
Greyhawk (D&D game world)
Honalee (home of Puff the Magic Dragon)
Knots Landing (TV show)
Lake Wobegon (Garrison Keillor's hometown)
Manderley (*Rebecca* by Daphne DuMaurier)
Middlemarch (English town in a George Eliot novel)
Mongo (Flash Gordon's planet)
Mu (*The Lost Continent of Mu* by James Churchward)
Naboo (planet in *Star Wars*)
Narnia (*The Chronicles of Narnia* by C. S. Lewis)
Neverland (land in *Peter Pan*)
Land of Nod (where sleepy kids go at night)
Oceania (nation-state in *1984*)
Ork (Mork's home planet)
Oz (*The Wonderful Wizard of Oz*)
Santa Teresa (fictional hometown of Sue Grafton's sleuth Kinsey Millhone)
Shangri-la (magical land in a James Hilton novel)
Spoon River (*Spoon River Anthology* by Edgar Lee Masters)
Tara (*Gone With the Wind* by Margaret Mitchell)
Tuna (Texas town in the play and movie *Greater Tuna*)
Twin Peaks (town in the series created by David Lynch)
Utopia (book by Sir Thomas More)
Vulcan (Mr. Spock's home planet on *Star Trek*)
Wisteria Lane (street in *Desperate Housewives*)
Yoknapatawpha (county in William Faulkner novels)

Adano (Italian town in Hersey's *A Bell for Adano*)
Avalon (Arthurian legend)
Bacteria (country in *The Great Dictator*)
Brigadoon (Scottish village that materializes every 100 years)
Camelot (King Arthur's castle)
Centerburg (Homer Price's hometown in *Centerburg Tales*)
Derry (Maine town in Stephen King stories)
El Dorado (legendary land of gold)
Elbonia (country in the comic *Dilbert*)
Elysia (land of fallen warriors in Greek legend)
Erewhon (novel by Samuel Butler; an anagram of "nowhere")
Funkytown (1980 hit song by Lipps, Inc.)
Genovia (country in *The Princess Diaries*)

114 SCHOOL'S OUT FOREVER

116 MAKING HEADLINES

1. BODY SEARCH REVEALS $4,000 IN CRACK
2. DR. TACKETT GIVES TALK ON MOON
3. FEDERAL AGENTS RAID GUN SHOP, FIND WEAPONS
4. GREEKS FINE HOOKERS
5. MAN GOES BERSERK IN CAR SALESROOM, MANY VOLVOS HURT
6. MEN PICKY ABOUT NOSES
7. NEW HOUSING FOR ELDERLY NOT YET DEAD
8. ROBBER HOLDS UP ALBERT'S HOSIERY
9. SHOUTING MATCH ENDS TEACHER'S HEARING
10. YELLOW SNOW STUDIED TO TEST NUTRITION

116 SUBURBAN LEGENDS

1. **False**. There are hundreds of straight lines in nature, most notably in crystal formations and snowflake patterns.

2. **False**. First of all there is no Eskimo language, because there is no one group of people called "Eskimos." The word misleadingly refers to dozens of tribal groups living in the northern parts of North America. Most speak different languages, and they typically have less than a dozen words that mean snow.

3. **False**. What may look like grooming is actually removing dead skin (but they do eat it).

4. **False**. Suicides are pretty evenly dispersed throughout the year, but springtime actually has the most occurrences.

5. **False**. Although bats are similar to rodents they have more in common with primates (which include us) than they do with rodents.

6. **False**. There's no law anywhere that guarantees this. It's just a courtesy or privilege offered, not a legal right. (Some jurisdictions might even let you make a second phone call.)

7. **False**. There was a Channel One at one time—in 1945, when the Federal Communications Commission first allocated broadcast television frequencies. But later the FCC decided that TV was taking up too much bandwidth so Channel One was reassigned to use by mobile radios.

8. **True**. Recent studies suggest that smoking may slow the onset of Alzheimer's disease. In fact, nicotine injections significantly improved certain types of mental functioning in Alzheimer's patients.

9. **False**, mostly. At one time, back in the 1960s, some sets emitted excessive X-rays, but that problem has now been eliminated. As to the more recent concern of sitting too close to computer video display terminals, research continues. We'll let you know.

10. **True**. Eating a couple of poppy seed rolls or bagels can cause you to fail a routine drug test. Some drug testers and researchers claim they can separate "false positives" from the real thing, but this doesn't seem to be the case. If you get fired due to a borderline positive with no follow-up tests or corroborating signs of drug use, call a lawyer.

117 TILT!

The leftover letters spell: "I'd ask for a pinball machine, because with all that rocking back and forth, you'd probably be able to get a lot of free games."

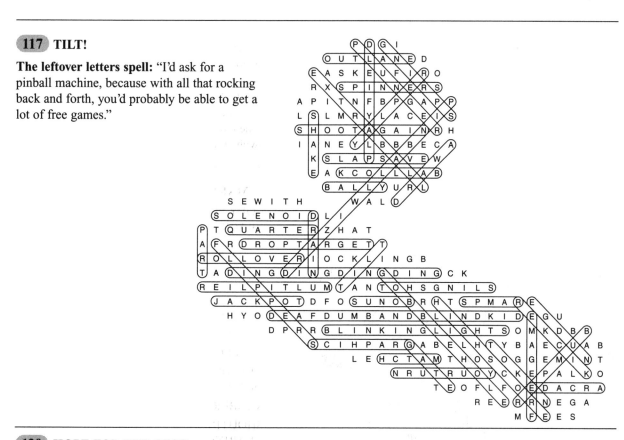

120 HOPE FOR THE BEST

1. Vice President Quayle thinks Roe vs. Wade are two ways to cross the Potomac.
2. The last time I played golf with President Ford he hit a birdie—and an eagle, a moose, an elk, an aardvark ....
3. Ronald Reagan is not a typical politician because he doesn't know how to lie, cheat, and steal. He's always had an agent do that.

118 WHICH HUNT

1. **The planet Jupiter** is larger than all the other planets put together.
2. Believe it or not, **rubies** are far more valuable.
3. You'll be relieved to hear that there are more **Americans who have visited a dentist at least once** (60%).
4. 95% of people put on **the left sock** first.
5. Forest fires move faster **uphill**.
6. It's much more likely to **survive** being struck by lightning; only 10% of the time is it fatal.
7. It's a close call, but there are more **people with non-type-O blood** (about 54%).
8. WITSEC has more **witnesses in drug cases**. Only 1 in 6 witnesses is connected to the Mafia nowadays.
9. **The U.S.** is bigger than the Sahara Desert, but only by about 100,000 square miles.
10. More children are accidentally poisoned by **toxic houseplants** than household chemicals.
11. **Denominations higher than one** account for 55% of the printed bills.
12. **Magnetism** is stronger than gravity.
13. **Super Mario Bros.** (40 million) has a slight edge over Tetris (33 million).
14. While there certainly are a lot of tattooed NBA players, **tattoo-less players** consistute the majority (70%).
15. The average traffic light is **red** 66% of the time.
16. **Girls' hearts** beat faster than boys' hearts.
17. **Cold gasoline** provides better gas mileage.
18. On average, a pet **guinea pig** will live twice as long as a pet hamster.
19. Hollywood makes more money from **video rentals** than ticket sales.
20. **Computer CD-ROMs** spin up to 100 times per second, compared to a music CD's 10 times per second.
21. The IQ of an **average stutterer** is 14 points higher than a non-stutterer.
22. 71% of **college-educated women** breastfeed, as opposed to 44% of non-college-educated women.
23. 75% of employees **attend** the office Christmas party.
24. **Married men** are twice as likely to be obese as single men.
25. The average person generates $2\frac{1}{2}$ quarts of **sweat** daily, compared to only 2 quarts of saliva.
26. You're more likely to be stung by a bee on a **windy day**.
27. The average person spends two years of life **on the phone**, and only six months on the toilet. (This could change, of course, if people started buying more Uncle John's books.)
28. It requires 21 pounds of milk to make **one pound of butter**, but only 10 pounds of milk to make one pound of cheese.
29. **Nonsmokers** dream more at night.
30. The odds that a stage or screen star is using a **stage name** is 75%.
31. It's a tie—there are eight of each on a dollar bill.
32. **The U.S.** has more time zones—China, despite its larger size, has only one time zone.
33. **Democrats** are more likely to own cats.
34. **"Too busy"** is the most popular reason for not voting.
35. **Falling from the peak of Mount Everest to the base** would take an estimated 2.5 minutes. Traveling to the top floor of the CN Tower via elevator takes 58 seconds.
36. **A soda can** can hold 90 pounds per square inch of pressure, three times as much as a car tire.
37. 74% of Americans **make their bed every day**, whereas a mere 5% never make it. (Or at least, that's what they *say* they're doing when confronted by pollsters.)
38. **One first-class meal** costs the airline $50. The price tag for ten coach-class meals is $40.
39. Okay, so the **Empire State Building** is taller. But not by as much as you might think: only 265 feet.
40. A **stone at the North Pole** weighs slightly more than the same stone at the equator.

---

126 CHEESE, LOUISE!

clogged sinuses
Monroe, Wisconsin
fell an ox
the Postmaster General
retch
a clothespin and a gas mask

he had no sense of smell
smoked whitefish
"Best Snack in the World"
bribing the judges with beer
a tie

121 LISTOMANIA

1. The Three Musketeers
2. The three daughters of King Lear
3. The Three Wise Men
4. The three components of the psyche, according to Freud
5. The three Fates
6. The three gods of the Hindu Trinity
7. The four sections of a symphony orchestra
8. The Big Four, representing the U.S., Great Britain, France, and Italy at the Paris Peace Conference in 1919
9. The four Brontë siblings
10. The six Axis Powers of World War II
11. The works of the seven days of creation, according to the Bible
12. The Seven Hills of Rome
13. The Seven Deadly Sins
14. The Ten Plagues of Egypt
15. The Twelve Tribes of Israel
16. The Twelve Knights of the Round Table

122 FAMILIAR PHRASES

125 A MYSTERY SOLVED

The acrostic: Perry Mason and Company

The quote: As a youngster, author Erle Stanley Gardner subscribed to a boys' fiction magazine, *The Youth's Companion*, and learned a lot about writing from the stories he read in it. *The Youth's Companion* was published by...

The clue answers:

A. PINATA
B. EDMOND HOYLE
C. RUNABOUT
D. RENEE FLEMING
E. YELLOW CAB
F. MATTHEW
G. A CHORUS LINE
H. SIBERIA
I. OUTBOARD
J. NETSURF
K. ADRIEN BRODY
L. NURSING
M. DITTIES
N. COSINE
O. OSCAR NIGHT
P. MAZES
Q. PHOTO SHOOT
R. AUTOGRAPH
S. NASTY HABITS
T. YEASTY

124 TROUBLE AND STRIFE

Ass: Khyber Pass
Believe: Adam and Eve
Boots: Daisy Roots
Car: Jam Jar
Check: Gregory Peck
Crap: Pony and Trap
Dance: Kick and Prance
Daughter: Bricks and Mortar
Dead: Brown Bread
Deaf: Mutt and Jeff
Face: Boat Race
Feet: Plates of Meat
Flying Squad: Sweeney Todd
Hat: Tit for Tat

Head: Loaf of Bread
Jewelry: Tom-foolery
Judge: Barnaby Rudge
Kid: Dustbin Lid
Lies: Porky Pies
Lodger: Artful Dodger
Mate: China Plate
Moan: Darby and Joan
Money: Bread and Honey
Mouth: North and South
Pissed: Brahms and Liszt
Pocket: Sky Rocket
Pub: Rub-a-Dub
Rent: Duke of Kent

Road: Frog and Toad
Shirt: Dicky Dirt
Sister: Skin and blister
Soap: Bob Hope
Stairs: Apples and pears
Stink: Pen and ink
Suit: Whistle and flute
Tea: Rosie Lee
Ten: Cock and Hen
Turd: Richard the Third
Windy: Mork and Mindy
Word: Dicky Bird

127 TOTALLY TEXAS

The leftover letters spell: Mexican Free-Tailed Bat, Prickly Pear Cactus, Petrified Palmwood, Lightning Whelk

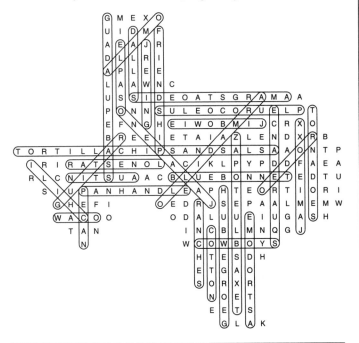

128 WHO SAID THAT?

136 WRIGHT AGAIN

1. I got food poisoning today. I don't know when I'll use it.
2. I have just received my degree in Calcium Anthropology—the study of milkmen.
3. Do you think that when they asked George Washington for ID that he just whipped out a quarter?

130 YOU KNOW THE OLD SAYING

Crazy as a loon: Loons are a symbol of the North American wilderness—and perfectly sane. The idea of their being "crazy" comes from the loon's tremolo call, which sounds like a strange laugh, but can be used to greet other loons or signal worry or alarm.

Strong as a horse: Horses have fragile legs and feet for their weight and size. This can make them prone to injury and lameness. If you've ever seen an ox at work, you'll know that "strong as an ox" is much more appropriate.

The noble male lion: The King of Beasts is actually something of a bum. His mighty roar is used to scare game in the direction of his mate, who is the real hunter. While the males sit around looking brave and noble, it's actually the female lions in the pride who do all the hunting.

132 TO YOUR HEALTH!

The acrostic: Invention of Dixie Cups
The quote: Because the inventor had in mind a disposable water cup that wouldn't carry germs, he called his invention "health cups." Luckily, his office happened to be in the same building as the Dixie Doll Company. Voilà!

The clue answers:
A. IMPETUOUS
B. NEEDLES
C. VILLA
D. EDDY DUCHIN
E. NOB HILL
F. TOBACCO
G. INFINITI
H. OVALTINE
I. NEON LIGHTS
J. OUTWIT
K. FENWAY PARK
L. DABBLED
M. INCHED AHEAD
N. XEROGRAPHY
O. IN THE CHIPS
P. ESCAPADE
Q. CELESTE
R. UMA THURMAN
S. PHIL SILVERS
T. STOMACH

131 EUREKA!

Archimedes (water screw, determined pi)
Charles Babbage (computer precursor)
Alexander G. Bell (telephone)
Karl Benz (gas-fueled car)
Louis Braille (alphabet for the blind)
Luther Burbank (Idaho potato)
Nolan Bushnell (Pong video game)
George W. Carver (peanut products)
Samuel Colt (revolver)
Seymour Cray (supercomputer)
Thomas A. Edison (phonograph and more)
Gustave Eiffel (steel lattice construction)
Philo T. Farnsworth (basic principles of TV, at age 13)
George W. Ferris (amusement wheel)
Henry Ford (assembly line)
Benjamin Franklin (lightning rod, bifocals)
R. Buckminster Fuller (geodesic dome)
Robert Fulton (commercial steamboating)
Bill Gates (PC software)
Elias Howe (sewing machine)
Robert Jarvik (artificial heart)
Hedy Lamarr (secret code for U.S. military)
Leonardo da Vinci (parachute, swing bridge, catapult)
Charles Macintosh (rubberized cloth – for raincoats, e.g.)
Guglielmo Marconi (radio & telegraph transmission)
Samuel Morse (telegraph alphabet code)
Alfred Nobel (dynamite)

Elisha G. Otis (elevator braking system)
Louis Pasteur (process to destroy germs)
Erno Rubik (cube game)
Igor Sikorsky (helicopter)
Levi Strauss (denim jeans)
Edward Teller (H-bomb)
Nikola Tesla (x-ray technology, alternating current, and more)
Earl S. Tupper (plastic food storage ware)
Alessandro Volta (voltaic pile – predecessor to the battery)
James Watt (steam engine improvements)
George Westinghouse (automatic electric block signal)
Eli Whitney (cotton gin)
Frank Zamboni (ice resurfacing machine)

134 IT'S A LIVING

C	A	R	P	E		A	H	A	B		J	A	W		T	E	C	A	T	E	
A	V	O	I	D		S	A	L	A		A	L	A		A	G	A	T	H	A	
B	R	I	T	I	S	H	S	O	L	D	I	E	R		I	G	L	O	O	S	
L	I	L	I	T	H		B	E	T	A		S	T	A	P	H		P	R	Y	
E	L	S	E		I	R	E		I	S	M		M	E	E	K					
		D	A	N	C	E	S	C	H	O	O	L	P	I	A	N	I	S	T		
R	N	S		B	E	A	N	E		E	S	T	E	E		D	E	N	I	M	
E	A	T	M	E		R	A	D		T	A	R	P		E	D	G	E			
A	C	R	E		H	A	I	T	I		R	E	F	E	R	S		U	S	N	
C	H	I	C	K	E	N	F	A	R	M	E	R		I	T	A	L			
T	O	P	C	O	A	T	S		O	A	T		C	O	M	I	N	G	T	O	
	P	A	N	T		J	U	N	I	O	R	S	U	R	G	E	O	N			
A	D	O		G	E	T	H	O	T		N	O	Y	E	S		I	N	G	E	
D	I	K	E		R	E	E	K		B	A	Z			C	O	C	O	A		
D	E	E	P	S		A	R	E	E	L		E	D	D	I	E		E	S	L	
S	T	R	E	E	T	C	A	R	C	O	N	D	U	C	T	O	R			
	E	C	R	U		O	T	O		S	I	E		U	S	D	A			
C	S	A		T	E	P	E	E		T	H	A	T		M	A	G	P	I	E	
H	A	R	M	O	N		S	C	H	O	O	L	M	I	S	T	R	E	S	S	
I	H	E	A	R	D		P	H	I		P	I	E	R		M	A	A	C	O	
C	L	A	S	S	Y		N	O	D		E	T	N	A		S	T	R	O	P	

137 SONS OF TOM SWIFTIES

1 – d ("Dat's de end of April," Tom said in dismay.)
2 – b ("I have a split personality," Tom said, being frank.)
3 – c ("I just came in through the door," Tom said, entranced.)
4 – j ("I'm crazy about hot dogs," Tom said with relish.)
5 – i ("I've been to Alabama, Wyoming, and everywhere in between," Tom stated.)
6 – h ("It's time for the second funeral," Tom rehearsed.)
7 – f ("Oops! There goes my hat!" Tom said off the top of his head.)
8 – e ("That just doesn't add up," Tom said, nonplussed.)
9 – a ("There's room for one more," Tom admitted.)
10 – g ("Where should I plant these water lilies?" Tom pondered.)

133 HEY, DADDY-O!

The leftover letters spell: "Real gone" means "amazing." "Subterranean" is a "hipster." "Sanitary" means "wonderful."

AD-LIB: To play the field

BEATNIK: A member of the artistic "beat" generation

BIG TICKLE: Something funny

BLOW YOUR JETS: Get angry

BOTTLE: Guts. A person who "loses their bottle" loses their nerve.

BUCKET BAGS: Purses shaped like a bucket

CAST AN EYEBALL: Take a look

CHARIOT: Car

CHROME-PLATED: Dressed-up

CLASSY CHASSIS: Nice body

COCA-COLONIZATION: Refers to the inroads that American commercial products, such as Coca-Cola, made around the words in the 1950s

COOTIES: Nonexistent germs

CUBE: Nerd

CUT THE CHEESE: Fart

DRAINPIPES: Tight pants with straight legs

FLABTABS: Ears

HI SI: High society

IGGLE: Persuade

INTOXIMETER: What Breathalyzers were called before that term was invented in 1960

KNUCKLE SANDWICH: A punch in the face

LARGE CHARGE: Something that's wonderful

LUMPY: Okay, not great

MADE IN THE SHADE: Assured of success

MAKE THE SCENE: Attend an event

MENTAL CASE: A weirdo

NERD: A social outcast

NOWHERE: Inferior

PANIC: Something that's very funny

PASSION PIT: A drive-in movie

PEEPIE-CREEPIE: A portable TV camera used to film in the field (derived from walkie-talkie)

PUNK OUT: Back down from a fight

RABBIT: Talk continuously; babble

RAGTOP: A convertible

SILVER JEFF: A nickel (it has Thomas Jefferson on it)

SIN BIN: Another name for the penalty box that hockey players have to sit in when they break the rules

SKIJAMAS: Pajamas that look like a ski suit

SLIP: Give, as in "Slip me five"

SMAZE: A combination of smoke and haze; similar to smog, a combination of smoke and fog

SUDSABLE: Washable with soap and water, as opposed to requiring dry-cleaning

TATT: Garbage; junk

TONY CURTIS: A haircut that mimics the one worn by the actor: combed back on the sides, forward in front

UNREAL: Exceptional

WIG OUT: Go crazy

WOCK: A bowl-shaped Chinese frying pan. By the 1970's, they were known as woks.

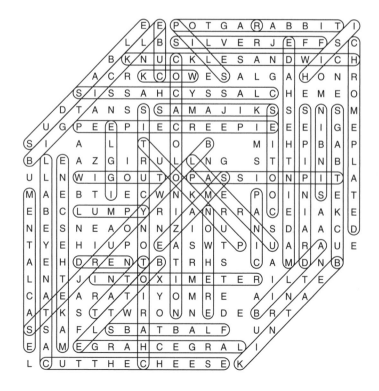

137 MORE LISTOGRAMS

7 Vegetables That Are Really Fruits:
CUCUMBER
OKRA
EGGPLANT
TOMATO
PUMPKIN
SQUASH
AVOCADO

The 7 Deadliest Dogs:
PIT BULL
GERMAN SHEPHERD
CHOW
MALAMUTE
HUSKY
WOLF HYBRID
AKITA

138 LIFE STYLES OF THE NOT YET RICH AND FAMOUS

1. a	10. b	19. b
2. b	11. both	20. b
3. a	12. a	21. a
4. b	13. b	22. b
5. a	14. both (!)	23. a
6. a	15. a	24. both
7. a	16. a	25. a
8. a	17. b	26. b
9. b	18. a	

142 DANCE, DANCE, DANCE

sitting atop a flagpole
up Pike's Peak
New York City
six
nine days
movie theaters
heart failure
on buffet tables on the dance floor
seven months
They Shoot Horses, Don't They?
the mid-1940s

140 PLEASED TO MEAT YOU

C	A	D	S		A	R	G	O		D	A	F	F	Y			P	L	O	W
A	T	O	P		H	O	O	D		O	B	O	T	E		B	U	E	N	O
Y	O	U	R	P	A	N	E	I	S	O	U	R	P	L	E	A	S	U	R	E
U	N	B	A	R			S	O	U	R				P	E	N	S	K	E	
G	E	T	Y	O	U	R	B	U	N	S	I	N	H	E	R	E		E	L	F
A	D	S			T	O	Y	S		I	L	I	A	D			A	M	I	D
			T	O	T	S			L	I	V	S		C	A	G	I	E	R	
	W	H	I	L	E	Y	O	U	S	L	E	E	P	W	E	L	O	A	F	
S	O	O	N	E	R			W	S	W			A	S	I	D	E			
P	R	O	M	O		M	E	S	A	S				R	A	G	W	E	E	D
A	S	H	E		W	E	D	R	Y	H	A	R	D	E	R		E	R	M	A
S	T	A	N	D	E	E			A	H	E	A	D		S	I	N	E	W	
			O	A	S	T	S		A	N	N		B	E	R	I	N	G		
	I	T	S	G	R	E	A	T	T	O	B	E	K	N	E	A	D	E	D	
T	N	O	T	E	S		G	A	R	B			O	S	L	O				
I	V	E	Y		F	U	G	I	T		S	H	O	E			P	A	D	
P	A	T		D	R	O	P	Y	O	U	R	P	A	N	T	S	H	E	R	E
	D	O	G	E	A	R			S	O	R	T			A	U	T	O	S	
W	E	T	A	K	E	A	B	I	T	E	O	U	T	O	F	G	R	I	M	E
W	R	O	T	E		Y	O	D	E	L		N	E	R	O		S	T	A	R
I	S	E	E		S	O	O	E	Y		G	R	E	G		T	E	S	T	

143 WEATHER SYSTEM

The leftover letters spell: ("The trouble with weather forecasting is that) it is right too often for us to ignore it and wrong too often for us to rely on it." —Patrick Young

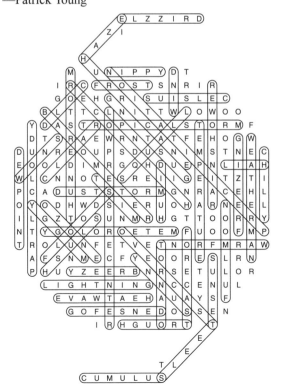

144 LOST IN TRANSLATION

The acrostic: China's *Wheel of Fortune*
The quote: Evidently some wires got crossed somewhere along the line, as the foreign version of this game show featured small boys strapped to a wheel trying to win prizes. Where and what was the show?
The clue answers:
A. COPPER
B. HOOFBEATS
C. INSIGHT
D. NEW AGE
E. ANALYZE THAT
F. SHOWDOWN
G. WHAT ME WORRY
H. HARD EIGHT
I. EAST SIDERS
J. EGGS ON
K. LIAM NEESON
L. OLIVES
M. FISH
N. FOWL
O. OOMPH
P. REVIEWS
Q. THE WILD WEST
R. ULSTER
S. NED ROREM
T. EASY STREET

145 SLIGHTLY IRREGULAR READING

Philaunderer
Palindromeo
The Fundead
Guiltar
Sitcoma
Siddhmartha
Idiotarod
Urinpal
Hippopotamush
Rescute

145 ALONE IN THE BIG CITY

a. 14

146 YOUNGEST & OLDEST

Joe Nuxhall played one game for the Cincinnati Reds in 1944, just shy of his 16th birthday. Bep Guidolin joined the Boston Bruins in 1942.

148 FAR ABOVE PAR

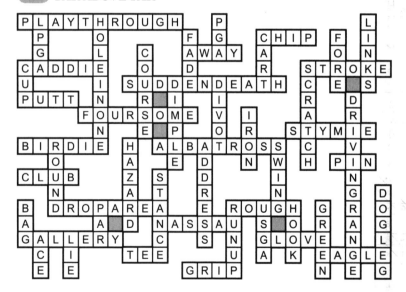

149 THE NAME'S THE SAME

1 – g (Dave Thomas)
2 – f (Sebastian Cabot)
3 – d (James Watt)
4 – e (Graham Greene)
5 – c (Jim Davis)
6 – b (Joe McCarthy)
7 – h (Cassius Clay)
8 – a (Muhammad Ali)

149 MYSTERY PLATE II

Maple syrup   Machine oil
Meat loaf   Ptomaine steak
Pancakes   Rubber patches
Powdered milk   Chalk
Salt and pepper   Sand and dirt
Soup   Hot water

150 AND YOU CAN QUOTE ME!

1 – b (Meg Ryan)
2 – a (Melanie Griffith)
3 – c (Charlize Theron)
4 – a (Christopher Walken)
5 – b (Catherine Zeta-Jones)
6 – b (Pamela Anderson)
7 – c (Halle Berry)
8 – b (Jon Stewart)
9 – b (Kim Cattrall)
10 – c (Stockard Channing)
11 – b (Simon Cowell)
12 – c (Arnold Schwarzenegger)
13 – c (Dame Judi Dench)
14 – c (Leonardo DiCaprio)
15 – c (Rupert Everett)
16 – a (Calista Flockart)
17 – b (Gwyneth Paltrow)
18 – c (Pink)
19 – a (Wanda Sykes)
20 – b (Wesley Snipes)
21 – b (Quentin Tarantino)
22 – c (Jennifer Garner)

151 BURIED TREASURE

The "Buried Treasure" inside each of them is a unit of currency: DINAR, YEN, FRANC, PESO, RIAL, EURO.

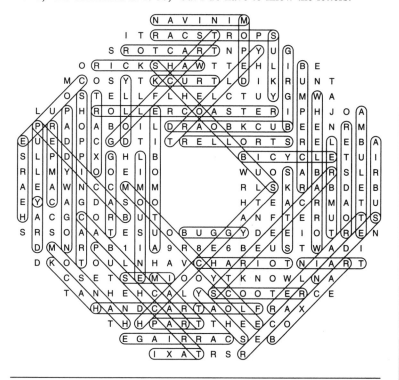

152 OUCH!

156 CELEBRITY FAVORITES

1 – a (coffee ice cream)
2 – b (French fries)
3 – b (McDonald's cheeseburgers)
4 – b (*The Wizard of Oz*)
5 – a (*Gone With the Wind*)
6 – b (writing poetry)
7 – a (interior design)
8 – b (*Little Women*)
9 – b (*A People's History of the United States*—but that's because he hasn't read the other one yet)
10 – b (*You Might Be a Redneck if…*)
11 – a (the Beatles)
12 – b (Donna Summer)
13 – a (big league pitcher)
14 – b (brain surgeon)
15 – a (teacher)

154 THE WHEEL THING

The leftover letters spell: "It's not the most intellectual job in the world," she confessed in 1986, "but I do have to know the letters."

156 STICKY SITUATION

b. Superglue requires moisture to bond.

157 KIND OF KINKY

On the Creation
In six days the Lord created the heavens and the earth and all the wonders therein. There are some of us who feel that He might have taken just a little more time.

On Attitude
If you have the choice between humble and cocky, go with cocky. There's always time to be humble later, once you've been proven horrendously, irrevocably wrong.

On Patience
If you're patient and you wait long enough, something will usually happen. And it'll usually be something you don't like.

On Rejection
Seventeen publishers rejected the manuscript, at which time I knew I had something pretty hot.

155 THE UNKNOWN COMIC

1. I haven't slept for ten days because that would be too long.
2. I would imagine if you understood Morse code a tap dancer would drive you crazy.
3. It's hard to dance if you just lost your wallet. Whoa! Where's my wallet? But hey, this song is funky.

158 LOONEY LAWS

```
BLINI  CUT  ORCS  ALTIMA
EATONIONS  FEAT  NEESON
DRINKMILK  FIREHYDRANT
SASS  ALE  GENE  RITE
     LUGES  WINDOWSHADES
STRIPEDSUITS      III
TEEPAD  NRA  WOODENLEG
ART  JOIE  WHALES  IVY
BRR  TREAT  RIOTED  PEER
 YOURBAREHANDS  LASSO
   REIN  ETC  ETON
SKUNK  FEATHERDUSTER
AIRS  STIMPY  QUITE  RUM
KEG  CHESTS  FUNT  VIA
ELEPHANTS  BRA  WISING
   IAN  PEELANORANGE
ICECREAMCONE  SIRED
OINK  POOL  SGT  IWAS
TRAINTRACKS  TIGHTROPE
ACCESS  NOAH  UGLYHORSE
SATRAP  SASH  NNE  ENDED
```

160 THANKS A LOT!

```
PAPA  PLED  RACE  ANTES
ALANS  LILI  ULAN  KOALA
PORTUGUESE  SOMA  ARCED
PERISH  GETSSTUCK  WOVE
   HOWE  SUI  STOVES
SPANISH  MAI  SIGHTS
PALO  TOUCHANDGO  EIEIO
ASCOT  STOIC  IRR  SALMA
SHANIA  EIN  ADEAL  NLER
 APOLLO  FDIC  ETAS
 POLISH  ETH  KOREAN
  SEMI  REIN  RUEFUL
ABBA  NINAS  EEL  ERICAS
LOAFS  UDO  ISAID  SELMA
ASTRO  MINISTRIES  LEAS
SCHISM  ETS  SWEDISH
 SKOALS  AHS  UKES
NCAA  BOTTLECAP  ATONCE
OLLAS  YURI  AUSTRALIAN
AETNA  ADIA  MRED  SETIN
MOSSY  LYON  PATS  GENE
```

162 ANIMAL PLANET

The national animals list (* = mythical):

Bald eagle (U.S.)
Barbary ape (Gibraltar)
Barn swallow (Estonia, Austria)
Bear (Russia, Finland)
Carabao (Philippines – an Asian water buffalo)
Condor (Chile, Bolivia, Ecuador)
Coqui (Puerto Rico – a frog)
Cow (Nepal)
Crocodile (East Timor)
Doctorbird (Jamaica – a hummingbird)
Elk (Norway)
Garuda* (Indonesia, Thailand – half-man, half-bird)
Gyrfalcon (Iceland)
Horse (Mongolia)
Hummingbird (Martinique)
Jaguar (Guyana)
Kangaroo (Australia)
Kiwi (New Zealand)
Llama (Bolivia)
Markhor (Pakistan – a wild sheep)
Oryx (Namibia)
Pelican (St.Kitts-Nevis)
Quetzal (Guatemala)

Red dragon* (Wales)
Rooster (France, Portugal)
Sisserou (Dominica – a parrot)
Springbok (Republic of South Africa)
Swan (Denmark)
Takin (Bhutan – a goat)
Tiger (India, Malaysia)
Two-spot ladybird (Latvia's national insect)
Vicuña (Peru)
Zebra (Botswana)

163 KIBBLE ME THIS

milk
the bones of dead sheep
huge stews
China
all of the above
hard biscuits

Spratt's Patent Meal Fibrine Dog Cakes
Medicated Dog Bread
Milkbones
horse
50,000
Chex cereal

Purina Dog Chow
table scraps
Lorne Greene
1,500
$11 billion

164 WOODSTOCK: THE WORD SEARCH

The leftover letters spell: "I think you have proven something to the world—that half a million kids can get together and have three days of fun and music and have nothing BUT fun and music. God bless you all."—Max Yasgur

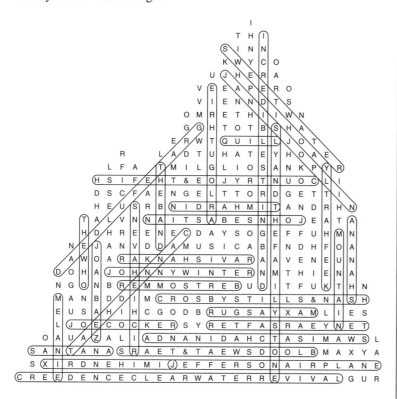

165 HOPING FOR HIGHER MARKS?

The acrostic: They changed their tune

The quote: Sixteen violinists from the Beethoven Orchestra of Bonn, Germany, sued for a pay raise on the grounds that they played more notes than musicians in the woodwind or brass sections. They finally relented and dropped the suit. "You might say...

The answer words:
A. TOSSES
B. HIPPODROME
C. EXHIBIT
D. YANN MARTEL
E. CUT TO THE CHASE
F. HYPNOSIS
G. ALOHA STADIUM
H. NONENTITY
I. GOLDFINGER
J. ELECTION DAY
K. DUSTIN HOFFMAN
L. THE ART OF WAR
M. HARVEY
N. EUGENE LEVY
O. IMPRESSIONISTS
P. ROBBERY
Q. TESTINESS
R. UNDER THE HOOD
S. NAYS
T. EDWARD NORTON

166 DO GEESE SEE GOD?

169 THE GREATEST

1. Only a man who knows what it is like to be defeated can reach down to the bottom of his soul and come up with the extra ounce of power it takes to win when the match is even.

2. I am America. I am the part you won't recognize. But get used to me. Black, confident, cocky; my name, not yours; my religion, not yours; my goals, my own; get used to me.

3. I hated every minute of training, but I said, "Don't quit. Suffer now and live the rest of your life as a champion."

169 SECRET RECIPE MAN

b. Asa Candler, Coke's founder, was Atlanta's mayor in 1917.

170 RENAISSANCE GUY

172 TALES OF THE KING
1. High. Elvis had 18 Billboard #1 hits.
2. Low. Elvis starred in 31 feature films.
3. High. Actually Elvis only made one TV commercial—for Southern Maid Doughnuts in 1954.
4. High. The 1993 Elvis Presley stamp had a face value of 29¢.
5. Low. 13 countries have issued Elvis Presley postage stamps.
6. Low. Graceland has an average 4 callers per day asking to speak to Elvis.
7. High. Actually, Elvis Presley never once gave an encore.
8. High. "Hound Dog" was written in about 10 minutes.
9. Low. Elvis owned nearly $60,000 worth of prescription sunglasses when he died.
10. High. The estimated value of a single pair of Elvis' underpants is $1300.

172 JINGLE, JINGLE
The quote: The Carpenters' "We've Only Just Begun" was originally a radio spot for a bank.
The clue answers:
A. SPARROW
B. INVOKE
C. NATTY
D. GALA
E. AUBURN
F. LOREN
G. OBJECT
H. NEPAL
I. GIFT HORSE
J. SIDEWAYS

173 YOUR MOMENT OF ZEN
1. President Bush announced we're going to Mars, which means he's given up on Earth.
2. In South Carolina, Senator John Edwards won handily, fulfilling his promise to win every state he was born in.
3. Yesterday, the president met with a group he calls the coalition of the willing. Or, as the rest of the world calls them, Britain and Spain.

176 TAKE MY PUZZLE, PLEASE
1. I'm so old that when I order a three minute egg they make me pay up front.
2. I knew the Savings and Loan industry was in trouble when my banker knocked on my door and asked for his calendar back.
3. You should see my (hotel) room. I put the key in the door…it breaks the window. When I complained, they gave me a room without a window.

174 MIXED-UP PEOPLE

177 PARALLEL HISTORY

WATERLOG
THE NORMAL CONQUEST
THE STOLE AGE
THE CIVIC WAR
THE DARN AGES
THE HUNDRED SEARS' WAR
THE IDEA OF MARCH
THE LONDON GLITZ
THE BATTLE OF THE BUDGE
THE WARS OF THE NOSES
THE GOLF RUSH
THE LINCOLN-DOUGLAS REBATES
THE LONE MARCH

180 REDUNDANT AND REPETITIOUS

The leftover letters spell: A <u>Russian cosmonaut</u> who was an <u>old geezer</u> felt he had <u>future potential</u> if he could <u>circle around</u> the earth for his <u>fellow countrymen</u>.

The word list:
AND ETC.
BABY CALF
BARE NAKED
CLOSE PROXIMITY
DESCEND DOWN
FIRST PRIORITY
FREE GIFT
FUTURE PLANS
HOLLOW TUBE
ILLEGAL POACHING
JOIN TOGETHER
NEW BEGINNING
NEW RECRUITS
OLD ADAGE
OLD FOSSIL
PAST EXPERIENCE
REFLECT BACK
SUCCESSFUL ESCAPE
SWIVEL AROUND
TEMPER TANTRUM
TOTAL EXTINCTION
VIOLENT EXPLOSION

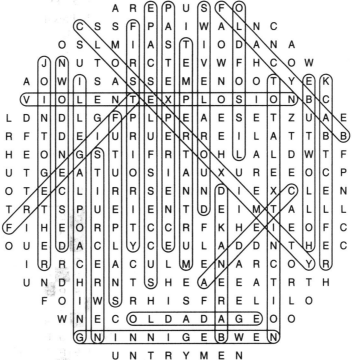

178 DON'T BE A LIRIPOOP!

185 HERE'S JOHNNY!

1. Married men live longer than single men. But married men are a lot more willing to die.

2. The difference between divorce and legal separation is that a legal separation gives a husband time to hide his money.

3. The best things in life are free, and the cheesiest things in life are free with a paid subscription to *Sports Illustrated*.

181 YE GODS!

Here's a list of our gods and goddesses and their ancient realms:

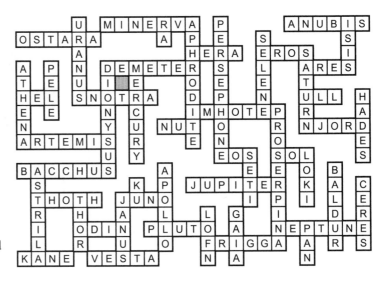

Anubis (Egyptian god of embalming; friend of the dead)

Aphrodite (Greek goddess of beauty)

Apollo (Greek and Roman god of the Sun, poetry, and music)

Ares (Greek god of war)

Artemis (Greek goddess of the hunt)

Astrila (Norse goddess of love)

Athena (Greek goddess of wisdom and defensive war)

Bacchus (Roman god of wine)

Baldur (Norse god of innocence, beauty, and peace)

Ceres (Roman goddess of the harvest)

Demeter (Greek goddess of nature and the harvest)

Dionysus (Greek god of wine)

Eos (Greek goddess of the dawn)

Eros (Greek god of love)

Frigga (Norse foremost goddess; goddess of the sky, marriage, and motherhood)

Gaia (Greek primordial earth goddess)

Hades (Greek god of the underworld)

Hel (Norse goddess of the underworld)

Hera (Greek chief goddess; goddess of marriage)

Imhotep (Egyptian god of wisdom, medicine, and magic)

Isis (Egyptian goddess of magic, motherhood, and family commitment)

Janus (Roman god of beginnings and endings)

Juno (Roman chief goddess; goddess of marriage)

Jupiter (Roman chief god; god of the sky)

Kane (Hawaiian god of earth, fresh water, and stones)

Ku (Hawaiian god of war)

Lofn (Norse goddess of forbidden love)

Loki (Norse god of fraud and mischief)

Mercury (Roman messenger of the gods)

Minerva (Roman goddess of wisdom and civilization)

Neptune (Roman god of the sea)

Njord (Norse god of sea, fire, and wind)

Nut (Egyptian goddess of heaven and the sky)

Odin (Norse supreme god; god of wisdom)

Ostara (Norse goddess of springtime fertility, and whose name is the origin of "Easter")

Pan (Greek god of the shepherds)

Pele (Hawaiian goddess of fire and volcanoes)

Persephone (Greek queen of the dead)

Pluto (Roman god of the underworld)

Proserpina (Roman queen of the underworld)

Ra (Egyptian foremost god; sun king)

Saturn (Roman god of agriculture and fertility)

Selene (Greek moon goddess)

Seti (Egyptian god of war)

Snotra (Norse goddess of justice, virtue, and self-discipline)

Sol (Roman sun god)

Thor (Norse god of thunder and lightning)

Thoth (Egyptian god of science and the arts)

Ull (Norse god of the hunt, snowshoes, and bows)

Uranus (Greek and Roman consort/son of Gaia and father of the Titans; god of the sky)

Vesta (Roman goddess of the hearth)

189 WOULD WE LIE TO YOU ONE MORE TIME?

1 – b (Paper defeats rock because ancient Chinese emperors rejected petitions by draping them over rocks.)

2 – b (The detergent in toothpaste temporarily modifies your taste system.)

3 – c (Mussolini had a handshaking phobia.)

4 – a (The ancient Greeks used parsley to mask garlic breath.)

5 – b (Area codes with lower numbers were assigned to bigger cities.)

182 GARDEN OF EATIN'

```
CAPOS  RIFF      ABITOFF
ALERT  ENLISTS   GUSHIER
SORBETGOURMET    ENMASSE
THESPHINX  EXILED  NEST
SAS  BOS   BEALL   TSK
     PAR  TRE SEAN NUDGE
MONICA WIRY  MUSE  AIR
BRINK MOOGOOGAIPANFAN
ARTE MART UVA  TAKEONE
SSE  SINO RIPA  RIVETS
   CONSOMMEDEVOTEE
RETARD MIEN  OMAR  DRE
EVILEYE LIU  ICAN  NOSE
VENISONPARTISAN  ACUTE
ERG PUZO  SHAD  PLAGUE
LIETO OLDE ANO  IFA
   WTS LIVID  SLA  IRS
PUCE PASSED  CATALONIA
SHOEGOO CREAMPUFFBUFF
SUSTAIN STEROID  AISLE
THISTLE  ANNS  STEER
```

186 "THE WHO?"

```
DECKS  BAMA  FLAGG  CAMP
SCHMO  AMIN  LYCRA  OREO
CHEAPTRICK ALTAR  PTAS
SORROW  ALICEINCHAINS
   TRADE EMO  DIOCESE
ANG  NAST ANDA  APE
FOOFIGHTERS URI  STRUM
RULES LALO FLING  IONA
ONFIRE BLUEOYSTERCULT
  NARC AGAR TUTU  EEE
BUTTERUP HRE  ARMBANDS
UNI LARA INGA  NABS
THEGINBLOSSOMS DIPPED
TITO DEATH EMIL  SCALE
SPOOK DCI PROCOLHARUM
  DEC ESPO NEVE  ELO
SKATERS  APT  METES
MARILYNMANSON  UNISON
OREM  POINT DEEPPURPLE
KANE TOSIR AMER  READS
ETAS STONY YOKE  ESTES
```

190 CLOWN ALLEY

```
GOURD THRU MCAN  HEEDS
APLEA MOOR AONE  OCTET
FANCYPANTS DRYBUTCHER
FLATLAND UNIT  SCLERA
  OIL ATLAS EMMA  RED
DUG GEL  RAZORBACKS
OPRAH ONO INUSE  ELBOW
ROUSTABOUTS BEST  ARLO
KNEE MORPH TENTH  SUER
SALAAM SEEME  RIGHTON
   HOMESWEETHOME
ONELANE HANOI  BEATIT
VERA ITSSO ENROL  LONE
EVIL AHOP GREASEJOINT
RECAP ONCEA AMS  EULER
  WINDJAMMER OFT  SRA
IVS VISA BURMA  ATL
NOTION ERTE  ETHIOPIA
FIRSTOFMAY CLOUDSWING
OCALA ORSO TENN  OLLIE
REPEL PITS SOSA  NYETS
```

194 REALITY TV WATCHING

```
ANNES SPUD ACED  BARBS
ROUGH TOTE TAME  IDARE
AMIGO ERAS ERIE  ROBIE
GETSOMECHIPSANDADRINK
  HINDU  ETTE  SWEDES
MORENO PARK  MESAS
OPEL GIVEOFF LAT  MVD
PULLUPANICECOMFYCHAIR
ESS NOMEAT CRU  HASTA
  JIBE TON  TAI  SARI
TUNETOTHERIGHTSTATION
ANAT YEA  BIO  TITO
ESTER  LGE RODENT  SPF
BETRANSFIXEDFORANHOUR
ORY PIN FOREIGN  ENCE
  ASCOT  ARTS  GADGET
SCATHE SWAT  NOMSG
WONDERWHYYOUWATCHEDIT
ENSUE HIER LIMO  OHARA
EGEST ERTE ALEE  RODEO
TALKS NTHS NESS  EGADS
```

192 MY OTHER CAR IS...

1 – ee (STARING)
2 – u (MULTI-TALENTED)
3 – ii (VILLAGE)
4 – b (AHEAD)
5 – bb (RADIOACTIVE CATS)
6 – y (PHARMACIST)
7 – m (FILM)
8 – gg (STOP FASTER)
9 – r (LEAVE)
10 – f (BUSY)
11 – p (HANG UP)
12 – dd (RELOADING)
13 – i (DESIGNER GENES)
14 – w (OUT BY ITSELF)
15 – d (BAD COP)
16 – n (GOOD GRAVY)
17 – cc (REAL POO)
18 – jj (WIFE)
19 – e (BODIES)
20 – a (ABUSE THE PRIVILEGE)
21 – h (CHOLESTEROL)
22 – j (DIAPERS)
23 – c (ATTITUDE)
24 – hh (THE LAW)
25 – s (LISP)
26 – ff (STAY OFF)
27 – l (DRUMMER)
28 – o (HANDBASKET)
29 – g (CHEAP)
30 – t (LOUSY HUNTER)
31 – x (PARTS)
32 – k (DRAG)
33 – v (NAPS)
34 – q (KILL)
35 – aa (QUITTERS)
36 – z (PUBLIC SCHOOLS)

168 OUI THE PEOPLE

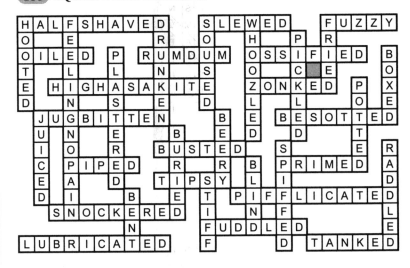

188 SQUIFFY AND SWACKED

193 ... A WORD SEARCH PUZZLE

The leftover letters spell: Horn Broken, Watch for Finger; I'm Only Driving Like This to Piss You Off.

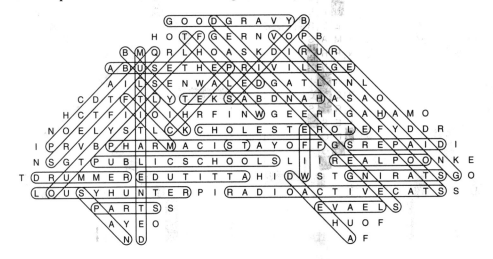

184 NICE HOUSE...NOBODY HOME

The leftover letters spell: "Slipped into the gene pool when the lifeguard wasn't watching" and "As sharp as a marble."

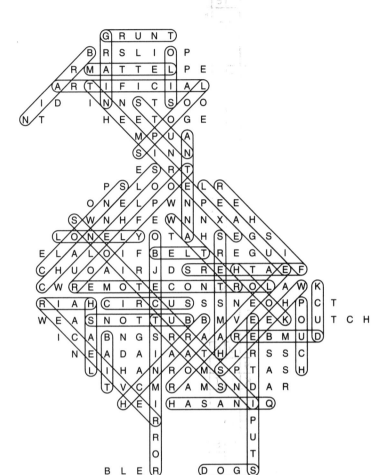

1. FEATHERS, DUCK
2. BELT, LOOPS
3. BUTTONS, REMOTE CONTROL
4. ELEVATOR, TOP FLOOR
5. WATER, INSTRUCTIONS
6. WHEEL'S, HAMSTER'S
7. BRAIN, LONELY
8. OBJECTS IN MIRROR, DUMBER
9. ANTENNA, CHANNELS
10. HAS AN IQ, GRUNT
11. FISHER, MATTEL
12. RECEIVER, HOOK
13. STUPID TREE, BRANCH
14. CLOWNS, CIRCUS
15. DOGS, LEASH
16. GRAIN, SILO
17. NUTS, POUCH
18. LEAGUE, HAIR
19. EXPERIMENT, ARTIFICIAL
20. SMART, BAIT

---

196 NOT THE WORLD'S HARDEST...

F	O	O	D	S	T	A	N	D	S	■	C	S	I	■	D	O	D	O	M	A
I	A	M	A	C	A	M	E	R	A	■	D	I	S	C	O	V	E	R	E	D
S	H	E	N	A	N	I	G	A	N	■	S	L	E	A	Z	E	B	A	L	L
T	U	N	I	N	G	■	R	I	C	H	■	E	R	R	■	R	E	N	E	E
■	■	S	T	E	P	O	N	T	O	■	N	E	A	■	L	E	G	E	R	■
M	I	S	S	■	D	E	N	■	A	P	P	T	■	V	E	E	R	■	■	■
E	T	H	E	R	■	Z	I	P	■	E	O	N	■	A	M	A	S	S	E	D
M	O	O	L	A	H	■	A	G	A	L	■	N	P	R	■	T	A	O	■	■
B	L	T	■	J	A	C	K	I	E	G	L	E	A	S	O	N	■	A	S	E
E	D	O	M	■	M	O	U	N	T	A	I	N	D	E	W	■	A	N	T	S
R	Y	N	E	■	M	O	S	T	S	I	N	C	E	R	E	■	C	M	O	N
F	O	G	G	■	I	N	T	E	R	N	A	L	E	A	R	■	S	I	F	T
D	U	O	■	I	N	S	I	D	E	S	T	O	R	I	E	S	■	K	E	W
I	S	A	■	T	E	K	■	A	T	E	S	■	D	O	S	I	D	O	■	■
C	O	L	O	S	S	I	■	E	D	H	■	E	E	L	■	O	P	T	E	R
■	■	A	S	S	N	■	L	Y	O	N	■	G	E	L	■	H	A	N	K	■
M	E	E	K	O	■	C	A	Y	■	P	A	R	A	D	I	S	E	■	■	■
A	T	A	L	E	■	A	L	S	■	E	B	E	L	■	N	E	E	D	T	O
J	A	V	A	A	P	P	L	E	T	■	O	L	I	V	E	R	R	E	E	D
O	P	E	N	S	Y	S	T	E	M	■	B	I	T	I	N	G	I	N	T	O
R	E	D	D	Y	E	■	O	S	S	■	S	T	E	P	S	I	S	T	E	R

---

198 ANYTHING GOES

B	A	M	B	I	D	R	O	S	S	■	B	R	A	S	S	■	W	A	F	S
A	S	C	A	R	E	D	Y	C	A	T	Y	E	L	P	S	■	I	N	I	T
L	A	B	R	E	S	E	A	R	C	H	P	L	A	Y	S	■	N	I	L	E
S	N	O	W	E	E	■	A	R	E	A	O	A	K	■	F	E	M	M	E	■
A	I	R	H	E	■	R	O	P	E	P	U	L	L	■	B	I	R	A	M	P
M	G	S	O	■	R	O	M	E	D	I	L	L	■	F	I	N	A	L	A	M
B	U	C	■	B	E	D	M	U	R	A	L	■	O	R	R	E	T	I	R	E
R	A	H	P	E	T	E	■	P	O	N	Y	T	H	A	T	S	I	N	G	S
A	N	T	I	L	U	N	T	■	D	O	N	W	I	T	H	S	O	N	I	A
N	A	S	C	A	R	T	A	G	■	I	D	I	O	M	M	E	S	S	E	S
■	■	■	I	N	G	R	E	A	S	E	X	V	I	I	I	■	■	■	■	■
W	A	T	E	R	G	A	T	E	D	J	■	T	I	N	S	H	I	V	E	R
O	R	A	N	G	E	F	O	N	D	U	E	■	P	E	T	O	L	I	V	E
B	R	I	D	E	O	F	L	A	S	S	I	E	■	R	A	P	S	T	I	R
B	A	N	O	N	R	E	D	■	A	T	E	A	C	A	K	E	■	I	L	E
L	I	T	F	I	G	S	■	M	D	G	I	R	D	L	E	■	V	A	P	A
E	G	G	D	U	E	■	P	A	S	R	O	L	L	S	■	M	E	T	E	D
K	N	E	E	S	■	H	E	R	A	A	I	L	■	■	M	U	T	E	A	S
I	O	N	E	■	V	A	P	I	D	N	E	E	D	L	E	P	O	I	N	T
C	B	E	D	■	T	H	E	O	Z	D	I	S	C	O	T	H	E	Q	U	E
K	I	S	S	■	M	A	S	S	E	■	E	T	S	T	H	I	R	S	T	Y

Be sure to check out more hot titles from

Available at bookstores, warehouse clubs, and in great bathrooms everywhere. Or visit www.bathroomreader.com.

Bathroom Readers' Press • P.O. Box 1117 • Ashland, OR 97520 • Phone: 541–488–4642 • Fax: 541–482–6159